The Finest Kind
Voices of Newfoundland and Labrador Women

Marian Frances White

Other Books by Marian Frances White
A Woman's Almanac
1987 – 1992
Not A Still Life:
The Art and Writings of Rae Perlin

The Finest Kind

Voices of Newfoundland and Labrador Women

Marian Frances White

Creative Publishers
St. John's, Newfoundland
1992

Appreciation is expressed to *The Canada Council* for publication assistance.

The publisher acknowledges the financial contribution of the *Department of Tourism and Culture, Government of Newfoundland and Labrador*, which has helped make this publication possible.

Cover: *Spring Thaw* – Acrylic on canvas by Tish Holland. 36" x 40" – 1987. Small reproductions of Tish Holland's artwork were used in the 1987 *Almanac*. Courtesy of Christina Parker Fine Art Gallery.

Title: *The Finest Kind* is a Newfoundland expression used in response to the greeting "How are you doing?"

Acknowledgements

Special thanks to the Canadian Employment and Immigration Commission who financially supported the *Almanac* since its inception and to the Newfoundland and Labrador Arts Council for a project grant to complete this work. I would like to extend much appreciation to Beni Malone who continually encouraged me to compile this compendium. The many women who contributed to the *Almanac* over the years are named individually in this book, however I would like to acknowledge the work of my co-worker, Sharon Brenton, who dove into this project on short notice, with all her care. Thank you all.

∝ printed on acid-free Sno-Glo offset paper

Published by

CREATIVE PUBLISHERS

A Division of Robinson-Blackmore Printing & Publishing Ltd.

P.O. Box 8660, St. John's, Newfoundland A1B 3T7

Printed in Canada by:

ROBINSON-BLACKMORE PRINTING & PUBLISHING LTD.

P.O. Box 8660, St. John's, Newfoundland A1B 3T7

Canadian Cataloguing in Publication Data

"The Finest Kind"

Includes index.
ISBN 1-895387-10-8

1. Women — Newfoundland — Biography.

I. White, Marian Frances, 1954–

HQ1459.N5F56   1992   305.4'09718   C92-098644-7

Dedicated to my mother
Florence White
who is "The Finest Kind."
With admiration and love for her stories.

Index

Foreword

Often I have been asked to put all the stories that I gathered for *A Woman's Almanac* in one book. While the annual agenda book worked well for its intended purpose, it always seemed a shame to discard the book at the end of each year. This compendium will offer easier access to the entire collection of profiles and will give the women profiled a more permanent place in our heritage.

When I first began research for the *Almanac* in 1986, it was a solo effort. I travelled around the province with my tape recorder and camera and gathered as many interviews as possible. Over the years, other women courageously got involved as researchers, tape transcribers and later as interviewers. I have always enjoyed the process of shaping the stories, so the final editing was still a solo task. As I wrote in the *1987 Almanac*, "The geography of this province has worked both for and against the planning of the Almanac. Stories were collected by personal interviews, letters, telephone interviews and women writing their own words." In whatever form, the intention was to offer women an opportunity to take pride in their survival and in their achievements.

The initial concept to produce an agenda book featuring the profiles of twelve women annually came about for two reasons. First, I had been using an agenda book since 1984 when I purchased one in Boston where I had been studying alternative survival skills. I loved the togetherness of this spiral bound book that opened flat on my desk and added some organization to my day. Secondly, I grew up with a mother who was a great storyteller and kept her family of twelve amused with her tales of people long gone, but never forgotten. She would often finish her story with the phrase, "My, the books I could have written, had I the time". I was inspired by her words and took them with me when I left home to study journalism in Ottawa.

When I returned to Newfoundland to 'live', I wanted to connect with women who were doing much more than merely surviving. Their words continue to inspire me. From these profiles I have learnt about perseverance and honouring of our lives no matter how simple or extreme the struggle might be. More especially, I have seen how numerous women in their senior years challenge their right to have independent and creative lives. However, if there was one recurring theme that sounded very clearly in these interviews it was the need for choice, whether that be in where we choose to live, love or work. In the *1988 Almanac* I wrote that "the values (of the women I have interviewed) show me that despite geographical isolation there is an endless determination to thrive (not merely survive), and to defy narrow stereotypes.

One of the personal delights each year for me in the *Almanac* was to see how some of the women I had profiled went on to make even a bigger mark in their community. To name a few: Suzanne Blake was the first woman to be a sports broadcaster in Newfoundland and went on to take a position with national CBC sports. Joy Burt broke the powerlifting world records in 1992, and was named—pound-for-pound—the strongest woman in the world. Nancy Riche continues to be powerful in her work with labour relations and Wendy Williams is, at the time of writing, a city counsellor in St. John's. I admire Patty Au who came here from China with very little knowledge of the English language. Marilyn John continues to fight for Micmac land claims on this island and Rose Gregoire has devoted many years of her life to the Innu's struggles in Labrador. The determination of these women has had a powerful impact on my own life. Most of all, I have learned that to live honestly is to live with the wind at my back, moving me forward. My work is enhanced by all these women and further fuelled by their courage and commitment to change.

The biographies of the women contained in this book also comprise the stories of artists, writers, filmmakers, social activists, crafts women, potters, midwives, singers, and women like Hope who cannot give her full name for fear of the repercussions from her family. I have included her story to remind us that there is still, as yet, not enough safety for women to tell all their stories. But there is hope.

Women pass on their strength to others through the example of their lives. While it has always been my intention to recognize and celebrate women's lives while they are still here to enjoy their achievements, I felt it was also essential to include the stories of some women who are no longer with us. These include Agnes Marion Ayre, a major amateur botanist and painter; Julia Salter Earle who was a defender of the working class in the pre-depression years of this province's history; Joan Morrissey, a singer and songwriter whose work has all but been erased from record, and Mabel Squires, a Salvation Army missionary in China who lived long enough to raise children and write some of her own biography.

Indeed, tangible recognition of women's achievements continues to be sadly remissive in the history that has been selected by historians. By 1990, I felt the *Almanac* was "a tool to help unearth the remnants of our foremothers' roles. It is reminiscent of their voices that echo through present day women who struggle for equality and sanity in a society that shows little remorse for its failures in these areas." This continues to be true.

The Almanac Compendium, *The Finest Kind*, is a celebration of women's accomplishments. It is also a tool from which to measure and acknowledge our own achievements, as well as a record of *our* lives, in our own words. Enjoy *The Finest Kind*, you never know what amazing part of your own heritage you might excavate.

MARIAN FRANCES WHITE
JUNE, 1982

Eva Ellen Abbott

1988 Profile

Interview by Marian Frances White

Situated on the isolated southwest coast of Newfoundland, Gaultois is a prosperous fishing community of some five hundred people. Yet the rugged coastline bordering the town reminds Eva Abbott of the contrast between this land and that of her first home in Pushthrough, where animals grazed and where she "dug many's a potato and spun more than one sheep's wool." Like numerous outport Newfoundlanders, Eva Ellen Abbott moved from her near-self-sufficient community of Pushthrough to the more economically viable community of Gaultois. Here there was a fish plant in which the men could work. Women left Pushthrough because their husbands, the fishermen, were promised more work in Gaultois, and consequently more money, with Joey Smallwood's resettlement program of the early 1950s.

To get to where Eva Abbott has lived for the past twenty-five years is not a simple task. One does not just take a ferry from the nearest port, Hermitage; one also has to walk along a mountainous road which the town's one vehicle, a pick-up truck, barely manages. At the end of this trail is Eva Abbott's home, perched beside an immense rock that serves as her doorstep. Abbott's story is an example of how a government, intent on development and economic profit, moulded more than the lives of fishermen—in retrospect, it narrowed and confined women's work to the home.

🍎   🍎   🍎

1

I was born in Pushthrough, Hermitage Bay, on April 23, 1909. My older sister still lives at Burnt Islands, but my younger sister died when she was sixteen. I went to a one-room school in Pushthrough. There were about fifty of us and we had two teachers who taught from grade one to eleven. When I was fifteen I finished school and went to work for the local minister. I worked like this for a few years, until he left to work in Corner Brook. He wanted me to go with him but my mother didn't want me to, so I stayed and found work with a woman looking after her children. I had a number of jobs like this and stayed with one woman until I married Benjamin Abbott in 1936. I was a Lilly before that. I never got nothing for my work except for a piece of clothing now and then and a place to stay. Everyone was alike in those days.

Pushthrough was a right comfortable place to live. My mother taught me what there was to do to take care of myself. I learnt at an early age to card wool, to spin it and then knit everything from socks to longjohns. You see, in Pushthrough we had sheep to look after; we had goats and we had hens and ducks. My mother worked the garden and I helped her. In that time I didn't know what it was to buy anything much; like eggs, for example, we had plenty of them. There was nothing fancy about our eating or our clothes that we knitted, but it was good living.

I moved from Pushthrough when I was fifty or so, like many people did with Joey's plan. I didn't want to come here to Gaultois, but everyone was resettling so I hung on until I had to leave and then I went. Coming to Gaultois was real different for me. Here everyone builds their houses on rocks, whereas in Pushthrough everyone had a garden and large meadows for the animals to graze. When I first came here, I said I would only stay the fall, but when the winter came and no one planned to return to Pushthrough, I didn't have much choice but to stay.

The business people here, the Garlands, asked me to work in their store. They built me this little house and I worked for them to pay it off. I settled in here against my mind, but I've made do. I've had my share of work. With the Garlands, I got seven cents for every sale I made. That was good for them times.

Gaultois hasn't changed much in the twenty-five years I've lived here. We still don't have much of a road, but the truck makes it up here with supplies. When I came here there were only nine or ten families. Just like in Pushthrough, we only had lamps to help us get around at night, but I never found that difficult until I tried to get around in Gaultois. I was always a bit nearsighted, so I'd sit under the big lamp that hung over the table. These days it's worse; I finds it most when I try to read, and I likes to read something most every day. It's good pastime, I finds.

At least these days there's a community hall where everyone can get together for a 'time.' There's a senior citizens' time this week, but I won't go now that the weather is here. It's difficult for the older people nowadays, at least here it is because you can't get down over the rocks so easy. I fell down a few years ago on the old bridge and ever since then my leg hasn't been the same.

I have an old fashioned sewing machine here that's as old as myself. My aunt, that's my father's sister, got her when I was born. She always told her husband, "When Eva gets old enough she got to have my sewing machine." So when she died in our house, I was given the sewing machine. At one time I used to make everything I wore, but nowadays my hands don't work as well as they used to. Still, I sews the odd piece of material.

I've had someone living with me since Benjamin passed away in 1969; they do for themselves and we share whatever there is around. I didn't have any children of my own, but I used to take care of children and make things for them just like I would if they were my own. If the people who stays with me leaves here, they most often ask me to go with them. But I don't go nowhere. I have plenty of relations in Halifax, and a good friend in Grand Falls that I lived and worked with in Pushthrough. I sees her when I goes there to get my eyes checked in the summer, and I still hears from her all year around. My dear, no one knows the letters I writes.

For all that's said and done, I haven't wanted to go live anywhere else. There's a boy in Halifax, my cousin's son, well, he's a grown man now; his father died when he was only five, and then his mother died that next summer, so I took care of him for quite a while, and last year when I was in Grand Falls he came up to see me and said he wished I'd make up my mind to go with him. But still, I don't want to go.

When I was younger now, I enjoyed getting in the boat and going anywhere along the coast. But even then I didn't fancy going off the island. But my sister, Effie Fudge, she's in her eighties, still expects me to visit her on Burnt Islands, so I suppose as long as I can I'll go across the water to see her. But other than that, I knows I'm here to stay.

Mani Aten (Mary Adele Andrews) Antane

1988 Profile
Original interview by Camille Fouillard who has worked with the Innu since 1983. It was translated by Mani Mat (Mary Martha) Rich who lives in Labrador.
Mani Aten Antane is one of some 9600 Innu— an extensive group of native people who inhabit the subarctic forests of Canada (Quebec/Labrador region) and speak related dialects of the Cree lan-

guage. Mani Aten Antane is Mary Adele Andrews Innu name. She was born in 1932 in the Quebec interior, along Mitshen-nipip, a small tributary of Mistashipu, or the Moirie River as we know it. One of eight children, Antane has fifteen children of her own, five of which were born in the country and the rest in Sheshatshiu where she now lives part of the year.

Antane's memories of her childhood centre around her life in Nutshimit—the country. Her life changed dramatically in the early 1960s when the Innu were settled to village life in Sheshatshiu. As soon as the village band council obtained decision-making power over community funding, a program was set up to assist families to travel by small plane to the interior where they could live off the land as they always had. As a result, Mani Aten, now a widow, takes her children and grandchildren to the land of her ancestors twice a year—from September to December and from March to June—to hunt, fish and trap, to live the ways of her culture where it still thrives in spite of many odds, the most recent of these being the low-level flying of NATO training jets.

ೱ   ೱ   ೱ

I grew up in the country and what I remember more than anything are the mosquitoes! In the fall and winter my family and I would live in Nutshimit (the country) and in the spring we would head for the coast. Sometimes we would go to Uashat (Seven Islands, on the Quebec North Shore) and other times to Sheshatshiu. We would come from the country, walking more than a hundred miles to get supplies like clothing, food and tent canvas.

We would haul up our tent in the morning, travel by canoe or toboggan and snowshoes during the day, set up camp at night and then continue on the next day. When we stayed in one camp for a while, the men would go off to check far-off traps or to hunt caribou. Women and children would stay near the camp. We would hunt small game and chop firewood. We would collect fir boughs for the floor of the tent, cook, make clothing such as moccasins and mitts, and lace snowshoes. And then we would move on again.

If we were travelling from Uashat we would travel directly north up through Menmik-hipi and then to Mitshikamau Lake. My father's land was around Mitshikamau Lake which is now part of the Smallwood Reservoir. My husband, Matthew Ben, and I lost most of our hunting territory, canoe, traps and caches in 1963 when the Reservoir flooded. We were not forewarned. When we travelled from Sheshatshiu, we would travel to Mitshikamau either west along the Mistashipu (Churchill River) or northwest along the Naskaupi-shipu. In the spring when the rivers were breaking up we could not travel and we could stay awhile at Mitshikamau where we had left our canoe. Once, in the fall, I remember my sister and I had to travel a day by ourselves to get supplies for our family. We slept the night by the river and lake and although it was a long journey, I was happy to do it.

In Nutshimit we travelled to hunt the caribou. The caribou is the most important food for us, the Innu. Sometimes we would go up the Mushau-shipu to Mushuaunipi (Indian House Lake) to celebrate the Muskushan (the feast of the caribou) with the other families. Here, we would boil the crushed bones of the caribou and share the cooked marrow. This is a sacred food. The feast would be followed by a drum dance where everyone, the children and the old people, came together to celebrate our success at the hunt.

These days I go to Nutshimit in the spring or fall. The best place to go is where we can hunt caribou. That's the best time for me. I would like it more, though, if the caribou, like the Mealy Mountain or the Red Wine herds, weren't restricted by wildlife regulations. The caribou used to be free for us in Nutshimit. We have never overhunted the caribou, but the government refused to see that it is our right to hunt as we have done for hundreds of years. Last spring, the elders decided it was time for us to go again to the Mealy Mountains to hunt the caribou. We see this as our right, not as breaking the law.

My children and grandchildren like the country more than they like Sheshatshiu, and so do I. But Nutshimit was a different place with the low-level flying jets. I've been frightened. One day when I was alone looking after children, everyone ran into the camp terrorized and crying. I was afraid too. The plane was so low I could see the face of the pilot. I was overflown at Andrew's Lake by two jets, and once they came when the children were still sleeping. It's a terrible thing for the children. Once our life was very peaceful and now we have to live with these jets that fly so fast (800 miles per hour) just barely over the tops of the trees.

The jets chase away the caribou and because of this it's difficult to hunt them. We believe all the animals of the forest are being affected by these jets and by the pollution from the exhaust of their planes. We never had trouble getting trout, but now the good lake trout are dying from the exhaust. In the springtime, when the animals are having their young, many die for the same reasons. It is dangerous to go out on the lake nowadays. One spring, when my son Eric went out to check his net, his canoe almost tipped over when the jets suddenly flew over. Some children have fallen out of canoes, and the exhaust makes them sick. If this continues, Nut-shimit will not be so beautiful, but I know the Innu will still want to go to the country because that is our home. I don't like those planes and they don't belong here. That is why I set up my tent along with four other families, at the end of the Goose Bay airport runway last spring.

No one has told me why this training is going on, but I would like to know. It seems they are playing war and it will be like war if the NATO base comes to Labrador and Quebec. I know that much. Here animals will be killed and the land will be destroyed. I don't see any good coming out of that.

LINDA BODDIE

Patti Au

1988 Profile
Interview by Marian Frances White
Patti Au was born Chiu Shuet Lin on November 26, 1944 in Canton, China. At a young age she and her sister studied dance there and today her sister is a well-known Chinese dance teacher. At sixteen Au moved to Hong Kong, where she trained for three years as a teacher, and taught grades two and five.

In 1970, at the age of twenty-six, Au took her first flight—from Hong Kong to Tokyo to Vancouver, then to Toronto, and finally to St. John's. Immigration laws at that time stated you had to marry right away or you would not be able to stay, so within one month of her arrival she married her husband, Wing, at Gower Street United Church. She and her husband have five children, four girls and one boy. When she first came to Newfoundland, Patti Au worked at a restaurant in the Goulds where her working hours were 9:00 am until 2:00 am; for the past seventeen years she has worked at the E 'n' W Restaurant on Water St. in St. John's, a restaurant that she and her husband now own. Her life is indicative of hundreds of Chinese who immigrated to Canada, though she is quick to point out that those who come here with a knowledge of the English language have better opportunities to work in their chosen field. Patti Au has a strong identity with her culture, and keeps it alive through her activities in the local Chinese community and her contact with her family in China.

❦   ❦   ❦

*W*hen I first came to Newfoundland I wanted to go back to Hong Kong right away. My family lived there and seventeen years ago there were not many Chinese people here. The buildings downtown made no view; I saw no colour and the houses really looked all the same. It was not the height of the buildings that made me sad, but the look.

6

The markets in China and Hong Kong are open six o'clock in the morning to ten o'clock at night, so people can buy fresh Chinese vegetables any time. I remember here you could only get cabbage, tomato, celery and vegetables like that. My husband and his uncle and family always tried to find Chinese food for me; they thought this would make me want to stay here. Today I still miss my food. Even in the restaurant Chinese not cook Chinese food; they cook Canadian Chinese food like chicken fried rice. Everyone love the french fry here—even my children want to eat the french fry more than rice and vegetables—but still I never eat french fries. I cook the Chinese way.

In Hong Kong I learned English in school, but just a little, so first when I come over here I didn't understand not one word. My husband teach me a little and his uncle show me the cash in his restaurant, but until I learned enough to work the cash, I just wash and work in the kitchen.

I think it would make it easier for other women who come here if they had people to talk to. Not far from this restaurant there is a woman who just came from China and she works in the kitchen. She never went to English school in China. I'm lucky that I knew a little. The first time I met her I understood what she was going through because I was like that when I first came over. I talked to her to tell her that one day she would understand well; I tell her to listen to the radio and watch the news. I understand eighty per cent of what is said now. I love to learn and understand what people say.

It seems Chinese people mainly work in restaurants and in laundries because there is not much more unless they learn English. I know when my children grow up they do not want to work in restaurant; that makes me happy. I work like this for seventeen years with not much time off. I work seven days a week, and when I had young children I took care of them between the time I worked in this restaurant. Sometimes that's okay, but sometimes that's awful because the baby wants milk and you hear the baby cry but you cannot leave the customers. I don't think it's good to work seven days a week, sixteen hours a day. Now sometimes other Chinese families come here after hours and we open restaurant for them. That makes for a social time.

In China life was very different. Even in Hong Kong everybody spoke the same language so people did more things together. My children understand me when I speak to them in Chinese; my oldest daughter, Michelle, answers me sometimes in Chinese, but my youngest son, Richard, only answers me in English. I see no future for the Chinese like this. They can read and write and talk well in English but if they do not have their Chinese tongue I think they lose our culture. They learn a little in school but that is like when I learned English in Hong Kong; I did not learn much because I did not speak English outside the school.

Right now in St. John's there is a Chinese community but for many years there was no place except where we work to be together. I used to stay at the restaurant because I had no friends. There were not many women my age but when more and more people came here I found lots of friends. It was hard to try to make friends with the Newfoundland people. Once they did not like the Chinese people because we were very different. It is so difficult when you do not speak the language. Newfoundland people really like to go out and drink and dance, and often the men and women do that together; but the Chinese don't like that so much. I like to dance but my husband don't like it, so we cannot enjoy that together.

My kids really like to listen to me talk of when I was young in China and in Hong Kong, but if I do not tell them, and if not much happens here like in China, they loose their culture. In 1983 I took Richard and Michelle to my home in Canton where I was born. Richard did not like it so much, but Michelle spoke Chinese and she enjoyed the stores and my family. I think it's too late when they are older to learn the Chinese way of life. A few years ago I taught my two daughters and a friend's two daughters a Chinese dance for the Chinese New Year celebrations. I made the dress for the dance just like in China because I know the dress they use for each dance, but when the Chinese New Year was over everything went back to the way it was. That's not so good.

Today I wish I could teach like I did in China. I really enjoyed the work in the Hong Kong schools, and I really enjoy the dance. The government tells you lots of reasons why you should come over, but I wish now I thought about it more before I come. I think some day I got to move to Toronto because there the Chinese culture is strong. They got a Chinese school and Chinese books and they learn when they are very young the Chinese culture. I hope the government will do more for the Chinese people. I know every year they give some money to help celebrate the New Year but they could help us more, especially with the new people who come in and do not speak English but must work right away.

Agnes Marion Ayre

1990 Profile
Janet Miller talks with Marian about her mother
Born Agnes Miller on Ground Hog Day,
February 2, 1890 in St. John's, she was educated
at Bishop Spencer College. Ayre, an avid gar-
dener and painter, was a founding member of the
Newfoundland Art Society. The Agnes Marion

Ayre Herbarium was built upon her collection of watercolours and pressed specimens of wildflowers of Newfoundland. Ten of her 1,800 original paintings appeared in the 1990 A Woman's Almanac.

❦ ❦ ❦

*M*y earliest memories of my mother are those of her sketching while the rest of us played on the beach. St. John's was almost like country then and in the summertime we lived out at Murray's Pond which was really countryish. It was great fun growing up with my mother. My cousin called her Gossy which I guess is short for Agnes; she'd say, it's always an adventure when you go with Gossy. And it was.

Mother didn't have a certain time of year she preferred. She liked all the seasons. On Saturdays we'd often go to Shea Heights; we'd take the streetcar past the railway station almost to Waterford Bridge Road and walk up, that was the best part. There was a beaver pond up there and we'd have a winter picnic. In those days you could light a fire outside and she'd take out the kettle and frying pan from her knapsack and we'd have a hot drink with sausages or something. That was beautiful countryside then. It wasn't just my brothers and I who went on these hikes, but lots of our school friends and their dogs and goats!

Many of the women of that time had been overseas in England or France as VAD's in the First World War, so they had to find things to occupy themselves after they'd seen a bit of the world. Mother was a lifelong member of the Current Events Club and the Ladies Reading Room and campaigned vigorously for votes for women in the 1920's. More than once they got the time-worn remark from men to "go home and bake your bread."

In many ways Mother was a self-taught botanist. Mrs. Jenny Knowling, who came from Wales saw the need for a list of Newfoundland wildflowers. She asked Agnes to paint the specimens she collected. Unfortunately, Mrs. Knowling was unable to continue and the illustrator also became the collector— a monumental task for someone who had never studied Latin or scientific Botany. When she had collected and painted enough material for a book she took it to the Gray Herbarium in Boston. There it was verified and classified by Dr. Fernald, the eminent authority on North American flora— he was quite impressed. Only one section of this vast collection was printed privately by L. Reeve and Company, Botanical Publishers. Unfortunately, colour was too expensive back then and all the colour had to be washed off her paintings. The remaining specimens were stored and are now at Memorial University, in the Herbarium named after her.

More than once we went up to Labrador on the old Kyle, that's the boat that is now rusting away at the head of Harbour Grace Harbour.

When the Kyle stopped to let off a passenger en route to North West River, mother would get off the boat and go looking for rare flowers. The Captain had to blow the whistle several times before she returned on board.

One weekend the family's meat supply was locked in her car at the Railway Station because she had dashed off to Clarenville to botanize. It was not unusual to get a call late at night to be told she was stuck on some back road where she had gone hunting for flowers. Once she called to say she was leaving for St. Anthony on the next boat which happened to be in thirty minutes. Her car was found on the dock with the engine still running. Often as the family drove along she would cry "Stop the car! I see a ... ". Many were the bogs waded through in search of some flower seen a hundred feet back. Her collection was added to by friends and acquaintances who brought her specimens found on their walks and fishing trips. In 1936, Mr. Andrew Murray found a white iris while fishing in Deer Park. This was the first of its kind recorded here and it was named Iris Murryanna.

My mother was from a small family. They would sometimes go to Scotland with her father to see his sisters and brothers. Her brother died in the first war, that only left a sister. They were very close. My aunt called her Bully and my sister-in-law thought it was because she was two years older and bossed her around, but I said, no, it was because her father used to sing folk songs and nursery rhymes to them and he said she sang like a bull bird. I looked it up and found it is a seabird with a high pitch.

Mother loved her vegetable and flower garden. In it as well as the annuals, she had lavender, gooseberries, Jerusalem artichokes, heather mint, savory, chives and dandelions for salads. We ate a lot of artichoke soup or just with a sauce. It had a nice smoky taste. She was interested in history and folklore and would tell us tales about the trees that keep fairies away. She knew what plants kept away flies and those that cured cuts and coughs. Although her main hobby was painting and drawing she had a great interest in history and corresponded with people from England, Portugal and St. Pierre about the origin of Newfoundland dogs, Labrador retrievers and unusual Newfoundland names—there were the Basque tombstones in Placentia to see and draw and whatever was the origin of the designs painted over the doors in Branch?

The year before she died she'd been in hospital in Toronto and the winter before that she'd been in hospital in England with cancer. I was eighteen then. My mother was always interested in landscapes but if she painted something that didn't come off as well as the real thing, she'd tear it up and put it in the garbage. Hers was a lively mind and although the only value she put on her work was the enjoyment it gave to herself and others, because of it she has left me and many others with wonderful memories.

10

Suzanne Blake

1992 Profile
Original interview by Cathy Porter

Suzanne Blake was born in St. John's in 1964. Music and sports have been the big influences in her life. Her father, Harold Stanley, was a professional senior hockey player. The family eventually settled in Grand Falls where he played with The Cataracts and worked at the paper mill. Suzanne's mother, Maxine, is a well-known musician, who directs choirs and teaches piano and voice privately in the Grand Falls area. Suzanne studied music at Mount Allison University in New Brunswick, and then Journalism at Carleton University in Ottawa. She began her Journalism career as a radio sportscaster in Charlottetown, Prince Edward Island. Later she became the Sportscaster with CBC radio in St. John's making her the first woman to hold that position on a permanent basis. There is only one other female sportscaster with CBC radio in all of Canada. In 1991 Suzanne Blake was the first woman to host a national world junior hockey broadcast on CBC radio. In December 1991 she covered the world junior hockey championship in Fussen, Germany. In January 1992 she moved to Toronto to be the new host of national morning sports.

GORD JOHNSTON PHOTOGRAPHY

❦　❦　❦

Growing up, my life was very much involved with music. At school I excelled in music—all my awards were in music—I don't have any athletic trophies at all, simply because there wasn't time. The sports I was interested in were things like figure skating or tennis—things that don't get as much attention as if I played hockey, or if I was a really good softball player. When people said "Suzanne Blake" they did not think of athletics.

I wanted to go to Mount Allison to study because it had a really good music department. I really enjoyed my four-year music degree there, but by going I realized I wasn't going to be a music teacher in the school system, and I wasn't going to be Artur Rubinstein. So I said, what do I do now?

While I was doing my music degree, I had worked at CBC stations home in Grand Falls and in Halifax in the summers. I thought maybe something would come of that, so I went to Carleton University and did my honours degree in Journalism. I decided to do this as my career, but my music is always with me.

11

In our radio course at Carleton, everyone got a "beat." I, of course, wanted arts and entertainment—as did half the class—but only two people could do it. I wasn't one of them. Then the sports beat came up and I said, "well, I guess I can do that." I went out with a football player, Peter Blake, at Mount Allison, who I ended up marrying. I also played tennis and figure skated. My dad was a hockey player, so I'd have a clue at least. I put up my hand. I was the only one who did, so I got the sports beat! And that's how it started.

Sports journalism is really fun because it doesn't feel like work—I get to go to hockey games! I felt a little uncomfortable at first, because it's an area I hadn't dealt with before, and I was expected to know exactly what I was talking about. In most cases, I do know exactly what I'm talking about, but there's always that doubt because I wasn't a star hockey player growing up. But I read a lot and I ask a lot of questions. I ask Peter questions all the time when we're sitting at home, and I ask my father questions about things I'm not accustomed to, like hockey strategy.

I feel more and more comfortable as a sports reporter, but it's the kind of thing—especially where you're a woman—where you don't get confidence from anyone else but yourself. Nobody says what a great job you're doing, except your mom, and she does it as often as she can. It's the kind of work where you have to get your own confidence within you and say, "maybe I did a good job today," or "I really know what I'm talking about." It's the same as if I covered legal or medical issues; we don't all go into it knowing everything there is to know. But it is a lot of fun!

As a woman in sports reporting, what you say and what you think doesn't necessarily hold as much water as if it came from a male mouth. When you think about it, that doesn't make any sense because they don't grow up knowing any more about sports than we do.

I remember when I first got my job as a sports reporter, a boyfriend of a friend of mine just didn't think I could do it, and he was quite adamant that I not take it. That's about the only time I've gotten upset about my position, but it only made me more determined to forge ahead. You just go out and do your job and prove them wrong.

In P.E.I. I would be the only sports journalist that the coaches called "dear," because I was the only woman. I very rarely go in dressing rooms. I've been asked to go in—that's not a problem, but I find the players are more than willing to come out to me, and I can get a better interview because it's one-on-one. So that's probably the only difference I find ... I have to wait a little longer because I don't go into the dressing room with the "boys"—the other media guys.

Perhaps the only other disadvantage is that I'm not "one of the boys," so I'm not down at the bar hanging around with them on Friday or Saturday nights, and I don't play in their league, so sometimes I don't get all the inside information. So, it's a little different, but hey, I stick out in a crowd, and then I get singled out, usually for good reasons, so it balances out. But you sort of have to watch your step, and I always try to make doubly sure that what I'm saying is correct, because I know twice as many people will be ready to jump on me, if I'm wrong, than if I was a male sportscaster—that's been my experience anyway.

Cassie Brown

1988 Profile
This story, told through interviews between Marian and Cassie's daughter, Christine, exemplified the truth that Cassie Brown's contribution to Newfoundland literature is as enduring as the sea.

Born into the Horwood merchant family at Rose Blanche, Newfoundland on January 10, 1919, Cassie Brown identified with the sea at an early age. As a teenager, Brown was an avid reader and wrote fiction and radio plays. A five-time winner of the provincial Arts and Letters Competition, she was also involved in amateur drama with the St. John's Players, a group that awarded her honourary membership and adapted two of her radio plays to stage.

Cassie Horwood married Donald F. Brown in 1945 and had two children, Derek and Christine. She wrote a weekly column for The Daily News from 1959-66. Between 1962 and 1965 she also wrote for, edited and published her own magazine, St. John's Woman, that later became Newfoundland Woman. After reading Joey Smallwood's Book of Newfoundland she became interested in the 1914 sealing diaster in which seventy-eight men froze to death. A fifteen minute story for one of her Newfoundland history radio dramatizations became the groundwork for her first book, Death on the Ice, the success of which was phenomenal. Published by Doubleday, it sold 100,000 copies between 1972 and 1980. On September 23, 1987 Cassie Brown was inducted into the Newfoundland and Labrador Hall of Fame.

In 1976 Brown, an honourary member of the Newfoundland Writers Guild, published her second book, A Winter's Tale: The Wreck of the Florizel, and followed with Standing Into Danger in 1979. Just before her death on December 30, 1986 she completed her fourth book, an autobiography, Who Is Amalthea, as yet unpublished.

🐢 🐢 🐢

$\mathcal{M}$y mother was always writing, and as a child I thought that a boring way to pass your days. I used to tell myself I didn't want to be like my mother in that way and she never pushed it on me. She would say, "You do what you want but I *have* to write. It's in my bones, my molecules and my atoms." She was not only an inspiration to her family but to the public as well. She was a teacher and wrote about what she learned. Because of this she was always secure with herself since she didn't know how to be anything else but that.

I wanted to write music and my mother believed in me so much that she would continually say there would be nothing I couldn't do if I really wished it. She spent hours teaching me how to carry a tune because I couldn't sing and yet I wanted to. I don't think I really appreciated how much patience that took then, but today I look back and admire her even more for that.

My mother felt honoured to be chosen to write books about sea diasters, even though she was sometimes unwell while doing the research. If someone asked why she was writing what some considered a man's book she would say she felt she could do justice to it, and that she did not choose the book but that the book chose her. "It was as though these men who had already passed over to the other side were saying *Gotcha!* I was there. I was on the ice with those men," she would exclaim. Sometimes I would get up and leave when she talked like this, but other times I would stay in total fascination of this woman who called herself "the sea."

It was my mother's unlimited thought that allowed her to write such books as *Death on the Ice*. Her power came from her pen; there she felt the sea—spiritually, physically and mentally. She saw the sea as a whole, as a being that she could talk to and feel it answer her. She would come back from a walk by the sea sparkling, because she too had become one with it. Cassie would carry beach rocks in her car so as to have some of this sea energy with her when she drove about. Whenever questioned about it she would look surprised and say, "But you know I love the sea, and these rocks are of the sea, and so am I; these rocks have a life of their own and so do I." I would sometimes tell my mother that I thought she sustained her life by writing about the sea. She had an anaemic condition, and believed the sea had great healing power. After she finished writing her three most serious books, her anaemic condition had balanced itself out, strange but true. "I am too tough to surrender to the unknown," she would say. Her awareness of her task in life was so strong that she couldn't surrender "until the last word I have to write is written."

Cassie Brown seemed to have this great understanding of *why* things happen the way they do. She taught me how to contact that inner being within myself which took a great deal of patience; I was very rebellious. I was a slow learner and mom was an amazing teacher as well as my best friend. I had no other way of learning except by listening to her and

14

learning through her. I'm sure a lot of the diaster in her life was transmitted into her books because there is something about her disaster writing that was very healing, not only for her but for all who read her books. It was a part of her basic philosophy to turn the negative into positive and to transmit her frustrations into something creative. This was precious to me in my earlier years because I learned to write about inspirational things and I knew that if I wrote about things that were really upsetting me, I'd recognize the cause within myself. Writers, she believed, needed to accept this process and go with the flow.

My mother travelled on the sea and nearly drowned in Rose Blanche when she was about five years old. As a child she was drawn to the sea and would lie down on the wharf and look into its depths. However, she was not allowed to go near the wharf alone. One day her fascination drew her further from her home until she found herself on the dock. She started to sweep the dock to justify being there and before she knew it, swept herself right into the sea. Although none of the fishermen could swim a stroke, they formed a human chain to rescue her. What Cassie remembered of this near-drowning incident was the size of the pillars beneath the surface that kept the dock afloat!

My mother felt she had to write for Newfoundland, yet in the same breath she also felt the environment here limited her. Cassie could see that Newfoundland women had a lot of colour and had colourful stories to tell if someone was interested enough to listen. Mom was interested. There were many heroic things that happened here, but people would just tell of them as though they were commonplace. She could see they weren't.

Cassie Brown was very non-judgemental and for that reason didn't care what other people thought. She would discuss astrology with her sister, Joan, and thoroughly enjoy their different viewpoints on the why and how of things. Cassie's destiny was to be one with her universal mind, her God-source, and in that sense she very much fulfilled herself on earth.

Mother believed she was here to touch people and she did that through her books. She was mythological in many ways, and talked of carrying around a picture in her mind of this great, great teacher that she believed is in all of us, that is in the wind, and that tests us. She would say, "I'm having a mad love affair with my greater self, that greater self who gave me life!"

Sketch by Janice Udell

15

Lois Brown

1992 Profile
Interview by
Marian Frances White
Lois Brown, the eldest in a family of three, was born in Corner Brook on June 24, 1956. She lived in Corner Brook, Botwood, and Edmonton before moving to St.John's with her family. Brown attended Booth Memorial High School. She studied drama at the University of Alberta and in 1980 enroled in Memorial University to complete her B.Ed. In the mid eighties, she became involved in Neighbourhood Dance Works and began performing her own material in such shows as Cleaning up the house and Cult of the Personality. She taught theatre and literature for six years at Prince of Wales Collegiate. In 1990, she completed her master's thesis, and is now trying to recover her creative spirit.

ॐ   ॐ   ॐ

I remember once staying in Corner Brook with my grandmother for the entire summer. I was no more than five. We ate lunch at a table in her garden. Not a lawn table, a real table. The best part was she let me wear hot pink nail polish "as long as you don't tell your father." Nana and Pop Burt lived in a wonderful world of secrets, stories and weird ornaments, and clocks and hatches. They were so proud of me for no reason at all. I loved them with all of my five-year-old heart, and cried and cried not to have to leave when my parents came to get me at the end of the summer.

At home things were often strict and serious, especially on Sundays. Dad was the one great refreshing thing in the midst of it all. He is an independent thinker. So any given Sunday, he usually objected to the sermon; repudiated something in the Bible, and finally disagreed with something he had just said himself. From the time I could speak, he asked me to give my opinion on just about every idea that came into his head, even though that was almost always the beginning of a long, loud argument. He took me trouting.

His mother, Granny Brown, was a preacher in the Salvation Army. Granny Brown's house was always in a streel, like her long dark hair, which according to the Army tradition of the time, had never been cut. Both my father and I had sat in our own separate childhoods, watching

16

her braid and twirl her hair into a bun and clip it in place. She never seemed to care that her hair, like the continually accumulating stuff in her house, was soon all over the place.

In contrast, my own mother seemed almost obsessed with housework. She told me once she wishes that keeping the house spotlessly in order had not seemed so important to her. She wished she had spent more time with me and my two brothers, when we were children. I think we would have liked that, because my mom is full of play. She likes to say to me in her prophetic way, "Wait till you read my diary." My mom keeps a diary which I like to imagine contains ALL the secrets and mysteries. And I guess it really is the key to a lot of things that I still don't understand about my mother and myself. I've hit that age where I remember back, find myself—a part of myself—and console and coax the child-me to grow up.

It is my mother who taught me to appreciate a shiny glass and shirts, ironed and wrinkleless. One of the first things I created for Neighbourhood Dance Works was called *Cleaning up the house*. In it my character Laureen protests: "And vistors. I had the furniture completely wrapped in saran and they still took a chair as an open invitation to sit down. I had to have it all hauled to Robin Hood Bay and incinerated." In *Dancing on the Roof*, it was for my mother that I hung sparkling clothes and scarfs, postcards, valentines, and books on a clothesline stretching upwards through a LSPU Hall sun-set into a starscape, and asked the audience to believe with me that when I pulled on this clothesline, I was sending these ordinary things on into the universe.

With *Dancing on the Roof* I started to, not "think of," but "apprehend" a completeness in physical reality. I always sensed lots of subjective realities creating big archetypal realities—like a whole bunch of theme parties. But now, I SAW that chairs and grass and sky exist with a singularity that has nothing to do with chairness, grassness, or skyness ... BUT alas ALAS just for a micro-moment. Like my character Irene winding her way through the confusion with her toothbrush in her boot, usually I still wondered "Am I the only one in this hospital of life suffering from excess interpretation and hooked up to an IV bag of meaning?"

I honestly think there is meaning and a GOD-GODDESS-force, but the explanations, and even the visions, I come on are barely satisfying. Sometimes, I have put the force of all my efforts and attitudes into peering through a fog, only to use myself up in not seeing at all. Sometimes I look at something so intensely, the looking creates chaos rather than clarity. I forget what I'm doing, get tired or unhappy with what I have, and end up looking at my shoes. The good thing is my shoes have become very clear to me.

Okay. I'm 34 years old. I don't have any children of my own. Obviously, I would know if I did, although I have always had a rather tenuous grip on reality. And that tenuous grip—trying to get a hold of what amounts to a whole lot of shimmering colours—makes me one of the crowd. On the other hand, the fact that I'll admit to tenuous-gripping at the slightest provocation makes me one of those people you'd rather not sit next to on an airplane. But hey, this is a break-through year and I have come to think of the tenuous grasp as flexibility. Like my character in *Inside Stories*, I, too, "am reaching a higher degree of flexibility and acceptance. Anybody says anything to me I say, 'Whatever ... '

'Tea or Coffee?'
'Whatever.'
'Supper at six?'
'Whatever.'
'Logic has it's transcendental root in primordial subjectivity.'
'Whatever.'

In *Inside Stories*, I was a businesswoman pushed unwilling out of the egg-shaped womb of a giant woman, re-born, briefcase in hand.

In the nick of time, Tetley has put eggs and tea together, introducing a round teabag, the feminist teabag. At last, we can finally have a politically-correct cup of tea.

I taught at PWC for about six years. I struggled to provide a situation in which students could have power and be caring. I challenged my students with the opportunity to be autonomous; they challenged me right back. When Ken Tizzard was a student of mine, he underscored the central tenet of my teaching; he told me "Don't underestimate the importance of having an adult take you seriously." My students taught me to take their failures as serious attempts to achieve success. Then, I learned to encourage them to accept failure as part of a process that directs us to re-examine the question and come up with a better solution.

This is a gut-wrenching, mind-boggling, heart-rending process. Last year, I had THE EXPERIENCE when one of my thesis' readers demanded a complete re-write. As I read Geertz's famous writing on the Balinese cock-fight as recommended, I racked my brain to figure out what my reader thought this had to do with collective creation in the high school. I was completely confused and the same time furiously re-writing. I had help, but in the end I had to decide that my story about teaching was worthwhile enough to tell in a way that was acceptable, as well as comprehensible, to both me and, since I knew very little about my rejecting reader, any other. I finished re-writing. My thesis was better. My rejecting reader accepted it and commended me for peering into what could have initially appeared only a frightening fog. I guess fog is another recurring theme in my life.

Of course, being a sixth generation Newfoundlander, fog is cultural as well as thematic, and good for the complexion .... I always figured that's just because no one can see you.

My favourite memory is standing at night looking down at the stars reflected in a rippleless pond with a friend I love. My favourite memory is looking up at an egg moon with my best friend, so that now, when we see an egg moon, it is for us the return of that first egg moon. My favourite memory is Jeff saying that star is out to lunch.

I continue to choose between life as epic and scientific ... or as momentary and ecstatic ... or as getting out of and staying in bed.

LINDA BODDIE

Joy Burt

1988 Profile
Interview by Marian Frances White
A native of Corner Brook, Joy Burt was born November 4, 1956. She completed high school education at Herdman Collegiate and went on to trades school. She later attended Sir Wilfred Grenfell College, and while there began weight training. Burt, however, did not do any powerlifting until 1985 when she moved to St. John's to complete a B.A. degree at Memorial University. A single mother with one daughter, Emily, Burt lives on a set income and has to meet the extra costs involved in obtaining world class powerlifting equipment.

From the beginning of her powerlifting career, Burt has caused a stir because she competed in open competitions and in her very first competition came in second. The road to a world championship in most sports is a long one; in powerlifting you have to qualify for the national team, and then it's fairly direct. Burt more than qualified. At the Canadian Powerlifting Championships in January 1987 she won the title with a total combined lift of 908 pounds.

Burt was named 1986 Provincial Athlete of the Year. In May '87, in Perth, Australia, she became the World Powerlifting Champion when she lifted 402.25 pounds, setting a Canadian and Commonwealth record in the 56 kilo class. In 1989 Joy won a Gold Medal at the World Games.

On Sunday, May 31, 1992, Joy added to her already impressive trophy collection when she was awarded the Gold Medal for her class (56 kilo), at the World Powerlifting Championship held in Gent, Belgium. On Friday, May 29, she lifted 198 lbs. in the Bench Press, 457¼ lbs. in the Deadweight and 380 lbs. in the Squat, for a total of 1035 lbs. In accomplishing this Joy set a new world

*record and two Canadian records. Pound-for-pound Joy Burt is the strongest
woman in the world! She has set no limitations on her avocation, powerlifting.*

🍎   🍎   🍎

*W*omen's interest in powerlifting is growing, perhaps because it's a relatively new area for women to discover their strengths and capabilities. I never thought of myself as a competitive person, but once I saw the possibilities I wanted to see what others were doing and I wanted to improve my lifts. Most of the women I meet in these competitions are not tied down by the more traditional way of life, though there are those who like that too. I've met women who are lawyers, Olympic weight lifters, doctors, and many, like myself, who are still going to university.

I was brought up fairly traditionally and probably would have been someone entirely different if I hadn't come to St. John's. That changed a lot for me, not just as a powerlifter but in my life as well. The period in which I was brought up and went to school was one when attitudes and roles were slowly changing. A lot of people my age were thinking along the lines of marriage and children, but I resisted marriage until I was twenty-two and that seemed really late to most people. I wasn't married long, however, when I decided that was not for me. I had a baby right away so something positive came out of that experience. Emily is one of the best things that ever happened to me.

I could see education was a route to independence and my parents were very supportive while I went through all these changes. I'm not saying that education is the only way, but I think you have to have something so that you're not dependent on a man for your fulfilment. If you don't, there is little hope of doing things for yourself, or doing things that you really like to do. Most of my classmates are between eighteen and twenty-two. Somedays they ask, "How can you do this? How can you do weight lifting and go to university full time and raise a child?" I'm not sure sometimes—especially when I see that the most they have to do is go to school—but perhaps I'm motivated to go on because of what I've already seen. I certainly don't have much time for knitting or baking bread by the time I get home and get our supper and do assignments, but it's all a matter of what you see as a priority in your life.

Training is not something you can do by yourself. My coach, Walt Forsey, is there to make sure I lift properly so I don't get muscle injuries. The coach's job is a pretty important one. While training as a powerlifter, I don't get into all these protein body building supplements. I eat lots of carbohydrates and I've given up junk food. I think after you hit thirty junk food and bodies don't do well together anyway. I usually train five pounds overweight so that I have lots of energy, and if I should get sick I still have some reserve. Powerlifting is a lot of hard work, I train two or three hours every day, and I train strictly drug free. Drugs make you aggressive and give you the feeling of having more strength; that's why people fall into taking them. I consider them dangerous because we don't really know their side effects; there hasn't been enough research done over an extended period of time, yet amphetamines and steroids are already known to cause liver damage and hepatitis. That's enough for me!

When I'm in training I don't like to think about the actual competition a lot; I just try to concentrate on doing better each time I lift. There's a lot of pressure in this sport, pressure to repeat the great lifts you did in the last competition. Some days it's hard to get up psychologically for the training. Physically your body might be perfect, but mentally it's tough to always put your head in that space. That's also why people use drugs, to build up their mental power, and that's why you need a good coach to keep you motivated.

The people I train with are not intimidated when I work out, but I've found people in general have a strange attitude toward you. You get jokes thrown at you and everybody expects you to be this *humongous* person who has to turn sideways to get through the door! I've always played team sports like soccer, but when you move on to a sport where you're by yourself the focus shifts. It's just you and you know you're responsible for whatever happens out there.

A lot of people say that local powerlifters are getting so much publicity lately because I'm a woman. I don't deny that much has changed since women got involved, but I think the changes have been for the better. Some people think it's odd work for a woman, but I try not to let what other people think bother me. Sometimes you get a photographer who wants you to lift some guy to prove how strong you are, or who wants you to wear these fancy outfits body builders wear—which I don't—but outside of competition I don't feel I have to prove anything. That's not what powerlifting is about—it's about strength. I tell myself I'm not lifting for those people, I'm lifting for myself, because it means something for me. More than being chosen as champion, what really matters is that I'm enjoying what I'm doing. It's nice to be recognized, and it's nice that people think you're the best in the world, but when I see another competitor beside me I see what she's doing as great as well. To me it seems you win if you do better at that competition than you did before.

I'd like to continue powerlifting for quite a long time yet. Each year the best lifter is chosen at a competition and last year the best lifter was forty-two, so I've got a few competitions ahead of me yet. I don't think you can say that careers and sports, or virtually anything for that matter, are specifically for a man or a woman. I see it as finding something you enjoy doing and accepting that challenge no matter what the obstacles might be.

Moya Nora Cahill

1992 Profile
Original interview by Maura Hanrahan
Moya Nora Cahill was born January 10, 1961 in St.John's. Moya did her early schooling at Pius X, Belvedere and Holy Heart. At Memorial University she studied under the co-operative engineering program, specializing in naval architecture and marine engineering. She worked in Norway for two years in the offshore oil sector and in Montreal she was part of the management team responsible for the construction of a magnesium plant in Quebec. She is now president of her own engineering company, MNC Consultants Ltd. Moya speaks both French and Norwegian fluently. She lives in St. John's with her husband Paul Gaudet.

ẽ ẽ ẽ

*E*ngineering is not the first thing a girl thinks about doing because peer pressure is geared more towards home economics. Home Economics was taught at Holy Heart High School; biology for people who were interested in the sciences and chemistry for people who were going into nursing. When we were going to Holy Heart the school didn't offer a physics program and we had to get over twenty-five girls who were interested in order to make it feasible for them to put off a program.

I was always interested in how things worked, why they worked and the mechanisms behind them so I knew that engineering was what I wanted to do. It also came from my family background. My father had his own company even though he is not an engineer; he's an electrician. So I was brought up in a contractor's home; always listening to my father talk about bids and tendering, the unions and whatnot. So I guess I got involved that way.

I remember looking back to my grade nine yearbook. They asked what were your ambitions. I said "mechanical engineer" and underneath they said "probable fate: greaser." One thing about it, if I say I'm going to do something, if I tell enough people, I know I have to do it. So I had already committed myself to engineering and I was going to go ahead with it. My poor mother was heartbroken. She would say "Now you're sure you don't want to do nursing"?

We started out with one hundred and twenty people in our class and out of those, twelve of us were females. That was quite a lot compared to the previous years. Of those twelve, four had been in my physics class at

22

Holy Heart. After the first two years they were all gone and I was the only one left.

It's terrible to say, but because you are female you have to work harder in a male-dominated world. It's a very different setting because all my life I went to school with girls and I didn't know how to interact with guys. The engineering school is renowned for its rowdiness and drinking and partying, but I didn't get a lot of sexism from the guys and not even from the professors. I didn't consider that a problem at Memorial. The problem was how to react and where to draw the line: should you go out with the boys or should you stay home and study? I got involved a lot with the Engineering Society, organizing things and being on the board. I got involved with the pubcrawls and the beer bashes; that's how I felt was the best way to get through the program.

The boys were raunchy though, they were. When they had a stripper in I didn't agree with that. I didn't watch it, I left. I didn't condone it and I would say "Okay boys I don't think this is a great idea." It was really tacky. Every engineering work site I've been to, they always have pictures of nude women. I don't know why. You are not going to change them overnight.

In school there was almost no problem being female. In the workforce the biggest problems were the facilities; for example, they couldn't hire you because there were no female bathrooms. So I didn't care, I would say "I'm coming in," they would all scatter and I would put someone on guard at the door.

Now I work eighteen hours a day, every single night I'm here at the office, but I'm happy, I love it. It's really only since the announcement of Hibernia that I started getting back involved with the St.John's industry. I knew the only place I could make a change within the industry was to do it in Newfoundland. Here it's small enough that you can be responsible for small changes. I thought this was somewhere I could put a little bit of me back into the industry. I want to get involved with training New-foundlanders how to transfer technology so they can work on the site and start to develop their own expertise rather than having the French, English and the Americans come in and say "Well, in Texas we do it like this." There are a lot of technical environmental issues which have to be dealt with in Newfoundland. What are we going to do with our harbours for example? Is it worthwhile to put in treatment plants or recycling plants here?

Right now I have four people working for me. I have others working with me on joint ventures in Quebec, Halifax, France and Britain. If you come and talk to me next year I will probably have thirty people in this office because these things are really starting to blossom here. I've got fifteen things happening right now. I'm looking at developing training programs for oil spill response which is a two million dollar venture. I'm on a roll now and I don't see the roll stopping for quite sometime.

JANETTE LAANING

Charlene Caines

1992 Profile
Original interview by Marg Penney
Charlene Caines was born in St. Anthony, on Newfoundland's Northern Peninsula in 1967. She grew up, one of four children, in a single parent family. (Her father passed away when she was young.) At age six she became permanently blind as a result of an accident. Caines studied at the Halifax School for the Blind for five years and returned to Plum Point to complete High School. She has studied English at Memorial University of Newfoundland and later took computer software courses at Key-In Technical College, as well as Electronics at the Cabot Institute. She works at the CNIB as a Technical Services Counsellor doing both inventory and computer consulting. Caines is a single parent to a five year old son. She is also on the Board of Iris Kirby House, a shelter for battered women and children, and was instrumental in forming the Action Committee on Accessibility to Transition Centres.

ẽ ẽ ẽ

I found the school system in rural areas of this Province more accommodating to a blind person. Being so far away in the boondocks my teachers did a lot of work over and above their jobs because there were no teaching assistants like they have in St. John's. I studied subjects like biology, geology, physics and chemistry which have lots of diagrams and charts. Because I couldn't see, the teachers would have to take a pizza wheel and draw them backwards on paper so they'd be tactile. People have some bizarre feeling that blind people can't do sciences. I was the first totally blind person to be integrated into and graduate from the school system in Newfoundland.

I came to St. John's when I was seventeen to go to University and I studied English because I was bored and didn't know what else to do. I was more interested in partying and meeting people than studying, like everybody else who comes in from a rural area. I found the University much more resistant; they wouldn't let me take math or honours french. If I had 20/20 vision I would have studied the sciences, not the arts.

24

Right now I'm most interested in computers. I take computers apart and carry screwdrivers in my purse to change computer cards. What I do is mainly electrical, more like a computer technician. There are about fifteen people who do what I do across the country and I'm the only female as well as the first totally blind person to work in this area. We have national conferences to keep in touch. I've gone to Halifax to get recertified in Xerox Kurzweil Imaging Systems and to Toronto to do a four week technical training course, so it's a continuous challenge which I like.

Blindness can be a perceived disability in my repair work when dealing with sighted people because they don't think I can do it. When I'm setting up cables and plugging things in, they get nervous. So that's a big problem, but it's not a big thing. As long as the system is turned off and the batteries taken out, no one is going to get fried. Once you pop the top on a computer system, there's a motherboard and accompanying boards with some outlets, the power supply, hard drive and a few controls and cables. There was some resistance to my working with computers initially, especially since it's not something people want a woman doing anyway.

I like what I'm doing but I don't want to work with the CNIB for the rest of my life. I'd like to mainstream a bit more. I got involved with access to Transition Shelters, when I realized the obstacles in the way for people with specific needs. The building in St. John's was not accessible. I kept thinking that if I were in a battering situation, accessibility should not prevent me from getting into Kirby House. Finally, we were successful in obtaining money and implementing a game plan and the money; we had to widen doors, enlarge the bathroom and make ramps. A TDD machine (Telephone Device for the Deaf) has been donated by Taxation Canada, so communication is not as big an issue as it was before. The long term goal is to cover all the areas of accessibility and communication, but the immediate obvious needs were to make it wheelchair accessible. The changes necessary for a visually impaired person are mostly lighting.

There's not a lot you need to do for a totally blind person. I mean, I don't have a specially designed apartment. If I'm at a friend's home, the first thing I'll do if I'm cooking supper is ask how their stove is laid out. If accessibility for blind people is part of the work to be done at Transition Shelters, they would have to adapt their kitchen by marking the buttons on the stove with something tactile.

Most of my time is taken up with work, or this "womanstuff" I'm doing now, or raising my little fella, Rick. I have my own apartment, just the two of us. My life is the same as any other single parent, I would think. The biggest problem is money, daycare and babysitters.

Attitudes about blindness can be a problem, but that can change. As I found at the Network Dinner, sponsored by the Provincial Advisory Council on the Status of Women, blindness is the most feared disability by sighted people because they find it hard to walk up to you and say, "Hi, how are you?" I would assume it's because the world is so visual and a blind person is perceived as having no appreciation of that visualness and therefore you figure they're not on the same plane as you. But that's not the reality because there's no problem about where you can't go or what you can't do. Blindness is not as confining as some other disabilities. Most people say "You're a strange person, you're a thumb in a land of fingers and you're not supposed to be here."

Some restrictions for all people are self-imposed, but that's a personality disability and a social disability, not a physical disability. If you don't have the guts to get up and do what you want that's a whole other problem. It comes down to what you'll accept and how far you can be pushed before you say, "Look I'm not going to take it any more." People will push you to the very bottom of the pile if you let them, whether you have a disability or not. I mean, how many people live and die with nothing. Nobody's going to do it for you, that's what I've learned. I think it just comes down to how badly you want something.

LINDA BODDIE

Mary Margaret Cantwell

1991 Profile
Interview by Marian Frances White
Mary Margaret Cantwell, nee Heffernan, was born on January 4, 1914 in Maddox Cove. She taught at the Cape Spear Lighthouse—the most easterly point in North America. Cantwell remained there for four years, earning fifteen dollars a month. She also taught for six years in Petty Harbour where she earned fifteen dollars a month. In 1941 she resigned teaching when she married Frank Cantwell since that was the tradition of that time. However, Margaret Cantwell taught their six children at home in the lighthouse until they went to boarding school in St. John's. In the mid sixties lighthouses began to be automated and in 1972, a year after her husband died, she took up permanent residence in the west end of St. John's.

🍏 🍏 🍏

I was delighted to be the one to teach the Cantwell children; that was long before I had Cantwell children of my own. I taught the children of the lightkeeper and the assistant lightkeeper. There were twenty-six rooms at the lighthouse and I used one of them for teaching.

By the mid thirties, schooling had changed a lot from when I was young. We had slates in Maddox Cove to write on and those awful slate pencils. We would bring a small bottle of water to school each day, shake it up and put soap in it to clean the slate after we used it. Thank goodness they were gone by the time I taught school. I couldn't bare the scratch of the slate pencil! After school they'd go out and play on the hills behind the lighthouse and in the Fall they'd pick berries. I loved picking berries with them and often I'd bring them home to my mother in Maddox Cove. I would go home most every weekend, and I didn't mind walking, though sometimes I'd get a ride on the horse and wagon. In the wintertime we had the horse and slide to help us get around.

Between teaching at the Cape and then six years in Petty Harbour, I spent a good ten years at it, and I loved every minute of it, but I didn't mind giving it up. I resigned teaching at Petty Harbour in June 1941 and was married September 25th of the same year to the man I met ten years earlier when I was the teacher of his nieces and nephews at the light station. You see, we couldn't keep on teaching when we got married. I'm delighted for the changes nowadays, you can teach and still have a family. My situation was a little different because I went back teaching my own children when they were ready for schooling.

When I returned to the Cape as a married woman, I found many changes. The Lightstation was the same routine, but the younger folks had moved to St. John's to work. Due to the outbreak of World War II there were buildings everywhere for wartime purposes and dwellings for the military. A fort which was started in late '39 was just about completed and big guns were put in place. They were only used a few times for testing. The remains of the guns are still there in the National Park. We had the advantage of attending church services on the fort or going to a movie using a special pass for admission.

Of course, we enjoyed all this while it lasted, but everything was dismantled when the war ended, except for the guns. The children were then too young to remember any of this, when they were old enough we explained why they had the benefit of a large playground, a swimming pool for summer days — it had been put there for the soldiers.

Besides teaching my four daughters and two sons, there were lots of things to keep you busy. We had sheep and we'd sheer them, card their wool and hang it on the line to bleach. We used a lot of it to make eiderdowns, we never bought anything like that. We hooked rugs from pieces of cloth that were no longer any good for anything else; we made quilts and some of the children's clothes.

27

The children were always told not to go too near the cliffs. They often tell me now things they did and of how my husband used to take them picking marshberries and cranberries down steep cliffs. They were used to living there and going to those places that others didn't dare, but even when I'd go out to pick berries with the children they'd call out, 'come down, there's loads of them here,' but I declined the invitation.

I was never nervous out at the Cape. Now I never liked wind, even when I was home in Maddox Cove. If I woke in the night and found that it was blowing hard, I'd be afraid to go back to sleep. I always had a dread of the wind and the ocean, still I looked at it all my lifetime. I had a few wakeful nights at the Lighthouse during storms. Once a big pole with high voltage that was running the lights and blew the whistle, fell over on the Whistle House. We lived up in the old Lighthouse then and with the force of the wind you couldn't open the doors to go in or out. Luckily we were quite a distance from the fog alarm building, but still the sparks and pieces of wood flew everywhere. All we did was stay away and put up until the wooden building was burned.

We always had a good supply of provisions put aside for the winter months like sacks of sugar and flour. I did all the cooking even when I was teaching my own children. See, when I first started with my children, I wasn't paid for it. I started to teach them as they came ready for say kindergarten and I'd teach them at the dinner table. Well now, my husband, Frank, always peeled the vegetables, he was a great help like that, yes.

There was never a dull moment. We took the children for car drives when we had time off, so we never felt isolated. By that time roads were greatly improved and we were only a short drive from the city.

The children did well in school, but by the time they got to grade eight and nine, I often worried if I was doing the right thing by having them there and not with other children in a regular school. I often woke at night thinking that Helena was getting to be a big girl. I'd say, I wonder should I have her in town going to school? And she didn't even want to go the evening she left. Once they were there, I don't think they minded it, you know. If it were my own feeling, I would feel right out of place but I don't think they did. I didn't find any of them a problem to teach, I really enjoyed it.

New modern homes were built for us in the early fifties and we moved from the old lighthouse, a short distance away but nearer to the fog-alarm building. Our eldest son became principal keeper when his father retired.

I'd go back there again if things were like they were then. I've gone back there now two summers for two weeks and last summer for three weeks. My husband didn't want to leave the Cape. When we finally did buy this house in St. John's, he didn't live to move in. All the family came in to town just after Christmas that year and we were to follow, but he took sick and never recovered. I felt sorry leaving in July 1972 after thirty years at Cape Spear as a teacher, wife and mother.

My life there was definitely a different life. A lot of the old things we had passed from one Cantwell family to another were stolen one day after we moved from the old lighthouse to the new one, but no one can take my memories, I have enough of them to last a lifetime.

Rosann Cashin

1989 Profile
Interview by Marian Frances White
Born Rosann Earle in St. John's, Newfoundland on Jan. 24, 1940, Rosann Cashin graduated from Our Lady of Mercy when she was fifteen. Cashin obtained a Bachelor of Arts degree from St. Francis Xavier University in Nova Scotia and an education degree from Mount St. Vincent University. She married Richard Cashin in Halifax where they had their first child, Heidi. When they returned to live in Newfoundland Cashin began what she terms her 'post-graduate education' in politics when her husband became a federal Member of Parliament. She returned to Newfoundland after he was defeated in the '68 election and began her media career in broadcasting and reporting. Cashin also produced such programs as The Morning Show, Radio Noon and On The Go. She was later honoured with awards for her research on such topics as Labrador: The Land We Gave Away. Cashin also worked for CJON as legislative broadcaster for the House of Assembly and was president of the Legislative Press Gallery for two terms.

Her successful media career continued until she was ousted from her job following the CBC technicians strike, organized by NABET. Cashin was told she was let go because her husband, who had been appointed a director of PetroCanada, was too high profile. She took the case to the Human Rights Commission and won two tribunals which stated she was discriminated against because of marital status. These decisions were later appealed. Several years later, she won her case in the federal courts.

❧   ❧   ❧

*M*y first memories are of St. John's during the Second World War. The blackouts imposed because of the war were extremely frightening for a

29

young child, but the succession of military people who came to my home made life very interesting. They told me stories about the war—about Hitler and the Allies. I can't remember a time when I wasn't politically aware. During the Confederation debates when I was eight years old I used to sit glued to the radio when the news was on. I rode my first two wheeled bike around Rawlin's Cross for days covered with Responsible Government posters and cried when Newfoundland joined Confederation.

The social activist atmosphere of St. Francis Xavier University had a lasting impact on how I think today. I was fifteen then and soaked it all up like a sponge. When I finished my degrees I was on my way to teach at a private girls school in Port-of-Spain, Trinidad. At the same time, I fell in love with and married Richard. When he entered politics I spent a lot of time in the House of Commons listening to the debates. Lots of political people came to my home and we would have great discussions about how politics works, how the bureau functions and how the press interprets it all. It was a time of minority government so I spent a lot of my time on the campaign trail. Life was too busy and too disjointed for me to consider other work since my time was divided between two cities—St. John's and Ottawa.

When we returned to Newfoundland I finally had time to consider my own career and began work with CBC. I was scared to death when I first went on air but I had had a lot of public speaking experience when I was President of the Parliamentary Spouses Organization in Ottawa, so I lost my jitters quickly. In the early seventies after the birth of my daughter, Maria, I moved to the newsroom at CJON TV and Radio. I acted as liaison between the Gallery and the Speaker, covering the Newfoundland Legislature and spent so much time reporting on politics that I was approached by a political party to run, but I declined.

The documentary programs I did when I returned to CBC Radio allowed me to indulge my interest in Newfoundland's economic situation. I did an historic and economic study of the development of Churchill Falls from its inception as a topic of conversation between Smallwood and the Rothchild's, to the tragic economic deal with Hydro Quebec when the resource was virtually given away.

After thirteen years in media work, my career came to an abrupt end when my husband was appointed to the Board of PetroCanada. CBC management said I could no longer broadcast because his profile was too high, particularly in the resource area. I found CBC's position ridiculous since there was no question of conflict of interest. After all PetroCanada was a crown corporation owned by all of us. The real bias, of course, for the CBC decision is what I've always called the "chattel syndrome." In other words professional women are not to be viewed as separate from their husbands, but somehow an extension of them. A rather unpalatable nineteenth century concept to be voicing near the end of the twentieth century, when two career families are so common.

The Canadian Human Rights Commission ruled that the CBC had discriminated against me on the basis of my marital status. However that decision was set aside by a review tribunal who agreed with the decision, but who said CBC were justified in doing so because of a possible public perception. In other words, institutionalizing public prejudice. The case went before the Federal Court of Canada and the Supreme Court as a Charter case. (Update on this case since this story was published in 1989: In 1990 the supreme court ruled in her favour. CBC was told that it would have to reinstate her position and pay her legal fees, as well as reimburse Cashin for all monies lost from wages.)

The one good, immediate thing that came out of being fired was that for the next few years I devoted a lot of my attention to my daughter who had never known me as a non-working mother. Eventually I found work with the Human Rights Association who were looking for someone to present a human rights program in the school system. More recently, I have been the Chair of the Board of Governors Snowden Centre at MUN. In the Fall of '87 I went to the University of Orissa, Bubaneshwan, India where we are doing communications and international development through video. We are teaching extension workers at the University of Orissa how to use video as an educational and developmental tool in their Extension work. When I left India I went to an elephant festival in Bangkok, Thailand with a friend of mine, Marget Davis. It was wonderful until we were riding one and were charged by another. Thanks to that I got to see Bangkok in a wheelchair—needless to say, I will never ride an elephant again!

My experiences have taught me a great deal and I've tried to impart what I have learnt onto my daughters. I find it incredible that some young women still in high school continue to think that a prince charming is going to come along and from then on everything is going to be wonderful. Eventually they will realize, as I have, that life presents unforeseen challenges to each of us.

Sketch by Janice Udell

31

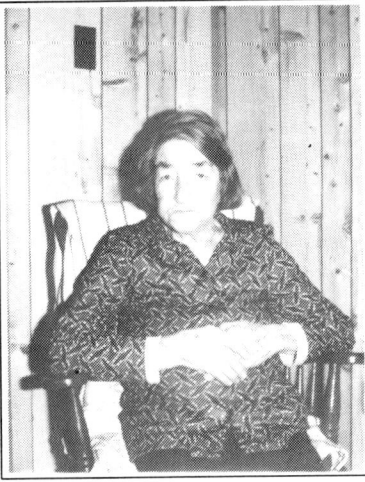

Constance Chrétien

1987 Profile
Original interview by
Marie-Annick Desplanques.
(The French written in this story is typical of the
Port au Port Peninsula.)

Constance Chrétien was born in Cape St. George
on June 14, 1913. The only girl among nine
children, her parents, Joseph Lainey and Marguerite Cornect, were francophone—one from
Acadia and the other from France. Like her
brothers, she did not have a chance to go to school
and although she does not know how to read or
write, she knows all the joys and pains of life out-
doors. She and her husband, Henri, had sixteen children, two of whom died
when young. While raising her children she also took care of the farm and of the
two cows while her husband was off to sea. In her leisure time she sings and
plays the accordion. She has been a widow for several years and now lives with
her granddaughter.

Constance Chrétien est née à Cap St. Georges le 14 juin 1913. Les parents de
Chrétien, Joseph Lainey et Marguerite Cornect, étaient francophone, l'un d'-
Acadie et l'autre de France. Elle était la seule fille parmi neuf enfants. Comme
ses frères, ell n'a guère eu la chance d'aller a l'école et bien qu'elle ne sache ni
lire ni ecrire, elle connait les joies et les peines de la vie au grand air. Constance
et Henri, son mari, ont eu sieze enfants, dont deux sont morts jeunes. Alors
qu'elle élvait ses enfants, elle s'occupait aussi de la ferme et des deux vaches,
pendant que son mari était a la pêche. Chrétein est veuve depuis plusieurs
années et vit maintenant avec sa petite fille.

🍂   🍂   🍂

I grew up in a French community, Cape St. George, and never heard
English spoken in my younger years. Most women around me worked on
the farms while men were out fishing, but I fished *and* farmed. I went
fishing in the morning and milked cows in the evening. I did everything
men did and when I would come back home, I had to do the housework
while my brothers relaxed. In those days women's life was much harder
than the men's life.

With all this work, there was not much time left for leisure, but
women would get together and spin. That was the time for stories too!
Some of us would card, some would spin, and some would knit. There
were no men, only us, only women. When we were finished we would
drink homebrew and joke around and I would play my accordion. I
learned to play that myself.

Franco-Terre Neuvienne

J'ai grandi dans le communaute francaise de Cap St. Georges. J'ai jamais entendu parler anglais quand j'étais jeune. Le plupart des femmes alentours travaillaient à la ferme pendant que les hommes pêchaient, mais moi je faisais les deux. J'allais à la pêche le matin et je tirais les vaches le soir. Je faisais tout pareil comme les hommes et quand je rentrais le soir, je faisais le ménage pendant que mes frères se reposaient. En ce temps là, la vie des femmes était bein plau dure que la vie des hommes.

Avec tout ce travail, il n'y avait guère de temps pour les loisirs. Mais les femmes se réunissaient pour les "fileries," et là elles contaient des contes aussi. Il y en avait qui cardaient d'autres qui filaient et qui brochaient. Il n'y avait pas d'hommes, rien que nous, les femmes. Quand on avait fini, on buvait du homebrew et on blaguait, et je jouait mon accordéon, j'ai appris ça moi-meme.

Dorothy Clarke

1990 Profile
Interview by Marian Frances White

LINDA BODDIE

Dorothy Clarke was born into the Antle family in St. John's on July 11, 1937. She lived in the Battery with her sister and brother and attended St. Joseph's School. Most of her summers were spent in Paradise where the air was considered drier for her mother who had tuberculosis. Clarke's mother died when she was six. Her family moved to Paradise when she was fourteen; however, they commuted daily to school in St. John's with their father who worked there.

For seven years Clarke worked as a Chef at Chateau Park in Mount Pearl. In 1978 she became a foster parent and since then has given care to thirty-two children besides raising her own family of four. On November 11, 1987 Clarke and four other foster parents got together to reinstate the Avalon Newfoundland Foster Parent Association that had died out five years previously. She has served as the President of this association which lobbies and directs questions at government to help improve the present conditions for both foster parents and the children they have in care. Dorothy Clarke continues to live in Paradise with her husband and two boys who are in their care.

❦   ❦   ❦

33

The way I see it, children are children no matter where they have come from. The only difference is the needs of foster children are greater. I found that if you sat down and talked to them and made them feel that they were just as special as your own, then they thought of you as their family. In that way they don't feel left out or that they are just boarding.

When I first became a foster parent I received just over a hundred dollars a month, it has increased a bit since then, but there is never enough money to give the kids what you want to give them. I mean, you can't put your own children in school dressed in Levi jeans and Nike sneakers and have a foster child getting on the bus with a pair of jeans too short or too long. They stand out like a sore thumb and people spot them as foster children. Over the past ten years I have seen a lot of needless hardship for foster children.

After a decade of fostering over thirty children, I seldom look forward to the day when the children go back with their natural parents because I've seen so few of those cases work out. I feel that Child Welfare should have someone investigate those children that are sent back home up to six months or even longer. I don't mean appointed visits, because then everything is prepared, I mean drop in on them from time to time. I've had children with me who did not want to go home, who went home for two or three years and are now teenage pregnancies. They can't be put back in foster homes, so they are in homes for unwed mothers or living with their boyfriends for as long as that will last. Probably a year or so down the road that child will end up in care; so the trend is repeated. More money needs to be spent on hiring social workers to have a follow-up on these children.

Because only a week's notice is given before a child is returned home, some foster parents feel they have to stand off a bit from their foster child. The child leaves, but you're the one left behind. Regardless of how long you've had a child, you do become attached. Their problems become your problems.

Every child that comes into foster care is a special needs child because that child has been taken from his or her family. Foster parents need to be trained so they will know how to cope with a child's problems. The foster parent needs help to learn how to survive from day to day with children who have often learned that how to get attention is by throwing a tantrum. We now meet every last Tuesday of the month at the Social Services building in Mount Pearl. There we can discuss our concerns and borrow books on fostering. Our association is also trying to obtain an emergency phone for foster children who are being abused and are afraid to call from their home. It's such an important tool to have, yet we are one of the few provinces in Canada who do not have this service.

Child Welfare is an over-burdened system, which means the social workers have case loads up to a hundred. Obviously, we need more child welfare workers who are trained to deal with foster children. When you're talking of fostering you are talking of meeting children with all kinds of problems from families who have separated or a parent died, or the child has been abused or the adoption has broken down. I have known more than one child from an adoption breakdown. You take it, those children are rejected by their birth parents, probably they have been in foster care, they are rejected by them, then they go into adoption, that breaks down, so they are put back in another foster home. What help is there for that child—little. And these children are our future, yet through no fault of their own they will probably end up on the street one day.

The law says that at age sixteen a foster child can leave fostering. That is too young. You wouldn't say to your own child, you're sixteen today, you can leave now. Anyway, you would take them back if it didn't work out, but not so with fostering. If they come back it is as a boarder, whereas if that child stays with you, all education is paid even through university. I think they should stay in care until they are at least nineteen.

If foster parents have a child in care for a few years and they grow to love that child, then they should be given first priority to adopt. We are lobbying to make a subsidized allowance available for adoption because presently once you adopt you are on your own financially. If you are an average working class person with a few children of your own, it is next to impossible to put them through university along with the child you've adopted. Some of that financial concern should remain with the department of social services.

I think that in place of many of the group homes there should be more foster homes because group homes are more like an institution or an orphanage and it is very impersonal. It's run by staff and it doesn't have a family atmosphere. Payment for one child in a group home for one month is more than a foster parent receives in six months. But I know that some foster children do need special care above the love he or she will receive in a family setting. It is sad when you realize that foster children are given no special allowances for Christmas time or special occasions like birthdays.

Many of you could be Foster Parents. If you are the type of person who has time, love and comfort to give a child who has some problems, call me at 782-1547. Let's face it, fostering is for the children. The only benefit we get is knowing that we did something to help a child in need. We need a lot more foster parents. A lot, lot more.

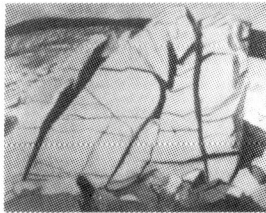

Lise Sorensen

Margot Davies

1992 Profile
Compiled by Maura Hanrahan

"Hello, Newfoundland, this is Margot Davies calling from the BBC, London." Margot (Margaret) Rhys Davies never discussed age and so we do not know how old she was when she died in 1972. We do know that she is fondly remembered by hundreds of Newfoundland soldiers who were stationed in London during World War II. Her weekly BBC radio program, "Calling Newfoundland," was part of many Newfoundlanders' Sunday morning ritual for thirty years. Born in Newfoundland to British parents and educated partly in St. John's, Margot considered herself a Newfoundlander long after she moved to Britain in her adolescence. Margot suffered from anorexia nervosa which ultimately caused her death. Below are recollections of Margot by artist Rae Perlin, excerpted from Perlin's biography Not A Still Life: The Art and Writings of Rae Perlin *by Marian Frances White. Accompanying this is one of Margot's poems written between 1940-41 from the book* Poems by Margot.

❦ ❦ ❦

*F*rom the moment that I first met Margot in the lobby of the old BBC building on Oxford Street I felt that we had known one another for years; there is nothing unusual about that since it is how everyone reacts, who has just met her. Now I want to say that my first impression of her was totally different from what I expected. Her voice coming over the BBC in wartime always suggested to me a rather largely built girl, the English 'athletic' type; the Margot I met was thin as a reed, with brown hair that curled, and eyes that sparkled friendliness. She was clutching a bunch of catalogues and greeted me as if we had been meeting every day for lunch.

If Margot herself had 'butterflies' (in the studio when recording for radio) they were well concealed by concern for her 'guests,' and her endeavour to put them at their ease. She accomplished this, I think, by her attitude towards them, and to everyone else, by seeing them as individuals; everyone was important to her, as well as what they had to say. This didn't always guarantee a good interview and sometimes the speaker struck dumb by mike-fright had to be rescued by desperate ad libbing from Margot. She told me of a horrible situation once when a speaker arrived late, an older man, and she had no time to prepare the interview; only to push a script in front of him while they were already in the studio. He made frantic signs and the awful message was that he couldn't read. As she rushed from the room to think about what to do, she said she had to fight an uncontrollable fit of laughter. By the time she returned, the interview went 'calmly' ahead, minus script.

More seriously; she felt she was fortunate to have a job she liked, which allowed her to work in her own time, meet lots of people, who did all sorts of odd things, go to the theatre (for which she once studied), and in short, be 'herself.'

Margot's memory was always phenomenal; she could recite reams of poetry, which she loved. Whereas most of us remember a sonnet or a few lines from school days, Margot could go on for pages. "I love words," she said to me. But Margot's memory was not only for words. She never forgot anything (except injury) or anybody; people once met were remembered forever.

Much has been said of her kindness to servicemen from Newfoundland; not much is known of her generosity which extended to infinity … she would chase all over London to see some lonely retired stage actress, and once when I had a problem with an old age pensioner while doing 'meals on wheels,' Margot solved it for me. [One of the people I delivered hot meals to was] a little old lady who lived in a small cottage in the midst of a drab industrial district. She pleaded with me for bread puddings for her ailment, which she said our custards did not cure. Where was I to get bread puddings? I confided in Margot and a few days later I was stopping off at Margot's to pick up several trays of puddings Margot had prepared the night before. The little lady's gratitude knew no bounds. She and Margot should have met, for there was something a little 'fey' about both of them.

Nobody has said anything about Margot's attachment to Christian Science, and I think that would have bothered her; she believed very firmly in Mrs. Eddy's teachings, probably because her own views were somewhat similar. She believed in the 'immaterial' rather than the 'material,' and no doubt this had much to do with her neglecting her physical self to the point of the malnutrition that was eventually to cause her death. She needed a 'high' to keep working, which also accounted for her going all night without sleep; so many of her letters ended with 'it's five a.m. and I must get to bed.'

On occasion, around a cafe table, we would talk about religion, or life after death; while some of us had different opinions from outright atheism to open-mind, Margot always 'knew'; how did she know? There was a sparkle in those blue-grey green eyes that were ever on the verge of laughter. I for one, never doubted that she did know, any more than I doubt now but that the transition from human and physical frailty was a simple one for Margot.

POEM XXVII

O the vastness of creation!
Little creatures, do not think
That thou art the only nation!
Link to link and link to link
There are other worlds and planets,
Other stars and moons and suns,
Where life stretches forward, upward,
Where the spirit streams and runs
Into infinite delight,
Nearer nearer to the Light ...
Think not a forbidding gravestone
Closes life and traps the dead,
While the body is beneath it
Soul is singing overhead.
Stones are star-dust, bodies emblems
Of each separate soul,
As the whole created glory
In the emblem of God's soul;
But as dust creates the atom
And the atoms form the stone,
So do human souls in glory
Sink into and form the whole.

Never are there any dead,
Dead are simply spirits fled –
Open your untutored eyes,
See them smiling in the skies!
                    MARGOT DAVIES

Sally Davis

1988 profile
Interview by Marian Frances White

Sally Davis was born into the Jacobsen family on December 23, 1914 in Seattle, Washington. She attended the University of Washington at Seattle, graduating in 1937 with a degree in zoology. In 1936 she married Charles Davis. With their two children, the Davises settled in Cleveland, Ohio, where, in 1958 Davis took a library degree from Case Western Reserve University, and worked in several school libraries. Twenty four years ago, their children grown, she and her husband moved to St. John's where she worked in several libraries and served as a school library supervisor for the provincial Department of Education.

In 1975, the beginning of the decade of striving for the rights of women, Davis helped develop the St. John's Status of Women Council but maintained an interest in seeking peace. In 1984 she and her husband travelled to Ottawa as part of the Canadian Peace Petition Caravan Campaign, carrying 11,000 Newfoundland signatures to join with some 420,000 other Canadian signatures - all asking for an end to the arms race. Known for her keen insights into global politics, she has been instrumental in bringing public awareness to the need for world peace through her work with the Newfoundland and Labrador Peace Network, and currently the St.John's Ploughshares.

Beginning in September 1986 Davis and her husband spent a year working at the Addis Ababa University in Ethiopia in the field of Biology.

❦   ❦   ❦

Looking back on my life I wish everyone could have had my opportunities such as to grow up on a farm, having musical training, to go to university, to travel a good bit, and to have lasted through thick and thin to my present age.

I grew up in north western United States in view of a 14,410 foot mountain called Mt. Raineer. My father immigrated from Denmark, my mother from New England. My father was a pioneer in the early settling of Seattle and my mother a school teacher who was living in Montana before coming to Seattle. I remember her telling me she rode horseback to get to her school. My father ran a lumber and fuel small business, and had horses to haul his products around the city when he first opened his business.

When I was about five years old we moved a short distance away to a village on Puget Sound where I believe I had the best of all environments. Besides viewing Mt. Raineer from my bedroom window, clouds permitting, and swimming in Puget Sound in the summer, my father developed a beautiful farm growing fruit and vegetables and setting up lovely grounds around our farm house. I had playmates nearby but still was given some chores to do since my father had his business to run in town. Gardening has always been a hobby with me throughout the following years.

Our farm was tucked away among neatly laid out large Japanese farms and I went to school with the children of the farmers. My mother made sure that the Japanese children in my grade were invited to my birthday party when I was growing up. Years later, during World War II, the Japanese living in western United States and Canada were forced into concentration camps and their beautiful farms confiscated—only because they happened to be owned by Japanese. I tremble to think how my childhood friends must have suffered from this unjust treatment.

Thinking back I realize now what an important role parents play in shaping the lives of their children. I was taught to be friends with everyone no matter the race, creed or ethnic origin. On the other hand my father having come from a very democratic country taught me to believe that the profit system was the root of all evil, and some other bits of knowledge such as - Do right because it is right, not because it is expedient. My father died in 1937, and so missed out on the event of the establishment of the United Nations and the Universal Declaration of Human Rights adopted on December 10, 1948. He would have been happy to learn that his country of birth was one of the 35 signers of the Helsinki Accord in 1975 and the first to set up their government based on these Accords.

In our small village my parents worked hard for its advancement. My father helped to set up a fire station. Oddly enough we were the first to test it out because of a chimney fire. My mother set up the first library obtaining books from the library in Seattle which discarded books from time to time.

It was fun helping her check in and shelve books. My first taste of libraries no doubt influenced me in later years to become a librarian.

Of course teachers influenced me, one of whom was a high school history teacher. It was the period in history when Gandhi was active in India mobilizing the masses to call for independence from Britain. Students were to make a cartoon based on an historical event and I chose to make it on the struggle for freedom in India. Maybe a seed was planted by that cartoon making effort. In later years I joined the Women's International League for Peace and Freedom, an organization which was formed in 1915 to try and prevent World War I. It now is world wide with its headquarters in Geneva and I still belong although the closest Canadian Branch is in Ottawa.

My married life which took place over 50 years ago took me away from my beloved mountain to California. Mt. Raineer was now more than ever nostalgic to me. My sister who was four years older than I had died in an airplane accident at age twenty-seven. Her famous mountaineer husband risked his life to climb to the top of Mt. Raineer by himself to leave his wife's ashes there.

After receiving his PhD Degree, my husband decided to spend some time researching at the Scripps Institute of Oceanography in southern California. From there our moves took us to central U.S. and next to Chesapeake Bay on the eastern coast. World War II was upon us and by then we had one youngster. There was the worry that my husband would be recruited into the army therefore he sought work in a powder experimental plant near Washington D.C. It was at that time we had our second child, just in time to take the train to move to Florida to take up teaching positions in two locations. Cleveland, Ohio was our next stop where we remained for 20 years, long enough to make many friends but too long to put up with the pollution and heavy traffic.

On a very windy freezing day in May my husband landed in St. John's to apply for a position at Memorial University. The Marine Sciences Research Laboratories (now the Ocean Sciences Centre) had recently been established and my husband thought it was where he would like to apply. It was a real test of his fortitude as he hung on to the rope along the walk to the Centre to keep from being blown out to sea.

Those were the days when the war in Vietnam was dragging on.

Our own son was among the American forces, although his role as a dentist, meant he was not subjected to the horrors of fighting. We had been a part of many demonstrations against the war while living in Cleveland. It was great to join in with Newfoundlanders in demonstrations outside the American Embassy soon after we moved here in 1968.

In the following years we took many trips to other parts of Canada, Central America, or to western and eastern Europe. In my case it was to attend women's, political or peace conferences. In my husband's case it was Limnology (scientific study of freshwaters) conferences, or to do research. I stayed behind the year he spent in northern Norway to take care of our Newfoundland dog and our home located on a pond in St. Phillips. Otherwise I went along to learn how other people live and enjoy seeing the sights.

Then came an offer in 1986 to go to Ethiopia in Africa, a continent we had yet to visit. We found someone to take care of our home and our dog and off we went to the capital, Addis Ababa, to work for the University. My husband trained students in Invertebrate Zoology and in aquatic ecology. I worked in the library in the same department. I was recuperating from open heart surgery at the time and since the climate was ideal, it was a healthy place to be especially since back home they were having snow storms that surpassed any seen for years, so we were told.

We found living in Ethiopia fascinating. It is a story within itself of a country which has not stood still since it overturned 2000 years of feudalism 10 years before we arrived. There has been a change of government since we were there and we hear conflicting reports since that happened. It's very difficult to keep up with events in many countries these days - even our adopted country of Canada and Newfoundland.

I have had a full life and perhaps I'm supposed to retire and fill my days with relaxing pastimes at this time. But I think Robert Frost has said it well in his verse that goes like this:

THE WOODS ARE LOVELY, DARK AND DEEP,
BUT I HAVE PROMISES TO KEEP
AND MILES TO GO BEFORE I SLEEP.

Jennifer Lynn Dick

1992 Profile
Interview by Marian Frances White
Jennifer Lynn Dick was born in St. John's on July 27, 1966. In the summertime of her teenage years she studied dance in Belleville, Ontario with the Quinte Dance Centre, leading into a full year at the School of Dance in Ottawa and later trained with the Royal Winnipeg Ballet. Upon graduation, after three years training with the Toronto Dance Theatre, she made her dance/theatre debut in Ann Ditchburn Jergen Lutz's film, "A Fairy Tale," followed by Theatre Passe Mureille's "Rigoletto." In 1989 she began performing full time with the Desrosiers Company touring Canada, United States and Europe. She has performed in New York, at the National Arts Centre and the Opera House in Ottawa, as well as three seasons at the Premier in Toronto. In July 1991, the Company performed at the Speleto Festival in Italy.

❧   ❧   ❧

I like to work and relax at the same time if that is possible. My mom put me in dance classes at an early age to get me out of her hair because I was a demanding child. I was adamant about doing things my way and if what I was being told didn't sit right with me, I would sit and do nothing at all until I figured out what it was I wanted to do. That can create problems when you are living with other people. When I was twelve I decided I wanted to be a dancer and studied dance every chance I got.

By the second year of training in Toronto I knew I was not going to fit into the dancer mould, but I was determined to learn from that experience. There were times when I couldn't get up the energy to go to class, so I would take a month off and go on my adventures and then I would come back to the discipline. It was really hard to get back in shape after being away, but I was finding my own set of rules and living by them regardless of the consequences. My decisions were neither right nor wrong, but just what I had to do at that time. However, there is no running away from the self.

When I was seventeen I took a year and half off from dance because a knee injury I had as a child returned, and I had to have my knee reconstructed. I was told I probably wouldn't dance again. At the time I was pretty burnt out on the demands of trying to be a professional dancer, so that felt ok. I felt for the first time that I truly was on my own dealing with this traumatic point in my life. Fortunately, it became a positive experience for me because I realized that it was up to me to make what I wanted out of my life. I began to trust myself and trust where I was in that time and place. I was finally beginning a search for the inner Jennifer instead of trying to fit into the mould of the perfect dancer that I had been struggling with for years. I was always really thin but I also scrutinized myself to the nth degree which I know was harmful to my psyche.

I came back to Newfoundland and got involved with the work young people like Sheilagh O'Leary, Rhonda Pelley and Dana Warren were doing and helped form Ploughshares Youth. We all felt a great need to get active in political issues and with what was happening with the youth of the Province. Of course, it wasn't too long before I could also return to the self which was the dancer.

As a political activist I often felt helpless and hopeless. I knew I couldn't go around screaming and yelling and standing in front of commissions all my life, when what those in power see is a cute female in a black beret getting all passionate in public. Finally I decided to take that energy to the stage and make it a performance that would make the viewer think as they walked home.

Over and over again it kept being reinforced in me that "Thank God I'm a Newfoundlander," otherwise I saw people crack up under the pressure. Dancers, or any one involved in strict physical discipline cannot allow themselves to get involved in substance abuse because it takes its toll on the body and a lot of people in the arts tend towards that. This is one thing that continually challenges me. However, I had taken with me the strength of a hardened place like Newfoundland which helped keep my sense of humour alive and that got me through a lot. Having lived with so many grey days on the Island, all the sunshine I got in Toronto kept me going.

No matter what style of dance you eventually decide to do, classical training is at the base of the work and that's where my efforts were concentrated for quite a while. I was able to continue my training with the support of my family and scholarships that were for the first time being opened up to women. When you think of women dancing, most people automatically think feminine, yet it's a very male-oriented business since a lot of choreographers and artistic directors are men. I was fortunate in that I studied the Martha Graham technique. I could really feel the difference in her choreography and I really felt myself grow as a woman.

As a child I use to think I was going to spontaneously combust. I heard somewhere that this was possible and I latched on to the idea until I became preoccupied with this possibility. I realize now that I have this highly explosive energy and I could either self destruct or focus it in a positive way. It takes incredible energy to discipline myself, but that's what I do on stage. I'm lucky to have found an avenue to express this vibrating energy because it can be disarming to people. Desrosiers was not afraid of the fire he saw in me, so we have found ways to get it out and use it on stage.

I am nearsighted which means I can't see things that are far away. I always think this is analogous to how I am as a human being. I've had to teach myself to move back and look at the larger picture. Dance gives me this perspective because I have to constantly look at my transitions as well as the whole picture. There is fear within me and I have to work with that and keep pushing it to evolve my vision and that of the company which I think is to fill our lives with incredible images and beautiful tapestries. To do this you have to be in tune with yourself physically, mentally and spiritually. The final product might be less political, as in my case, but more universal.

I've attained much of what I want to do in dance, but once you are on top of a hill and see the ocean and the mountains far away, you realize there are a whole other series of goals and efforts to take on. The other night a lady drove me home and commented on how outrageous I was and how she wished that she could wear her hair this way. I was stunned that she would rather have her hair another way and was not doing it. What's the point if we aren't living out who we want to be?

I wanted to be a strong dancer, a strong female dancer and I wanted to cross boundaries and I wanted to lift men and I wanted to lift women. I did a duet with a woman, it was quite a high experience; she threw me around the stage and we just went wild with movement. It beats me out but I love it. Peggy Baker, whom I love to watch, eats space, and Louise LeCavalier throws these guys around and throws herself around—it's a ballet of rock and roll. Ballet will always be my first love, but I become restless with it really quickly now. The guys I work with are really supportive and encouraging. Build those arm muscles, they say. Women aren't taught to jump, but since being with this company I am learning to do all these moves that women are never taught.

People either have a vision or they don't and if you have a vision then you are going to be totally inside that vision until you follow through with it. There will always be hardships along the way sidetracking you, but the important thing is to follow the sign posts inside yourself and learn to trust in yourself. If you fall on your face, fall on your face and pick yourself up and go again.

It's been therapeutic to clear my mind of all this, to see where I am right now and to go on from here.

Maggie Dominic

1992 Profile
Compiled through letters between
Maggie Dominic and
Marian Frances White
On July 15, 1944, in Corner Brook, Maggie Dominic was the first of three daughters born to a Lebanese father and a Scottish mother. After graduating from school and having already established a passion for theatre, she went on to study at the Art Institute of Pittsburgh. Shortly after graduating she moved to New York City in 1964. In 1968 she was honoured with the Langston Hughes Poetry Award. She has con-

Christmas – 1989 – N.Y.C. at a home for children with AIDS

tributed to numerous exhibitions, such as the Costume Exhibit she designed in 1983 for the New Jersey Library for the Blind and Handicapped and the Artists Respond to AIDS exhibit held in New York in 1990. Dominic continues to live in New York where she writes and contributes to art exhibits. She works in the costume department of New York Theatres on the set of "As The World Turns" and is a principle dresser with the Metropolitan Opera.

ễ ễ ễ

I have yet to meet a woman, either in Newfoundland or New York who had a television perfect, "Brady Bunch" life. Almost all women are coping with traumas, past or present and are in need of support and encouragement. As each woman is healed from whatever is hurting her, she is then able to turn around and help her global sister or brother. It is imperative that we help one another because in doing so, we heal the whole planet.

My childhood was like most people's, a series of ups and downs. There was a period of a year or so when we lived in a cabin in the woods, quite far from my school in Corner Brook, and I rode into town at six every morning with the egg man in his delivery truck and waited at my aunt's for school to open. I saw many beautiful dawns that year. There was no running water in the cabin in the beginning and we used to brush our teeth and wash our face in an icy stream behind the cabin. There weren't many families nearby and I think this is where I first began to get in touch with the artist and the writer in my soul. Even though I was a child I can vividly remember walking through the woods alone and knowing the names of spruce and pine and birch and silver maple and watching the way the sunlight slid through boughs and branches and made shadows on the ground. Nature was my friend. I was never afraid of it, not even the storms.

I went to Catholic school for twelve years. I will always remember grade two where I was one of seventy students in the basement furnace room that we used as our classroom. My earliest memories are of different houses. We seemed to move a lot. I went to church every Sunday and religion is still an important part of my life, but I've expanded my own concept of religion to include human rights, honesty and non-violence. Looking back on it now, my teenage years in Corner Brook were so simple and innocent compared to my daughter's in Manhattan with crime and drugs and homelessness and hookers and the need for the absence of innocence.

My love for art and design has always been a big part of me. Soon after arriving in New York City in the late '60s, I was fortunate to make friends with a group of young people involved in experimental theatre. The group included Bette Midler, Bernadette Peters, William Hoffman, Pulitzer Prize winner Lanford Wilson and Robert Patrick and many others. We established an Off-Off Broadway circuit with no production money and did shows in coffee houses and churches or wherever we could find space on Friday and Saturday nights. Most often we performed at the Caffe Cino which was to become the home of Off-Off Broadway for ten years. It was about this time that I went full fledged into theatre, writing poetry and articles for magazines.

To give an accurate picture of those days would be to imagine a family in its highest form. At the end of each show at the Cino we took turns passing a hat in the audience and whatever we collected we shared at the end of the week. We shared our hopes and dreams, our highs and lows and, most importantly, we cared about one another.

In more recent years my extended family includes AIDS victims. Since 1982 I've lost over twenty friends to the tragedy of AIDS—all gifted theatre people. My daughter and I have designed six panels for the AIDS MEMORIAL QUILT and I continue to work with several groups, trying to raise the public's awareness of this growing epidemic.

Newfoundland is my yardstick for everything. I feel that I've taken a very magical extension cord from Corner Brook and simply plugged it into New York. I wanted my baby to be born on the Island because there's something very special about being a Newfoundlander. We're a rare breed, there are so few of us. In 1969 I came home from New York, where I had been working for almost five years, and gave birth to Heather Rose with the help of the same doctor who delivered me. We had to move back to New York, but I can still feel a late summer breeze in Corner Brook (if I really concentrate away from traffic). Memories of the land, mountains, wind and icy trees comfort me on days when I feel I am living in a war zone with nice restaurants. After a particularly fast-paced month I go to the big map of Newfoundland that I have on my wall, unplug the phone and meditate on the Bay of Islands.

Barbara Doran

1988 Profile
Interview by
Marian Frances White
Barbara Doran was born
December 4, 1946 at St. John's.
She worked as a secretary until
she married at nineteen. Later,
as a single parent with two
small children, she started work-
ing as a lab technician, killing
rats; and attended her first
consciousness-raising group.
She was the first graduate of
Memorial University's
Women's Studies program, and
a founding member of the

Women's Centre in St. John's. She acted as its coordinator and lobbied for the current Transition House in St. John's. Working as a freelance broadcast-jour-nalist at CBC, she produced a "Woman's Report" for CBC for several months—until management found her biased (i.e. pro-choice) and cancelled her program. She then worked for "On the Go." Doran moved to Montreal in 1984 to work with the National Film Board on The Next Step, *six films on the plight of bat-*

47

tered women. Since then she set up MORAG PRODUCTIONS where she has produced and directed several films and videos, including most recently The African Market Women Series and A Harbour Symphony, which was presented at Cannes, 1991.

Doran describes her basic approach to life, among other things, as that of a feminist socialist. "We can have women mayors and professors, but it's a sham if we forget the women on the bottom who are not getting a meal. We're all in it together."

ॐ   ॐ   ॐ

$\mathcal{M}$y mother was certainly the driving force in my life. As a widow with eight children, she was burnt out at a very young age. This was before social assistance. To keep the family going she worked at the American base and ran a small corner store (the profits of which were quickly consumed by her eight children). She continued to raise us under the myth by which most women were raised; that is, that one day you're going to get married and then a man will look after you. With that myth in mind, I married at nineteen and when that didn't work out, after five years, I found myself thrust upon the world with two small children and very little training. I inherited a lot of my mother's strength and began to see through the myths she had passed on to me.

Going to my first consciousness-raising group was quite an eye-opener for me. They helped me see my capabilities and feel okay about myself again. In those early days of the fledgling women's movement, most of us really didn't know what we were doing. We knew we had been wronged on many levels, but we barely knew where to start.

I remember in 1975, when we were lobbying for matrimonial property law reform, a few of us put out brief after brief and press release after press release telling everyone what we wanted to see changed. We went to see one minister as part of the lobby. After we finished reading the brief, he looked at us and said, "Now, just let me get this straight. You're asking me to give my wife fifty per cent of the house if we get divorced, is that right?" And I said, "Yes, Mr. Minister." To which he replied, "My wife! My wife who sits home on her big fat ass all day long looking at soap operas! Get out of my office, I'm a busy man!" In the face of such opposition it took us five years to get money from the federal government for a transition house in St. John's.

I feel a lot of roots in Newfoundland within my family, my friends, and in the women's movement. So, whenever I'm in St. John's and I walk into the Women's Centre, all those memories flood back to me. Coming back to Newfoundland with my films is like a kid coming home from kindergarten with a drawing to show mommy.

I was working at CBC when Gerry Rogers called me from the NFB in Montreal to ask if I wanted to do research on a film about battered women.

I've been working in film ever since. What makes film exciting for me is when it has the desired effect. The Studio D films are not meant to be limited to a feminist audience. The film *The Next Step* and the ones that followed on *Counselling the Sexual Abuse Survivor* are made to suit professional training needs; that is, social workers, doctors, the RCMP, attorneys and Freudian therapists. I've learned a lot from the people I've worked with during the past few years, particulary the women at Studio D, the Women's Studio at the NFB. They were anxious for me to learn and they gave me the support and the confidence I needed to do the work. I think if there is one singular thing that will help women get ahead it is this cooperative attitude.

Of course, what you aim for in film, and what you get, are often two completely different things.

Taking part in the production of the film *Speaking of Nairobi* was as much an eye-opener for me as was my initial debut with the women's movement. It gave the crew a sense of what was going on globally with women. What I saw in Nairobi was a lot of common ground among women all over the world; even though a woman's concerns in Africa are different than mine here in Canada, her sense of herself as a woman and her sense of herself within the society in which she lives are not all that different.

I think this common ground is happening here as women get less rigid in their definition of what is a feminist and as we accept women coming from different political trains of thought. We need to concentrate on this rather than on who's the better feminist and who's purer than who. We need to get on with the real work of linking up to the point where it reaches a global level. I saw this in Nairobi and I realized that women are no longer concerning themselves with issues that are directed towards women—daycare, equal pay, maternity benefits, and access to abortion. They're doing that, but they're also taking up issues surrounding women who are living in occupied territories, women who are living under apartheid, women who are living in politically-torn countries, and women who want their voice heard in the economic development of a country. When you have that kind of expansion and that kind of political involvement, it's harder to separate the women's movement from the global political movement. Going to Nairobi and documenting such an important event means that there is something tangible for future generations of women to work from.

There is nothing stagnant about working in film. I've travelled across the country with the *Sexual Abuse Survivors* films because I want to try to balance the backlash that all this information on child abuse has created before everyone gets too paranoid to touch one another. It's a difficult task, but I do know that we cannot raise a generation of victims by being paranoid and over-protective. Yes, we have to arm our children with the information, we have to speak openly about our bodies, we have to make them feel strong enough to say NO and give our kids a sense of privacy about their bodies. They have to be told they have the right to speak up when something happens that makes them feel unsafe or uncomfortable. But I think we have to be careful not to have too puritan a reaction. I'm always worried when my teenage daughter, Erin, is walking home at night in Montreal, but I won't keep her in. After all, that's what *Take Back The Night* is all about.

I need to wake up every day with a new mountain to climb. I get that in film. I like the freedom it gives me and the necessity for constantly coming up with new ideas. I'm stimulated by it, and also know that if I screw up there's no one to blame but myself. That's both scary and rewarding.

Courtesy of ALISON FEDER

Margaret Duley

1987 Profile – consisted of an excerpt from Duley's Highway to Valour. *Here Margaret's niece, Margot Iris Duley, writes* Reflections of an Admiring Niece, *June 4, 1992.*

Margaret Duley was born in St. John's in 1894, and died in 1968.

Given that her books were written nearly fifty years ago, Duley's determination to develop independent, searching female characters placed her ahead of her time. She published four novels, The Eyes of the Gull, Cold Pastoral, Highway to Valour, *and* Novelty On Earth, *as well as a number of essays and short stories. Margaret Duley is not only Newfoundland's first native novelist but one who accurately describes the personal struggles of women no matter where they live.*

🐛 🐛 🐛

*A*unt Margaret is gazing down at my desk from the portrait on my wall. She is a powerful presence. Her flashing, deep-set brown eyes fix me with an inquisitive gaze, a piercingly intelligent gaze, yet there is kindness there too and a recognition of human frailty. Her black hair impeccably coiffed falls in soft waves brushed off her high set brow to reveal a dramatic widow's peak, a feature which pleases her. She is a woman of intriguing contrasts: brilliant and whimsical; dramatic and conventional; mercurial and introspective; cutting and compassionate; a bon vivant and mystic.

My memories of Aunt Margaret are those of a child and a young woman. I adored her as a child. As a woman I have a deepened admiration for what she accomplished and against what odds.

Twenty-four years after her death from cruelly debilitating Parkinson's disease she still leaves a vivid impression.

In my early years we lived in the same house at 51 Rennies Mill Road; then for the next decade, after my parents had moved to 7 Monkstown Road, she was still only a hop and skip away, and I was a frequent visitor for she was an engaging companion. After she became ill, my mother Florence Duley, brought Aunt Margaret to our house and looked after her for as long as that brilliant mind was reasonably alert. Her final days were spent at St. Luke's Home.

She was a wonderful aunt. She had a wonderful capacity to amuse children (and adults too). She could enter into a child's world without condescension and talk as apparent equals. She did, however, have a very exacting sense of what constituted good manners. She indulged me, however, when other adults in my life were worried because I had invented an imaginary playmate. She entered into the fantasy and we invented stories. She even pushed my invisible companion in an empty swing at Bannerman Park and bought all of us ice creams at McDonald's Drug Store on Rawlin's Cross. She was kind enough not to point out that I ate my playmate's as well as my own.

In her own youth she had been part of the women's suffrage movement. Her novels are implicitly feminist: the dilemmas of a talented or insightful young woman constricted by society lie at the heart of *Highway to Valour* and *Eyes of the Gull*. She also took great risks in dealing with divorce, abortion and woman's sexual feelings, topics that even her advanced suffrage contemporaries had been publicly silent about. As early as 1928 she argued the case for equal pay for women together with Emily Sterling, a former Principal of Bishop Spencer College and Margaret McDonald, the Executive Director of the YMCA, against a formidable male team of debaters which included Raymond Gushue, later President of Memorial University. Their's was a wildly unpopular position at the time, and they lost. But she never lectured me about these things. Indeed I found out some of this later through my own historical research.

She was a keen observer and an inveterate people watcher, and on her walks, which were frequent, she taught me a great deal about both the creative imagination and about seeing below the surfaces by observing her own vivid imagination at work. She might overhear a snatch of conversation on the tram or at McMurdo's soda fountain and it became a window into another world for her. It would turn up in a yarn later in the week. I wish she had written down her tales of the remodelling of 51 Rennies Mill Road which starred the plumber ("me darlin' ye needs them nipples lagged") and other craftsmen. She could keep a room in stitches.

51

She was a great entertainer and she dearly loved a party. She could easily have been an actress; indeed, she had studied at the London Academy of Music and Dramatic Art. A career on the stage was unthinkable for a young woman of her class in St. John's, and I suspect that grandmother Tryphene Duley who was a staunch Congregationalist put her foot down. In a sense Aunt Margaret's theatrical career became one of entertaining a drawing room. She knew reams of poetry and scenes from Shakespeare by heart. Often she would give them a melodramatic, comic rendering.

There was also a very serious, deeply spiritual side to her nature. Her evolving religious beliefs also put her light years ahead of most of her set. She broke with her Congregationalist upbringing, and read widely in theosophy, Hinduism,, Buddhism and Christian Science as well as European philosophers including Huxley. She was drawn to the notion of reincarnation and the belief that the "karma" we acquire through good or bad deeds dictates the circumstances of our rebirth. However, she continued to practice elements of Christianity—such as teaching me the Lord's Prayer, in French, I might add, for she loved the sheer poetry.

Aunt Margaret was a free thinking, free spirited, outspoken and charismatic personality in a society where this was not encouraged, especially among women. Given the odds, I am astounded that she found her literary voice. Her publishers included Macmillans, Methuen, Hutchinson's and Arthur Baker. One novel—*Novelty on Earth*—was translated into Swedish. She was reviewed favourably by critics in *The New York Times Book Review*, *The Times Literary Supplement*, and *The Manchester Guardian*. It saddened and frustrated her that she received comparatively little attention at home, and she was mocked by some erstwhile friends as "too grand." For all her elegant flamboyance, she was a sensitive person. One wonders what else she might have accomplished in a more sympathetic age. She was a woman years ahead of her time.

Julia Salter Earle

1990 Profile
Recollections of Julia Salter Earle by her daughter-in-law, Ethel Earle.
Interview by Marian.
Born in St. John's on September 20, 1877 Julia Salter was educated at the Methodist College and in 1903 married Arthur Edward Earle. Earle did not give up her name, she became Salter Earle and her son, Alton, was also given both names. In 1918 Earle, who was an engrossing clerk for thirty-five years, became the first President of the first all female union, the Ladies Branch of the

Newfoundland Industrial Workers' Association.
She was also one of the first women to run in
municipal politics. During the election a ballot
box was lost and she, herself, lost the election by
eleven votes. Salter Earle died in 1945.

🍎 🍎 🍎

*T*he first election I remember was when I was
a little girl living on Campbell Ave. Just across
the street from my house was the Newfoundland Butter Co. Julia was running for
election. I asked my mom, why haven't we got
a campaign picture in our window. "No," she
said "we don't need that kind of stuff in our
window, we have curtains."

The Butter Company was practically in our backyard across the
street. It hzd a high board fence and everybody was out with their chalk.
I joined in, and wrote in big letters Julia Salter Earle's campaign slogan
"Vote For Julia She Won't Fool Ya." When I was sitting down to supper
my brother asked me, knowin' full well what I had been up to that day.
He then went on to tell my mother what he had seen me do. "Where?" said
my mother. "Up on the Butter Co. fence." My mother said, "you can leave
the table, you'll have no supper tonight." When Julia later became my
mother-in-law, she said, "Well if I had known that, I would have went
directly up to your bedroom and took you downstairs and you would have
had your supper."

My late husband, Julia's son Alton, told me this story about Julia, her
husband and her children. They would be sitting down to supper—during
the Depression—and someone would come to the door looking for something to eat. Julia would excuse herself from the door and come into the
kitchen and if there were twelve slices of bread on the table, she would
turn around and say to her children "one slice is enough for you," and
she'd actually take the bread and butter and some of the hot meal they
were having and bring it out to whoever was at the door. No one was
turned away. She wasn't a good manager—she couldn't hang on to anything. Later when she lived with Alton and me—after she was widowed—
we would wonder what to give her for Christmas. Would we give her a
pair of stockings and put some money in the box for herself? We dared not
give it to her before midnight on Christmas Eve because she wouldn't have
it come Christmas morning. Minutes after we'd leave the parlour, we'd
hear the door and she would be gone down around Bannerman or Bond
St. and whatever she received herself for Christmas was given to somebody else.

One year we gave her two boxes of chocolates, split the cellophane and put money underneath it. We really thought she wouldn't do anything with it late Christmas Eve night, but we heard the door late in the night, and she came in singing as happy as anything. She had asked a store keeper to open up the store to buy something for a poor person who had nothing. Julia was not what you would call domesticated. She never went in for cooking or sewing. My husband said many times that though Julia had a family and loved every one of them, she should never have married and had children.

Nanny, as we called her, was involved in Cochrane St. United Church. She was just the whole cheese—whatever she said went. She wrote plays for the church socials and she used to want me to listen to all the lines as she walked around the living room going over and over each character until she got them right. She nearly drove me crazy, but she knew I'd listen even if I didn't want to. There were teenagers in the Church who asked her to arrange a Christmas social. Everything went well until she went to Church on Sunday; she came home and was breaking her heart in the parlour. The Reverend Barrett spoke to her about it and said she was teaching the young people wrong having boys and girls together. I seen her cry more than once. She'd wait until she got home to have her cry over what someone had said, though everyone saw her as the cock of the walk.

I remember a distraught mother contacting her concerning her daughter—an employee of a local firm who had been injured at work. The word "pauper" had been placed over her bed because of the family's bad financial situation. Julia consoled the mother and contacted the company managers stating "I want you to get out your little red book (that contained the employer laws of the day) and open it on Page 93. There you will find that you are responsible for her care while she is convalescing." She also added, "You have to do that much, but don't you think it would be nice if you sent down some flowers and a box of chocolates as well?" and the manager did as was requested.

During the Depression she led many strikes. On one occasion she stopped the strikers before they reached the Colonial Building and said, "If any of you are carrying liquor just get rid of it here." Many winter nights she left to visit needy families who had no food, and only squatters rights in the Mundy Pond area. We often worried about her. The roads were blocked with snow and the ice cracked beneath her feet as she walked across Mundy Pond, pulling groceries on a sleigh.

Nanny and I were from two different ends of town. Her way was not my way, but we never had words. I realize now what a powerful woman she was and that much of what she did was for the benefit of us all.

Carla Emerson Furlong

1991 Profile

Interview by Marian Frances White

Carla (Emerson) Furlong was born into a musical family which encouraged her studies in this direction. She first studied piano with Sister Mary Baptist at Mercy Convent before taking up harp. In the early 40's she travelled to Toronto to further her studies which were interrupted by the outbreak of World War II. During this time she worked in the cipher office in Pleasantville decoding messages for the navy. After the war she studied in New York at the Juilliard School of Music. She worked for five years in England and seven at the Toronto Conservatory before reestablishing her roots in New-foundland. She married Richard Furlong in the late 60s.

❦ ❦ ❦

I was born way back when we had street cars in St. John's. You could ride the town for five cents. Those were the days when money was money. It went around Rawlins Cross, down Queen's Rd., then to Theatre Hill and down Adelaide St. where it was met by another car going either direction on Water St.

My mother's family were Jameson's from Dublin, Ireland. My grandmother lived in Liverpool and I inherited her harp. It was brought over here by boat, just like everything else was in those days. I was sixteen the first time I touched a harp and loved its tone immediately. I had been studying piano with Sister Mary Baptist but she never lived to see me graduate. I was sorry about that because she was a dedicated teacher; the years of harmony and theory I learned with her took me right through Juilliard School.

My studies in Toronto were interrupted when I took up naval ciphering. The point was that some sailor could go to sea for every female that was doing some land work. Naval ciphering was tiring work mainly because of the shifts, but despite the war there was music to keep spirits lifted and the troops entertained. You could get a date even if you had two heads!

The first year I went to New York there were two hundred people waiting for harps, so I had to hire one. From then on I took my harp with me and would bring it home on long holidays. Coming from a small place New York can be terrifying; after the war it was harsh and sleazy, but I think it's worse now. Back then I most often went around by myself and felt relatively safe doing that, though I was always relieved to get home.

There were people at Juilliard from all over the world—Cuba, the

Phillipines, India and Europe. It was a very supportive atmosphere; our teachers became our friends. I studied conducting as an elective but soon discovered I wasn't cut out to be a conductress! Studying at Juilliard was a lot of hard work; you didn't have time for beating about New York but Sundays were kept for visiting museums, friends and seeing the sights.

After more than two years I had finished school and needed work so I went to Montreal, but the work for harpists was scarce there. I was offered work in England so I went and stayed for five years. The BBC used to have these radio shows and often they'd rely on the harp to change from one key to the other while they were advertising their product. So you had to know theory and modulation or you'd be crippled.

It was in England that I met Margot Davies. Of course, I knew her as a child in St. John's but I got to see how she worked on her program *Calling Newfoundland From Britain*. Nobody knows how much she did to help those down and out. She didn't get paid that much but she was dedicated to her work. The only thing that would upset her was if some house guest would try to tidy up; she had papers everywhere. That would upset me too. Some people find things in a mess and they know where they are; someone else comes in and thinks they know better.

When I returned to Newfoundland in 1962 I never looked back; I knew I was here to stay. Newfoundland is a place where you can build without everything being torn down. Your work can be submerged in a big city though I enjoyed my work wherever it took me. The competition and jealousy however, was fierce. I wasn't prepared for the help I received here in getting set-up to teach piano, theory and harp because I wasn't used to other people looking out for you. Anyone who plays harp will say that at some time or other they have had to play pieces in orchestra that are most unharpic, but for the most part I have enjoyed my performances and playing with the Newfoundland Symphony. The span of the harp makes for a long lasting, pleasing sound, yet the size of the harp and the subsequent difficulty getting it around to performances makes one lose one's religion over it. You never know when it arrives if you're going to find some strings broken or if it will be completely out of tune. Luckily, the North American harp is made to withstand central heating, whereas the European harps are made more for damp houses.

If there are any words of wisdom to be passed on to the youth it is for them to nurse their talents and to honour them and to not be temperamental. There was a time when you weren't a musician unless you were throwing things around, but no one has time for that behaviour anymore.

I'm glad for the way things worked out in my life, there's not much I would change. I enjoy performing, but mostly I enjoy teaching harp to young potential harpists. I will always play harp because it relaxes me and because I learn something new everytime I strum a chord.

Tineke Gow

1989 Profile
Interview by
Marian Frances White

M.F. WHITE

Born in Emmeloord, Holland in 1946, Tineke emigrated to Ontario in 1967. While working as a medical technologist, she obtained a BA in Psychology from the University of Western Ontario. There she met John Gow; they were married several years later and came to Newfoundland where John became an Assistant Professor of Biology and Tineke worked as a research assistant in the Immunology Lab at the Memorial University Health Sciences. Tineke's career plans changed abruptly after she gave birth to her second child, Emily, in 1979. Brain injured at birth, the prognosis for Emily's future was poor.

Against the advice of the majority of medical professionals, the Gows started Emily on a controversial program known as the Doman and Delacato program, developed some 25 years ago at the Philadelphia Institutes for the Achievement of Human Potential. The intensive neuro-motor stimulation program, also known as Patterning, is a comprehensive developmental program and requires a great deal of strength. Tineke started Emily on the program when Emily was thirteen months old and continued for the next four years. Five hours a day, seven days a week, Emily went through a battery of exercises to improve her coordination, vision, hearing, speech and to stimulate her cognitive development. This was done without the aid of an extended family.

Today Emily walks, talks, swims and attends Bishop Feild School in St. John's. She lives at home with her parents, her oldest sister Francie and two younger sisters Alexandra and Marieke.

❧   ❧   ❧

The most difficult decisions for me when I decided to start Emily on the program were to give up my job in the Immunology Lab and to ask for, and accept help, from so many people. I also knew that without the extra help the program would fail. However, even as a student in Psychology I had always wanted to work with mentally retarded children. It wasn't until the birth of Emily that I had to draw upon this earlier training.

Before I started working with Emily I became acutely aware of the differences between the principles learned at University and the actual practice of rehabilitation. As I went to the provincial rehabilitation centre I soon discovered that, for very young brain damaged children, most of the time was spent assessing the patient and little time was spent on rehabilitation. In the early years the "wait and see" approach prevailed. In the meantime our daughter remained passive, like a rag doll.

I had no real insight into what could be done until a friend, Pamela Henning, handed me a book, describing the Doman and Delacato program. That was a courageous thing to do. We found that people would gloss over the fact that Emily was badly brain injured; let alone suggest that maybe we could and should try to do something really constructive about it. It took about three months of intensive reading and discussions with my friends and with colleagues in the medical sciences before I decided to pattern. Patterning would require long intensive hours of rehabilitation. Our lives would appear to become centered on providing Emily with optimum conditions to grow and develop. The alternative however would be caring around the clock for a disabled child but without support from the community. I came to regard it as a job, just as a physiotherapist goes to work from nine to five. The volunteers were often very busy people, but they believed in what they were doing, They were interested, broad minded people, with varied ages and backgrounds. A friend, Rosemary Barnard, took it upon herself to coordinate the many volunteers needed to help us carry out the program. Emily thrived on the attention and I thrived on the moral support given by the volunteers. It prevented me from becoming the isolated parent of a brain damaged child. If we were to find that this was not the right thing for Emily, or the family, we were prepared to stop without any feelings of guilt.

We were not encouraged by the medical professionals to put Emily onto a patterning program. Later we were not encouraged by the educational experts when we tried to have her integrated into the regular school system. At first it was suggested that she should be in a special class with children with various disabilities, both mental or physical or both. We felt that this would not be the best environment in which to grow. A disabled child, even more than a normal child needs normal role models if integration into society is to be achieved.

Again there were obstacles to overcome. The regular teachers felt they were not trained to deal with children with special needs. However, once an Individual Education Program was set up the teachers became very supportive. Under the Individual Education Program Emily is integrated into a regular class, but, for a large part of her day, she has individual instruction from her teachers, or her aide, and under these conditions she learns at her own pace. Although in grade two, she functions at a much lower level than grade two in some aspects of her program. But, importantly, she is with her peer group, who accept her and in many ways understand her needs.

The most difficult times might still be ahead of us. There will be the teenage years, when Emily will have the same need for belonging, loving and being loved. These are issues which will be there for us to deal with someday. Far away maybe, but not far enough that we can afford not to think about them now. The facts are not encouraging. We understand that a majority of mentally retarded girls have been sexually abused. We as a family will always have to be on guard for her. If she were to become pregnant, and keep the child, what would happen, would she raise the child, or would I? If she would exercise her right to get married, who would be responsible and help her.

As we all treasure our independence, our long term goal for Emily will be independent living. How successful we will be only time can tell right now. However, many dedicated people will have helped her to succeed as best she can.

Many people have concerns about patterning. Some feel that a patterning program is too inflexible. We modified the program to suit our family. We feel it could be modified for other families, and ideally should be carried out within our institutions. With the average size family being small, with both parents often having to work for economic reasons, with an increase of single parent families and hospital budgets shrinking every year, who should care for brain injured children and try to rehabilitate them at the same time? Both the medical professionals, parents, and community should be involved in this. The program is not difficult to carry out. Also volunteers are available within the community. But such a program would benefit from cooperation between the medical profession and social services to help with organization and monitoring. Again, if the will is there it could be carried out, costing far less than the traditional methods with the possibility of better results. For us, the quality of life for the brain injured person and the family, both in the short term and in the long term, was of primary concern and we were prepared to go the extra distance to preserve it. Others probably would as well.

Rose Gregoire

1992 Profile
Interview by Marian Frances White
Rose Gregoire was born October
1948, in the interior of Labrador
where her family hunted and fished.
Delivered by her father, she is the
second youngest in a family of eight.
In 1987 she and three other women
began to organize meetings in their
community to deal with the problems
created by low level military flying

M.F. WHITE

and the excessive use of alcohol. Gregoire worked for several years as a nursing assistant in the Northwest River Hospital before she became a mother of four children. In recent years she has worked as counsellor with the Department of Social Services. There are some eight hundred Innu living in Sheshatshiu and the surrounding area.

❦ ❦ ❦

I spent most of my younger years in the country, Nitassinan, with my family. I remember my father carrying me on his back and being wrapped up on a blanket and sled and travelling for a long time.

Eventually we settled in the community of Shetshatshiu like so many of the other families who used to live in the country. My father went off drinking like most of them and I found that hard, especially when my mother followed. I was probably six or seven and a Catholic priest arrived there saying that I should go to school. He wanted the men to go to the country and the women and children to stay in Shetshatshiu. A lot of people listened to the priest because in those days he was almost like a god.

When I was thirteen or fourteen, I was left in the coummunity with my sister who was sick and couldn't go in the country. My parents had to return to get some supplies and I wanted to go back with them. We lived about twenty miles from Happy Valley Goose Bay and the road that we walked was right by the school window. I told her I was coming with her and she didn't say no. The priest saw me walking out of the community and tapped hard on the window, but I couldn't turn around, I just kept walking. I'd stay in the country from April to October and then I'd return to school.

I'm glad I learned English because it helps me deal with the problems in the community, but I want my kids to know their language and learn about their ancestors. This is not being taught in school although the Innu women who are now working in the schools are trying real hard to tell the kids of their culture.

I wonder today what kind of people we would be if the government and church didn't get involved with our people. I think they were not so interested in us as a people, as they were in what they could get from the country that we were living in. It wasn't all easy in the country, there was lots of work, but my mother called it the happy times because we had to make our own living and help each other. Today if I left home to travel to Quebec on foot, I'd probably get lost; she wouldn't have. I'd like to get back to that again.

Celebrations were not a part of our life like birthdays and Christmas, but if the present that you could give your family was being together and being happy and have some friends around and have a meal, then we had that. We didn't have turkey, we had beaver, partridge and rabbit. There

60

was a small tent where people stood shoulder to shoulder and there was no alcohol. Today Christmas is very different. My children expect more and it really breaks my heart because I don't have much. Celebrating Christmas started with the priest and when the military moved to Goose Bay they donated stuff to the priest who would get some people to wrap them and give them to the young ones.

Shamanism is lost because when the priest came he told the people to burn whatever they got; that it was the work of the devil and that really confused people. The people were divided between those who listened to the priest and those who didn't want to. I talked to the bishop recently about this and he said he wouldn't call shamanism the devil's work now but talked about it as a power from above that we had. The new priest is asking the people what kind of service they want and that is good, but it's too late because the people who live there are very much Catholic. Every new thing that comes to the community is confusing and causes problems because it is not our way. We sometimes don't even know our way any more.

Women started to organize meetings in the community because there were so many problems. We had a hard time I guarantee you because the leaders figured we were supposed to have meetings to organize meetings, not to do things. At first they thought we were trying to take leadership from them, so it took a long time for them to understand and give us support. We complained about the school system and we took a trip down to the bombing range because we wanted to see what was happening out there with the low level flying. When we came back we started asking questions of the leaders and that made them angry a bit. It took time for men to accept that women got a say in things too and have the right to say it.

I met my husband when he was cutting logs. He'd come from Norris Arm in Newfoundland. I told him I'd never move there and that's still true but I visits his parents sometimes. He might take a few of the children and go there himself for awhile, but I don't go. There's a lot of people like me in the community who are married to white men and I feel sorry for their kids because it must be so confusing. I've sat down with my children and talked to them about our history and what I learned from my parents because our history is an oral history passed from generation to generation that still needs to be told.

There are people who have mixed feelings about the military struggle because they have jobs all year around and they have school, but now that they understand the problems more, they can't help but support us. Over the years we've seen alcoholism and violence and suicide increase. Children are moved from home to home and that is hard on every one; they don't know where they belong.

Sometimes I feel like giving up. People say to the Innu that we don't hunt anymore, that we're lazy and aren't doing anything to help ourselves and yet if we go hunting we are harrassed by wildlife officials and the RCMP. My father didn't have that kind of problem and although he didn't have much education he knew that it wasn't good to overkill animals. The only thing that is legal to do is drink and they do, which is really sad. Most of my community are now on social assistance because they do not know how to live outside of the country. This creates a lot of problems in their minds; they feel disabled. Social services doesn't give them enough money to live a healthy life, just enough to get by. They can't pay bills and now because they are so lost, they drink whatever money they do get to forget about their problems.

What gives me strength is when I think of my parents and my children and other people's children. I'm frightened sometimes by what's happening around here and in Goose Bay where they burn PCB's. What is going to happen to our environment in the future? You can't believe them when they say this is safe. I'd like the Premier or Prime Minister or some MP's to go with a family out in the country and spend a week or two to see how we live and why it is so important to us. Only then will government begin to understand and take time to consider our side.

I'd like to thank the people who are interested enough to know us and I know some of them have not ever been to Innu country. This tells me that even with small knowledge of our people change can take place.

Naomi (Emmie) Gregory

1990 Profile
Original Interview by
Shelly Smith, Naomi's niece
Born January 28, 1901 as
Naomi Smith, she left home at
the age of fifteen to work in St.
John's as a domestic. In 1920
she left Newfoundland to work
in Moncton, New Brunswick.
Later she travelled to Boston
and New York to find suitable domestic employment. It would be almost two decades before she returned to her homeland.

ĕ   ĕ   ĕ

I left Newfoundland because I wanted to see the way people lived in another country and I wanted to make a better living for myself. When I was living at home all I knew was work, work, work and finally when I went to St. John's to do domestic service, I did everything there was to do from shining shoes to cooking. My parents didn't want me to leave home. They said I should stay because I had plenty to eat and drink, but I figured there was other girls that had gone away and it seemed that they were doing better.

I came to St. John's with Gladys Drover, a girl friend of mine whose sister, Albina, was working on Springdale Street. She got a job for her and for me. Her sister was probably to an afternoon tea and someone said they needed a maid and probably this friend of theirs said, well, my maid can get you one because out around the bay, there's lots of hard working girls.

In St. John's at that time an awful lot was expected of you, you were a slave to the people you worked for. I had to clean shoes, clean silverware, polish and clean and wash up the floors down in the basement because they had canvas there. She had a wooden table in her kitchen and that had to be so clean as a hound's tooth. You had to scrub it with a scrubbing brush. You got one night a week out and if you wasn't in at ten o'clock, you'd probably find the door locked on you, so you wouldn't get in at all. Most often I wouldn't get out until eight o'clock so that didn't leave much time for socializing. That was the case with all young girls in the city, and there were a lot of us; that was the rules, why I don't know. Gladys only stayed a month before she went back home, but I stuck it out regardless of how tough it was. Then one day I was going downtown and I met a friend of mine, Annie, she said she was going away up to Moncton, New Brunswick. I said you get me a job and I'll come, too. I said I wish I was going with you now. I would have just as soon stayed in St. John's if things had been better, but I suppose that was lotted out in my life, that I had to leave and go to some other place. Two months later I got this phone call come down to the Salvation Army Office. I didn't know what it was about and I had to ask for a couple of hours off and that's how I got away. I had to give two weeks notice and of course, she nearly blew her top, but I was determined to go. I had to go back to see the Salvation Officer again; terms had to be made out and they bought my ticket and made all the arrangements for me. I gave him the money and he bought my ticket. I had enough money scraped up to buy my ticket and when I went aboard the boat there were three other girls. One of them was a Salvation girl but the other two wasn't. When we got to Halifax, a Salvation Army girl met us and took us to her home and gave us all supper. We washed and done whatever we wanted to do and then she took us to the train and bought our tickets and put us on our way to Moncton and told us not to talk to anyone on the train. Now, that would scare you, you know. I knew no one in Moncton except the girl I asked to get a job for me. She was at the station when we got there.

I didn't like it much in Moncton and neither did Annie, so when she decided to go to Boston, I went too. Annie's cousin in Boston got us jobs. Her boyfriend was supposed to meet her in Boston, but when we got there, he wasn't there. We had no one in a strange country. We didn't know no more where to go than a lost cat. We had met this woman on the train and she asked us did we have someone to meet us, and we told her yes. But when we got there, there was no one and she looked at the address Annie had and said she had to go that way and we got on the streetcar with her and went out to Park Street and she told us where to get off. Now, she said, don't ask anyone directions where you're going unless it's a policeman and if you see a policeman and you get confused and can't find the number, you ask the policeman. So that's what we did and the policeman took us right to the door and Annie rang the bell. They were all strangers to me except for this one girl and the people that I went to live with were strangers to me, but they were the nicest people you ever met on earth. I wasn't scared.

The two of us lived in the same house as the Nelsons; she did the cooking and I did the nursework, they had four children. The little boy was nine months old when I took up the work and when I left he was going to school. I had to look after him and take him out for a walk every afternoon. But now, I didn't go out, like on the street, down among the people; I used to go in the backstreets because it was too confusing to go among people with William in the carriage. The family I worked for were fairly well-to-do; we lived around Jamaica Plains. Sometimes they'd go to Long Island or Cape Cod, and I'd go along. I was twenty-five then and I felt I was treated like one of the family. At that time Boston was a marvellous place to live, we couldn't have a better place. On our days off we'd go to Chelsea which was the Newfoundland section of Boston. We'd go to Birmingham Church there and visit friends. Annie married and I had her to visit and I made other friends. There were the Greens from home, the Rubys and Annie Benson over in Renews and the Martins. They're still up there, what's not dead now. There was an awful lot of Newfoundlanders in Boston. Sometimes we'd meet in Boston Commons or Central Park. Well, heavens, that's the one that's not fit to go in now—then you could go in there and lie down and sleep, not so now. That was Depression time and that's where half of the people lived. The States wasn't like it was today, it was a nice place to live then.

Some of the young women worked in factories, but that was harder work because you had to do piece work. One woman I knew, Francis Stone, she used to bring her piece work home with her at night. If you worked in a factory you had to find a room and you had to pay your rent but working in a house, doing housework, your room and your board was looked after besides your wages, so domestics made more money than the women in the factories.

Annie didn't like it so much in Boston either, so she went to New York, and I went with her. My sister, Ann, and my two brothers were in New York by this time. I worked in a house with three other girls. One looked after the children, there was a cook, an upstairs girl and I had to look after the dining room and wait on the table. They also had a chauffeur. The McAthens was their name; they were relations to John D. Rockefeller. They were wonderful and I liked it there a lot. I had to wear a black dress and a white apron when I was in the dining room; the other girls wore blue and white as nursemaids. When you left, you had to leave the clothes behind. I didn't have to go to the kitchen at all. The cook passed the food in the pantry and I took it in to the dining room. That's all I had to do, wait on tables and clean the silver. I had most every afternoon off from the time lunch was finished until supper was served. When the McAthens moved from New York out to Princeton, New Jersey, I went out there with them and I was out there for a few years and stayed until I returned to St. John's in 1933 to see my sick mother.

If I had stayed home in Island Cove I would probably have met someone and married and lived down there all of my life and I wouldn't have known anything about no other place, so I don't have any regrets, none at all.

Genevieve Hansen

1991 Profile
Original interview by June Hiscock
Born in Stephenville Crossing, 1911, the sixth of ten children, Gen Hansen grew up in Humbermouth, not far from where she now lives in Steady Brook. She was educated in Nova Scotia be- cause her infatuation with trains would
find her running away from school at the sound of the whistle. Hansen home- steaded in Newfoundland with her second husband. A 'Gen of all trades,' she fished, raised a family, managed a night club, scaled wood and in 1976, age sixty-three, became the first female fire fighter of this province. Hansen's Run, a ski slope on Marble Mountain in Steady Brook, is named to honour her ten year dedication to that resort. In more recent years she has been travelling with an elders hostel in Whitehorse and spent her eightieth birthday in Alaska. One of her favourite pastimes is exploring Klondike graveyards.

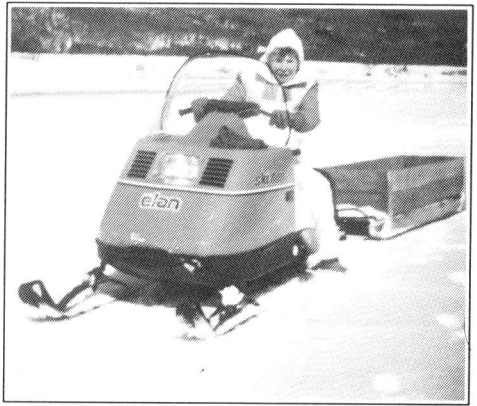

I've been fishing since I was three. I would often run away from school, spend all the day at Humber Mouth, catch a fish and fry it on a rock. I used to swim right across the Humber Mouth better than most of the boys.

The books on my shelves were sixteen dollars. I made that money one summer working as a timekeeper on a coal boat with one hundred and eighty men. My mother hated the idea, but decided to let me do it or I wouldn't go back to the convent school.

When I taught school on the Canadian Labrador there were eight families and seventy-two dogs. The Canadian government supplied one case of tinned tomatoes that I shared with the youngsters. What I missed most was music. Every once in awhile the men would get on one side and women on the other and rock back and forth making these sounds and singing folk songs. Everyone stayed where they were until spring; then they'd take up their bed and walk. Everybody left. In the winter you'd trap and in the summer you'd move out to the beaches to fish. I enjoyed it.

After that I did nurses training and worked as a nurse for fourteen months, but the first baby I saw born I took off and ran away. I was missing for three days. I had boys clothes on, my hair was short and I never stopped to think that my father would be worried. When I heard on the radio he was looking for me, I returned home.

I roamed around for a few years and later got married to a millionaire's son from New York. The first plane I went on was the first one I ever saw. It was a TWA that took fourteen passengers. It took sixteen hours to get from New York to Los Angles. I remember first when I came to Steady Brook from Los Angles in 1945, I had blue corduroy slacks on and people were shocked. I went back to Montreal to work with a shipping company when my husband was killed in the war.

Some years later I met my old boyfriend, Halfden, in Montreal. We married and came back to Newfoundland and boarded in Corner Brook for a year. I was scaling wood one day and I looked down into the valley and saw this little patch of land and said to Halfden, "That's the place I'd like to live." That was forty-some years ago and I haven't regretted it one day. You knew who was up in the morning by the footprints on the snow and by the smoke coming out of the stovepipes. Finally we got lights. I had the only telephone, you had to crank it. If there was a washout on the line after a storm, I'd have to go up and flag down the train with my red skirt cause I knew how to do it from when I watched my father. I always loved trains.

In 1947 I took care of my sister's little girl and in 1948 I had my first child, Jennifer, so that kept me out of the woods. In later years, I was the only one left with a wood stove and everybody used to come visit and crowd around the stove. I used to love baking bread and beans in the wood stove and only this year gave up using it. Thor, my son, said I'm too old to be carrying wood, so he got me a propane one. I have that little rangette there and the first chicken I ever cooked in it, I thought it was anaemic.

When I was in training to be a fire fighter, I found it a bit hard to keep up with the men pulling hoses and going up and down ladders for eight hours a day. By nighttime we'd be dirty black too cause we'd have to go through the smoke on that old ship with an oxygen tank on our back, but it was fun. In 1983 I was sixty-five and had to retire, but I'm still on call; when that beeper goes off any time of day or night I got to run.

I love reading old gravestones and I love helping my neighbour and I love children. There is not a day I don't wash extra coffee cups. The young people go away, but they always come back to see me. Another thing I love to do is read; I must have over two thousand books; when I lose one it's like losing a friend. My favourite books are historical novels, biographies, sea stories and adventures, but I don't read romance stories. I always loved riding motorcycles. I did that until recently. Anyone who came along on a motorcycle I bummed a ride. There's nothing like riding a motorcycle; I don't care what kind it is as long as it moves and the wind is in my face.

People are too self-centred nowadays; not giving to each other. I love poetry and a beautiful sunset. Does anyone look at the sunset any more? I love the sunrise. Sometimes the cloud formations are really fantastic. I spent time in northern British Columbia and loved seeing people coming out of the mines; the sun would be just shining on the copper dust on their backs.

The only way to live is to meet people, but people shouldn't keep so much to themselves. People are afraid to say I love you.

You know what I love most about Newfoundland—I love the bold colours. I remember first when I came here that old bathroom that I use for a washroom now, I had orange flowers on the wall and everybody was shocked. I like golds and I usually wear a lot of red. I always loved this place but I never dreamed, in my wildest dreams, that I would ever come back here to live. But when I saw this nice lazy old house, I knew I had to come here to stay.

Anne Hart

1992 Profile
original interview by Joan Clarke
Born in Manitoba, Anne Hart has spent much of her life in Newfoundland. She is head of the Centre for Newfoundland Studies at Memorial University library and has published several short stories, numerous articles and two fictional biographies, The Life and Times of Miss Jane Marple *(1985) and* The Life and Times of Hercule Poirot *(1990). Published in the UK and the US, both books*

have been widely translated. She has served on provincial and national library boards and in 1986 was presented with the Canadian Trustees Annual Merit Award.

❦ ❦ ❦

I had the misfortune to have my parents die when I was very young. This has always been a great sorrow in my life but my sister, my brother and myself went to live with an aunt and uncle in Nova Scotia who did everything they could to see that we lived a family life. I think of them often with enormous gratitude.

My aunt was my father's sister so I was taken at an early age into the culture of their family. The stories I heard from my aunts and my grandmother rang with the accomplishments of women. I have always regretted, however, that I have never really been able to retrieve the stories and myths of my mother's family. She was Irish, and though I've visited relatives in Ireland several times, and one of my sons has studied in Dublin, I still feel my daughter and I have been cut off from important foremothers.

I grew up in rural Nova Scotia and went to a two room country school, wood stoves and all. My aunt had one eccentricity: she was convinced that children spent too much time in school and only sent me in the mornings! I don't know how she got away with this, but I remember secretly studying for exams, a forbidden activity. As a consequence, I have always harboured a somewhat subversive view of schools and authority in general.

At thirteen I was sent to a girls' boarding school and at sixteen I went to King's College at Dalhousie. Here I studied for a degree in history and then for a degree of library science at McGill. After that I spent a year working in London and youth hostelling around Europe. England seemed a natural place to go. Like many Newfoundlanders, I grew up receiving messages that all good and interesting things of value were in the old country, as it was called. I have lived in England twice since then, and enjoyed it, but this sense of affinity has steadily waned away.

I have always wanted to be a writer and a lot of my time has been cluttered up with not writing. I have enjoyed most of my life, but if I could do it over again, I would somehow make writing the central part, however precarious. Nevertheless I love working in libraries, and the concept of libraries as tranquil places is utterly misleading from my experiences.

I came to Newfoundland in 1962 with my husband who had been appointed to the faculty of Memorial. Our daughter was then three weeks old and during the next three years I gave birth to two sons. There then

68

followed a strange blurred existence familiar to many women. I remember that many evenings, after the last child was asleep, I would get into the bathtub and read. The bathtub was my space. Wonderful! I enjoyed being a mother more when my children became teenagers and, now, adults. They are the best of companions.

When I first came to Newfoundland most of the people I knew were also from somewhere else. When my youngest child was four, Jessie Mifflin, who had led an epic life establishing libraries in the outports, offered me a part-time job at the public libraries headquarters in the Arts and Culture Centre. The coffee breaks were presided over by a memorable group of women who had worked for years at the old Gosling Library on Water Street. They seemed to know everything that was going on in St.John's and why. It was from them that I had my first real taste of Newfoundland. They were very astute, and wonderful story tellers. It made me realize that I was in quite a different culture than the one I had grown up in, and one I liked a lot more. One of the messages I got from these women, and about Newfoundland, was not to take life too seriously. Catastrophes pass.

I was fortunate that the first job I had at the university library was in the Centre for Newfoundland Studies. When Agnes O'Dea, a distinguished librarian and wonderful mentor, retired, I became head of the Centre. Over the years it has grown enormously, thanks to the writers and researchers of Newfoundland and the fanatic collecting zeal of the people who work in the Centre. I am extraordinarily lucky to work there.

I have always taken an interest in politics. I grew up in a conservative family with a capital C. As soon as I got to university, however, I was drawn to more left wing points of view and over the years I have worked on many an NDP campaign and advocacy cause. I've been lucky to live here during the formation of a strong feminist community. In 1972 my family and I lived in England, and I began to hear discussions about women's liberation. When I returned to St.John's, I was astonished to find that the women's movement here was way ahead of anything I had heard of in England.

When I look back on my life so far, including the years of being a single person again, I think I was lucky to have had children fairly early and a career afterwards. It mixes you up in the time frame in an interesting way. You are back where you might have been years before, which staves off mid-life crises wonderfully.

Lise Sorensen

Sarah Holwell

1989 Profile
Story formed by Marian with help from Laura Jackson

Sarah Holwell was born into the Elson family on January 10, 1928 at Porcupine Bay; a small winter settlement in coastal Labrador. The only girl in a family of nine, she travelled by boat with her family from their winter settlement to their summer fishing station on Spotted Island—a small three by five island situated on the southeast coast of Labrador; population approximately two hundred and fifty people at its peak.

In 1937 Holwell, age nine, entered Lockwood Boarding School at Cartwright where she spent four years and was taught much more than the three R's. Though the years were few there, she has many fond memories of life at Lockwood. At sixteen Holwell went to work as companion for a trappers wife while he was away on his trapline. At seventeen she was cook at the Nursing Station in Cartwright, then went to St. Anthony Hospital, situated on Newfoundland's Great Northern Peninsula, for two years as Nurse's Aide. When she returned to Spotted Island she married Jack Holwell.

The residents of Spotted Island were resettled in 1965. By then she and her husband had four children, two of whom died at an early age. In her adult life Holwell has been involved in women's health education programs, alcohol and drug abuse education, nutrition, and has taken courses in Home Nursing. Although she's never studied Native Crafts, like most Labrador women, she does a fair amount as a hobby and in 1986 her large embroidered "Mealy Mountain" scene of deer, trees, mountains and water was shown in a juried travelling exhibition, "Labrador Crafts: Where Cultures Meet."

❦   ❦   ❦

*L*ike most Labradorians my family fished and moved regularly from our fishing station, Spotted Island, to our winter homes some fifteen miles inland into the sheltered bays for about six months of the year. We moved into the bays in the fall by open boat loaded with almost everything we owned, then again in March or April by dog teams with the same load and with many loads of fire wood (there are no trees on Spotted Island). As children we loved and looked forward eagerly to each move; looking back I love the memories.

Spotted Island, home to the same people for generations, is surrounded by some of the most rugged shoreline and savage seas to be seen anywhere. It also had one of the best cod fisheries on the coast, as many Newfoundland fishermen can verify. They made up about half the summer population and their coming signalled the start of another summer fishery and many happy reunions. With Confederation in 1949 and the availability of new jobs, they gradually stopped coming, 'til sadly they came no more.

Though treeless, Spotted Island is beautiful in summer with wild flowers that cover the hillside and green grasses of many shades fill the valleys and gulches. Bakeapples, blackberries, blueberries and partridge berries grow rampant over hill and dale.

Education was hard to come by in those days and before the second Lockwood School at Cartwright came into being in the mid 1930s, I hadn't been to school at all. How privileged I felt when, in January 1937, we were advised by Nurse Poppelton who was passing through our tiny winter settlement on her rounds along the coast, that at last I was old enough and there was room enough at Lockwood for me. She picked me up on her way back two weeks later. We arrived at the dormitory about 7 p.m., tired and cold, having ridden all day by dog team. There is no way of describing my feelings; the delight, the excitement of finding myself at last inside the beautiful building of which I had heard so much from my brothers. It was a fairyland of bright lights, (like dozens of moons I thought) shining floors and lovely smells and lovely, lovely people. I was ushered into the large, bright kitchen, stripped of my outer garments and given hot cocoa by Sevilla (Martin) Bird who was one of the cooks and whom I loved at first sight, as did everyone in school.

There was such a backlog of children waiting to get into Lockwood that each child was only given up to four years there. Then they moved out to let another take advantage of these few years, which was for some of us a gold mine of knowledge. A great deal was absorbed in the limited time allotted. In order to get those few years of school, we had to be away from home ten months of the year and only saw some members of my family on rare occasions when they came to Cartwright for supplies. A high price to pay perhaps, but the higher price was having to leave after only four years. Eight years later, Jack and I were married and continued to live at Spotted Island where we were born and where we raised our children.

We had been living on Spotted Island year around for several years prior to resettlement. We had a teacher and had just built a one-room school for our thirty or so children. We had the possibility of a new phone system which at that time was a ship to shore type system. There was the likelihood of a new clinic (the old Grenfell one still stands there after seventy-five years. We bought it twenty years ago) and we had hopes of better fishing facilities and housing. The school had been used just one season—typical of senseless government spending. We might have been

71

living on the Island permanently in comfort and contentment instead of having to move, as of old, to winter settlements.

Our resettlement in 1964 and 1965 was similar to resettlement everywhere. Everyone suffered emotionally, physically and financially. It was especially sad for the older folks, many of whom had never been away from their home, except maybe to a hospital. *Torn Roots Sometimes Never Heal.* We were literally forced to leave our homes where we'd lived, loved, laboured and died for generations. Tho' we refused to even consider it and held on for a year, we knew we were fighting a losing battle when the government told us there would be no teacher, no medical services and no mail service—in short we were a forgotten people as far as government was concerned. Then there was the emotional trauma of trying to settle into a strange community with the feeling of being an outsider and not being wanted, which was very real for many.

After we'd moved it was rumoured our summer places would revert back to crown properties and that we could lose them to anyone that might want to fish there. This was the most devastating of all; however, as we continued to return each year to fish, we heard nothing further on the subject. Most of us still live there in summer—that never changed.

We suffered financially because many of these homes had previous owners and cost much more than the monies allotted to each family for homes, so many ended up paying out of pocket. Others were moved into unfinished, poorly constructed homes that cost the owners many hundreds of dollars to rebuild or renovate. We were to move to 'growth centres'—half of us were sent to Goose Bay, the other half went to Cartwright where, at that time, the only growth was in population (and misery for us) until a few years ago. There is now a fish plant, a Marine Centre and several small privately owned businesses, although only part of the community has water and sewage. The building of the new radar site and twenty odd miles of road has provided a great deal of employment for the community and will continue to do so until it is completed.

I know that I am speaking for every one of us when I say that we would not have moved had we our time back and we will always regret our weakness in not telling them to get lost, as we would now.

Hope

1990 Profile
Interview by Marian Frances White
This is the story of Hope. Because anonymity is the spiritual foundation in all the affairs of AA (Alcoholics Anonymous, a world-wide self-help group), we cannot give you any biographical information about the woman profiled in this story, but we hope it will offer some insight into the serious problem many

women face with regard to addictions.
Hope is one of hundreds of women who
cannot be named for fear of the repercus-
sions. It is her hope that this story will
add support for more detoxification
centres for women in this Province.

☙   ☙   ☙

I left school in grade eight to go to
work washing dishes in a Water Street
Restaurant, so I could help out at home. I got married at nineteen and had
three children, one after the other. The marriage was abusive, both physically and mentally, yet I stayed in it for fourteen years because I didn't
really know where else to go. I tried leaving a few times but I always went
back because there was security at home for me and my children. I
eventually got a divorce and although I was lonely, at least I wasn't living
in fear of him.

Two years later I met a man and I fell into the same pattern of
abuse—a few smacks here and there because he saw me look at someone
else meant he was jealous and that, I thought, meant he loved me. But then
one night he came home drunk and raped me. I wanted to take him to court
but was advised against it because I had been divorced and because he
lived with me. I didn't pursue it because I could see that it would hurt the
kids, so I had the baby even though it wasn't a product of love. It took quite
a while to break ties with this man but when I did, it was for good.

I asked Social Services to take my newborn baby until I got myself
together; they said no. They suggested putting the child up for adoption
but I didn't want to do that. At that time I couldn't feel any love for my
child, I think now that I was afraid of him. I honestly don't know how I
got through that period because I never did get any help. I remember
calling a revival line and they told me I was being punished for my sins.
Drinking hadn't yet started in my life.

Shortly after this I took a work project offered by Social Services and
I really felt good because things were looking up. I started going out for
an afternoon drink with my co-workers just to be social. Then the happy
hours took over, and eventually I was drinking almost every night of the
week. I was in my mid-thirties by then and having blackouts. I stopped
going out but I continued to drink alone. In a span of four years I became
a full-fledged alcoholic. I realize now it doesn't matter how long you drink
or how much you drink, it's what happens to you when you drink that
reflects the kind of problem you do have.

The last binge I was on was in '86. It was the worst tear I was ever on. I don't think that I drank any more booze, it was that I couldn't handle it anymore. I wasn't eating very much. I know now that I had DT's (delirium tremors) but I didn't know it then. I was seeing things and felt really sick so my daughter took me to St. Clare's Hospital. They told her to take me home because I was drunk. She helped to get me home and then she took care of all my needs. A doctor eventually came and gave me valium. Some people say it only takes forty-eight hours to detoxify but it takes a lot longer than that for some people. For the next three months, I couldn't even watch television, my nerves were shot. I needed peace and quiet and in our small apartment there was little of that. In desperation I called AA. It wasn't easy but I'm glad I found the strength to go. What drove me there was being afraid that I would start drinking again. There were nights when I couldn't sleep; I would walk the streets hoping to get run down because I didn't have the nerve to kill myself. But when I started going to AA meetings, I listened and slowly I started to realize that I wasn't alone any more. I had tried AA before but it only lasted a few months. I thought because I didn't drink for a long time I wasn't an alcoholic—I sure proved myself wrong. One thing I learned was that it does get worse and I could see what was ahead of me so I reached out before it was too late. I had to let go a lot of old friendships because they thought I wasn't an alcoholic. I realized that if they had been true friends they would have been more supportive. Now I go to parties late and I leave early.

You really need to do something for yourself when you get sober. There is life in sobriety. I started thinking about the men who have a detox centre here in the city. I also started thinking about all the women who were going to suffer like I did when I got turned away at the hospital. I joined up with an Ad Hoc Committee which was formed in 1986 that promotes the development of alcohol and drug treatment services for women in Newfoundland and Labrador. After three years of writing briefs and sending letters to government we are still waiting and hoping; meanwhile, women detoxify in hotel rooms or at home. There are co-ed detox centres in Port-aux-Basques and Corner Brook, but in Labrador and St. John's nothing has come of our requests. We are still hopeful. I think more women today are realizing they have drinking problems even though alcoholism used to be seen as a man's problem. I do know that many women who are in psychiatric units are indeed alcoholics and have no other problems except there is no other place for them to go.

I know now that I'm responsible for one person and that's me; everything else will fall into place if I can hold myself together. I've always been hard on myself but today I know that I have to let go of things in my past. I have to not worry about tomorrow but try to do the best I can today. Today I choose to be sober and my life has turned around a lot. I have good communication with my children, I have a companion whom I am comfortable with and I have a job that I enjoy. Sobriety means a lot to me today. I feel a lot better and I'm in control of myself, but for me to be content, to live life as best I can, I need to be involved with the program and go to meetings regularly. For anyone who thinks there is no light at the end of the tunnel, there is. I'm happy, after all.

Linda Hyde

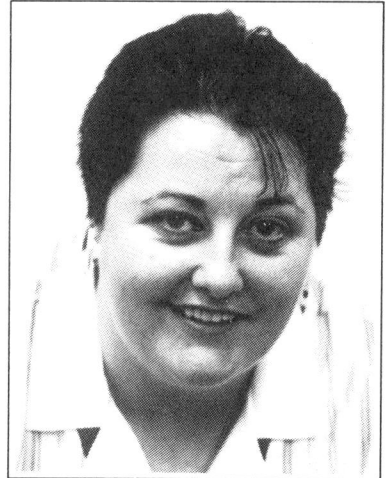

1991 Profile
Original interview by Cathy Young
Born into a fishing family, Hyde lived in Red Head Cove, Conception Bay, with her parents, five brothers and one sister until she moved to St. John's. She started work at National Sea Products fishplant on the southside hills in January 1978, and got involved with the fish union, now the Canadian Auto Workers, a year later and since then has served as a shop steward, president of her local, and executive member of her union board. She is an accomplished spokesperson for fishplant workers and presently runs a convenience store in St. John's, Helen's Mini Mart. Hyde continues to do vital work surrounding the issue of rate increases for public utilities.

❧ ❧ ❧

My mother spent twenty five years along side of my father splitting fish on the wharf, and in the evening time when it was split, we'd be salting it down. There was no weekend off, and there was no such thing as sleeping in on Sunday because if you weren't to mass you'd be killed; your life wasn't worth a darn. You didn't challenge it, you went to church. My mother never complained and my father never complained and there were seven of us home. I hated to spread fish, I hated to wash fish, and I didn't want to get my hands into fish.

I think my mother would have appreciated her twenty five years in the fishery a lot more if she had been paid, or if she could have gotten stamps from it. Then she would have been an equal partner with my father. But that was never heard of then. Women always worked next to their husbands in the fishery but with the deep sea fishery and $80,000.00 boats, women became more housewives. I think the deep sea fishery really took women out of the fishery for that period. There was no more salting of fish;

it was sold directly fresh. Women were needed again when the plants opened.

Right now we are in a crisis situation. The fish is not there. The companies are not willing to wait. They should wait for a few years for the stock to pick up, but they don't want to. I don't think National Sea should be allowed to pull up stakes in Newfoundland because they want to keep operating at ninety per cent capacity. No plant should close on a permanent basis, devastate a community or a group of people, wherever they live, and walk away to where labour is cheaper, giving the workers a few dollars severance pay after we've given them twenty years of our lives. We don't even have a severance pay clause in our contract.

We are not talking about subsidizing companies, we are talking about keeping communities alive. The Americans tell us what we can or cannot do. If their communities were in danger, they would be coming to us and looking for some fundamental changes in the free trade agreement. We would be looking at six months work.

But the fish is not there. The best scientists are the ones who went out on the boat and learned through traditional knowledge, not textbook knowledge, that the fish stocks weren't as great.

It seems as if the bad news has always outweighed the good news. There is always a bit of gloom with the bit of glory. This bad news is one way for the company to put pressure on the employees to produce more, and put pressure on governments in times of restraint to look for money and more quotas. Our premier wants to give them three million dollars of the taxpayers' money. If National Sea can tap into extra government money, from ACOA or somewhere, they will do it.

My employer, National Sea Products, was the biggest fish company in Canada. Fishery Products International, a Newfoundland company, operates at fifty per cent capacity during these hard times. National Sea resisted restructuring to keep control of the company. Now, when the fish stocks are down, National Sea will do what's best for National Sea, this conglomeration of several prominent Nova Scotian families. After making huge profits after the mid '80s, they just spent two hundred and fifty million dollars overseas. They have two plants in Argentina, they are in Uruguay, the United States, and they have a sales office in Japan. The bottom line is they should not be allowed to close a whole industry on their whims because they diversified, spent some money, and the profit margin is not what they want it to be for that year.

Society looks at fish plant workers with guarded indifference. We had one woman who went to a Sears store and tried to change her cheque, but Sears came down with a policy: "We don't change fish plant cheques." What's wrong with fish plant people? We have an awful tag on us. We are the best bunch of people, and we have been kicked around so often and dragged through the mud and stood the test of time and work so well with each other that it is not deserving.

Newfoundlanders are known as fighting Newfoundlanders. Maybe in the war people gave up their lives freely because Newfoundlanders would almost lay down their soul for anybody. But when it comes to fighting for what is our heritage, what is our way of life, and what we make our living at, we are not fighters. The fight has gone out of Newfoundlanders. The federal government looks down its nose at Newfoundland and the provincial government now can hardly speak up. You hardly know they are there.

The government gives licences to these companies, so I told Tom Siddon, then the Fisheries Minister, "Tell these people at National Sea to come back home, and don't be issuing new licences for factory freezer trawlers over in Argentina. If those trawlers were in the Janeway races, where everything is supposed to float, those trawlers would sink!" The government own thirty per cent common shares in National Sea, and they claim this money is nothing! I said to them: "Listen in here, my good friend, if I had a thirty per cent share in any company I would have a controlling interest. I could call in my markers at any time."

The time has come when we must fight for our livelihood.

Dorothy Inglis

1990 Profile
Interview by Marian Frances White
Dorothy Inglis was born April 15, 1928 in Calgary and grew up in Vancouver. A founding member of the National Action Committee On The Status of Women, Inglis moved to Newfoundland in 1972 and since then has been active in the feminist community. Dorothy Inglis is currently on leave of absence from The Evening Telegram, where for several years she has written a weekly column "Bread and Roses." She won the 1987 Robertine Barry (English) Award by Canadian Research Institute for the Advancement of Women (CRIAW).

❦ ❦ ❦

"*G*rowing up in the CCF" was the most important influence of my childhood years. My parents were early members of the Cooperative

Commonwealth Federation, the forerunner of the New Democratic Party, because they wanted to see a new kind of government emerge, one that cared for the needs of all people rather than for the rich and powerful.

My father was a minister and my mother was a nurse, and between them they knew a lot about human suffering. In depression years they opened our house to "the unemployed," as they were called—young men who had left prairie provinces to ride the freight trains to Vancouver hoping to find work or at least a warmer place.

There was no work for them in Vancouver either, and when they held demonstrations to force government action, the police moved in with billy clubs to disperse the crowd. Some of them used to come back to our house to discuss these injustices and I remember the despair my mother felt on their behalf. She would say that their only sin was in wanting jobs, but they were clubbed for saying so. It was a cruel system that played havoc with human lives then and now, but I've never forgotten my mother's and father's conviction that there could be a society that cared about people.

The CCF was more than just a political party. It was a way of life, a dedication to a better world. I used to love conventions as a child because so many family friends would come to town. It was a time of great oratory and even at a young age I was always content to go with my Dad or with one of my older siblings to public meetings to hear Grace MacInnis or Tommy Douglas or Gretchen Steeves hammer away at the inequities of the system and listen to their vision of a world that cooperated and shared resources.

And it was family, too. You could meet as strangers in towns across Canada but when the common bond as CCFers (or later New Democrats) was discovered there was instant rapport and welcome. It was the same feeling I got at my first meeting with Helen Porter and the Mount Pearl NDP club. I knew I was home.

The B.C. CCF was given a wonderful piece of property on Gabriola Island which was used for a summer school. Families and individuals went by the CN ferry to spend holidays there in July and August. Some would come just for weekends. It was a great spot where kids like myself could swim and climb the Malaspina caves and then join the grownups when we felt like it.

But as idyllic a playground as it was, the summer school was serious stuff as well. CCF Members of Parliament, Provincial legislators and other intellectual leaders, like the late Senator Eugene Forsey from Grand Bank, chaired study groups on the issues of the day and helped to develop social policies like medicare for the future.

In the early fifties I was on an arbitration committee for the Retail, Wholesale and Department Store Union. The contract before us was one of the first to ask for equal pay for women. We were just as astonished—as the company was appalled—to hear their nominee on the committee,

Senator Norris, saying that he agreed completely with the proposal. "Yes" he said, "of course the company will support equal pay for women, in fact I'd be inclined to give them a bit more." I was flabbergasted until I learned that his wife had been a suffragette and that he had always championed the rights of women. It's nice to know that some people can practice their principles in whatever setting they're in. I'm sure the company hadn't known of his commitment before they chose him for the job.

I was accepted for an in-service training program of the provincial social service, and sometime later had the unforgettable experience of being the first flying social worker along the rugged B.C. coast. The area I served was a lot like coastal Labrador or the South Coast of Newfoundland, with small, isolated fishing and logging villages. And then I met my husband-to-be who was teaching school in Cumberland, a small mining town on Vancouver Island. We married in the spring and in the fall both of us became students at the University of B.C. I had won a scholarship that allowed me entry into the Bachelor of Social Work year, and he was finishing his B.A. I was also pregnant and gave birth to my first son a week before final exams. It was a wonderful, exciting year.

In the early sixties the women's movement was starting to rise. Betty Freidan's book, *The Feminine Mystique, was causing quite a stir. We went from house party to house party where someone would say, "Dorothy, have you read The Feminine Mystique?"* and Gordon would say, "Read it? She wrote it!" It raised so many questions for men and women it couldn't be ignored. It was like a dam bursting.

We moved to Toronto in the late sixties where I was the stay-at-home mother raising our two sons and daughter and loving it, knowing that I was lucky to have a choice. I was working with the Voice of Women, a peace group that has remained active to this day. Kay Macpherson (who received an honourary doctorate from Memorial) was one of the original presidents of VOW who inspired us all.

She later became president of the National Action Committee which held its official founding meeting in the Royal York Hotel in Toronto in the spring of 1972 with over three hundred women present. Rita MacNeil sang. Iris Kirby, who is commemorated in the name of the St. John's transition house, gave the report on the status of women for Newfoundland, and since we were just moving to St. John's, she invited me to join the social action group at the YWCA.

Over the years here I have been involved with the Defenders of Signal Hill, a lobby group that worked to prevent commercial development in the park, an enthusiastic supporter of Historic Trust, a manager of an Oxfam Third World craft shop on Duckworth Street, an elected member of the Avalon Consolidated School Board, a founding member of the Georgetown Neighbourhood Improvement Program and of the St. John's Status of Women Council, a provincial representative and Vice-President of the National Action Committee (NAC) and a twice defeated provincial NDP candidate.

Since the early eighties I have worked with people for whom I have the deepest respect in the Coalition of Citizens Against Pornography. In my opinion no factor has had a more poisonous effect on our communities than the introduction of pornography. It's a subject that won't go away and today we are seeing the tragic effects of it reaching down into the lives of very young children.

I've really enjoyed writing "Bread and Roses," for the St. John's Evening Telegram since 1986 because it's given me a chance to present and explain some of the issues defined by the feminist movement. I hear regularly from people of all ages and backgrounds who begin by saying, "I don't always agree with you, but..." What they go on to say is usually a basic acceptance of the need for gender equality while they add their own modifiers. Mostly, I believe, people see the past injustices and want them remedied for their daughters and sons.

An Icelandic friend of mine, Gudrun Agnarsdottir, ended one of her letters with the admonition to "shake yourself so the seeds will fall." That's what feminists are doing and I like to think those seeds will sow equality and peace for us all.

SAND NORTHRUP

Fran Innes

1988 profile
Interview by Marian Frances White
Fran Innes was born on July 20, 1924 at Grand Falls, into a family of very strong women (the aunt for whom she was named continued nursing until she was eighty). After attending Grand Falls Academy, she received a B.Sc. in Home Economics from Mount Allison University. She worked as a Home Economist in the Home Service Department of Consumer Gas in Toronto. Two years later, she returned with her husband to Newfoundland and raised two children.

At age forty-five, having taken a refresher course at Mount St. Vincent College, Halifax, Innes taught home economics at Booth Memorial High School in St. John's. She was one of the organizers and the first president of the Newfoundland and Labrador Family Planning Association (now Planned Parenthood). In 1975, International Women's Year, she was a story editor for CBC's Here and Now.

In 1977 she was elected to a four-year term on St. John's City Council. Her main concerns were for good affordable housing, water and sewer for unserviced areas, daycare legislation and deferred taxes for senior homeowners in financial need. She is well known for opposing the destruction of traditional St. John's by large developers.

Innes is a pioneer member of the St. John's Status of Women Council, Past-president of the Newfoundland Writers Guild, and a member of the Writer's Alliance of Newfoundland and Labrador.

❦   ❦   ❦

I often say I was born a feminist. My mother was one of four sisters and my grandmother moved the family from Cape St. Francis, where my grandfather was lightkeeper, to Curling where she opened up a little business. She obviously served as a role model for her daughters, all of whom were independent women with successful careers apart from homemaking.

My brother and I were treated much the same in our upbringing. He had to do his share of household chores the same as me, and my father helped when he could. When my parents decided to send me to university they were criticized for wasting money on a girl "who would only end up married, anyway." They always replied, "Well, she has the brains so she's going to get her chance."

The war was on while I was at university and women were needed in munitions factories, on farms, and in fact everywhere, to keep things going at home. Women adapted easily to their new roles and thrived on the work. They had no worries about who would look after their pre-schoolers like today's working mothers; government and industry were quick to set up daycare centres because they desperately needed these highly productive women.

As soon as the war ended, they changed their tune. The closing of day-care centres and government propaganda literally forced women back to the home. "Don't take a job away from a veteran," was the constant theme. About this time, I graduated and went to Toronto to work as a home economist. I was engaged to be married and my boss continually harassed me about whether I was secretly married because they were no longer hiring married women, even in jobs not required by men.

After my marriage, I returned with my husband to Newfoundland where it was all but unheard of for married women to work for pay unless they had no means of support. Over the years, while raising my two children, I did a lot of volunteer work and became an active member of the Newfoundland Branch of the Canadian Federation of University Women. It's incredible when I look back now and see the progress made since then.

In the fifties and sixties, we lobbied for a higher standard of education for teachers beginning with a minimum of two years university and later a B.A.Ed. At that time, teachers were in schools without so much as grade eleven.

My involvement with Family Planning more than anything else made me aware of the constraints placed on women in all aspects of our society. The belief that I could do anything I put my mind to proved a lie. Society said, "Oh yes, you can do some things if you're not too pushy, but you can't be a bank manager or premier or church elder." Being at home and unable to participate fully "out there" in the real world does something to your ego. I suffered depression and finally realized I had to change my situation if I was to survive. Teaching restored my feeling of self-worth and gave me the confidence to pursue other concerns.

I had always been interested in politics and I have a real love for this old city of St. John's, which is always in danger of being destroyed by developers. I attended a conference in Toronto on "Women in Politics" and was inspired by N.D.P. politician Rosemary Brown who was one of the speakers. I realized the only way to change things was to get in and do it yourself, so on returning home, I joined a reform group. In the Municipal election of 1973, I teamed up with another woman and three men and ran as a slate, "Five for Change." Only one of our group, a high profile businessman, was elected. However, I learned how to mount a campaign, and although I took lots of abuse and was told repeatedly to get back home where I belonged and leave the business of running the city to the men, we made real progress in raising the level of acceptance of women candidates.

In the four-year interim before the next election I wrote articles and did freelance broadcasting on CBC radio. During International Women's Year (1975) I was invited to be a story editor on CBC-TV's *Here and Now*. I took the opportunity to air programs about family planning, rape, feminism, the law and how it affects women. I had to listen to snide remarks, and even had my name changed by a colleague from Fran to Frank on the report on "Women in the CBC." Despite all the flack, I persisted. I was working on a film on abortion when my contract came up for renewal. It was renewed verbally by my executive producer, but was never ratified and the film which was ready to be edited, was never shown.

I ran on my own in the next election (1977) and, with the help of feminists and other friends, I won a seat on Council. Shannie Duff was also elected, and Dorothy Wyatt was re-elected Mayor. It was the first time two women councillors were ever elected in St. John's. Having fought for greater accountability through a Ward System, I ran in a ward in the next election (1981). It was a mistake. The anti-choice forces mobilized against me and I lost my seat. It wasn't until the '89 election that another woman, Wendy Williams, replaced me, bringing the number of women elected back to three out of a total of nine seats. (Shannie Duff was elected Mayor and Dorothy Wyatt won a council seat.) the provincial record is equally appalling. Since Lady Helena Squires won a seat in 1928, only six other women have been elected to the House of Assembly (updated 1992). In the decision making process, it seems women simply don't count in our society.

Women will never count unless young women are willing to fight for more than the right to work for equal pay. Unfortunately, some young women think of feminists as radical, loud-mouthed, strident women whom they would not care to emulate. Other successful women reject feminism believing they have made it on their own. Actually, they all owe a tremendous debt to those early feminists. Without their personal sacrifice in the struggle for justice and equality, few women today would be the recipients of anything like equal treatment in the workplace.

I believe Media and Politics are the two most important arenas. Both exert tremendous power in our lives and unless women share equally in this power, we won't see much real change for generations to come. Yes, we may finally reach pay parity with men, and there will be more women in non-traditional jobs, but the important decisions about quality of life and whether we survive as a species will be left to the Ronalds or Georges, Brians and Mikhails of our planet.

Marilyn John

1987 Profile
Interview by Marian Frances White

Marilyn John has taken on the mammoth task of claiming aboriginal rights for the Newfoundland Micmac Indians. She was born on the Conne River Reserve, Bay d'Espoir on September 20, 1951. By 1973 she had been elected secretary/treasurer of the Native Association of Newfoundland and Labrador. The first group attempt to organize all aboriginal people in the province, it included the Nascapi, Montagnais, Micmac and Inuit. Over the next five years, as vice-president and president of the Micmac Band, she encouraged them to go back to their tribal systems. To determine the status of people living in Conne River John worked with the Department of Indian Affairs doing genealogy research. The 580 Micmac Indians were finally given Indian Status in 1984 under the Indian Act of Canada.

83

As international spokesperson for the Band, John has lobbied in Geneva to have the United Nations establish a statement of principles for indigenous people of the world. She negotiates for reserve lands, for Indian control of education, and for more say in the Indian social and welfare system.

ૠ ૠ ૠ

*A*s a child I was taught English as my first language. Later on in life I began to realize there was a part of my culture missing and I wanted to know what that was. I never learnt the Micmac language fluently because the old people around me were discouraged from using it. The Micmacs were even discouraged from saying their Catholic prayers in their own language. I would like to see the school systems changed to take into account the Indian culture.

Culture is a big part of the development of an individual; that is, knowing who you are and what you are. Because this has not been taught in the schools, kids today are caught between two worlds. To change this we have finally introduced the Micmac language as an extra-curricular activity in the schools. Up until our booklet on the cultural history of the Micmacs was printed everything that was written about us was written by non-Micmacs. We are finally beginning to express ourselves as we see ourselves.

As aboriginal people we see the right to land as one of our basic rights. The attitude that the Micmacs are not aboriginal to this island is ludicrous. The Micmac Indians have been in Newfoundland since time immemorial and once occupied a land mass of what is today known as Eastern Canada. They were a nomadic people and travelled back and forth between here and Nova Scotia. This is where the old mythology that the Micmacs were brought over here to kill off the Beothucks is slowly losing ground. In the research done on genealogy we have been able to document that both Beothucks and Micmacs lived in the same community but have not been able to document any major clashes or wars between them. It seems apparent that many of the people here today are a mixture of Beothuck and Micmac. Every summer an archaeologist comes here to do excavating and talks to the old people. He has documented so many similarities between them that he believes what other archaeologists have labelled as Beothuck could very well be Micmac. Today the government is saying that the Beothucks are the aboriginal people. I venture to say that if there were Beothuck people around today to claim aboriginal rights the attitude would be the opposite. I have come to recognize that peoples' attitudes are born out of ignorance. You have to teach people your history and make credible arguments for them to realize that what they have always believed is not necessarily true.

In June 1984 the Micmacs were finally recognized as Status Indians under Canada's Indian Act. Since then the Band's social conditions have improved greatly. However, when it comes down to reserve lands the provincial government tries to make things very sticky for us by attaching so many conditions to granting land for a reservation. We don't feel they have land to grant us because the land was ours to start with. We have aboriginal rights as the first people here. We are not a minority group but indigenous people, and the problems generated from other people who left their own country and came to ours ... we have problems because they came to ours. We feel we have the right to fish, hunt and to make our own laws and to develop ourselves in a manner that we feel is fit for our people.

Before April 17, 1985 if an Indian woman married a non-Indian man, legislatively she was cast out of the tribe and was not allowed to live on reservation land; neither was she entitled to any program of services of the Band. We negotiated Clause 12 1 B so that this would not apply to our women. Clause 12 1 B now states that even if you have intermarried we do not cast you out. However, we also realize that a time may come when too much intermarriage will seriously threaten our culture.

Employment is very scarce in Newfoundland and, to say the least, desperate for Indian women. It is especially scarce for non-professional women who have no training. It's not difficult to see the parallel between women with no education and also women who are young, unwed mothers. Because of this problem I have been working on a training program to bring women back into the workforce. We are using skills that are in the community like basket weaving, leather work, bead work and reviving the old art of doing embroidery with caribou hair. Employment and Immigration partially sponsors these programs. Under *Micmac Crafts* we sell our work all over Canada in trade shows. This project works well because some of the older people here offered to teach their skills to the younger generation.

As a counsellor for the Band I see the problems of child welfare and medical services as serious ones. The immune system of the Indians here does not seem to be strong, whether that is genetic or not I don't know, but it certainly seems to have a lot to do with diet and the kinds of food we eat. In my genetic research I have found that the people today are not as healthy as those who lived off wildlife. Now that we are federally funded we have more money to put into these programs.

I think as women, especially aboriginal women, we have a role to play in developing our culture and providing for our own people. We should strive to ensure that the life we want to provide for them is the best one possible. I am dedicated to improving the life and lifestyles of all Indian people and making the culture thrive and flourish where it would otherwise die. I think the answer lies in taking parts of our culture and using it in modern day situations. I don't think my work stops or starts regionally or internationally; you have to recognize the work on both ends to find the meeting point. Indian women have to start making this awareness grow so that somewhere in the middle we will all reach a happy medium.

Cathy Jones

1987 Profile

Witty and controversial with a rare ability to transform a stark stage into truer-than life scenes, Cathy Jones stands as an actress of impact. She is an original member of the infamous CODCO troupe whose stage and National TV performances have won them awards and international acclaim. Writing from everyday life experiences, Jones is sensitive to the burden laid on women for contraception, child care and relationships. She brings these issues to light through perceptive characters who inspire rebellion.

Born on April 16, 1955 in St. John's, she joined the Newfoundland travelling Theatre Company in 1973 while still a teenager. Before that year finished she was working with CODCO in their first show Cod On A Stick. *Her strong singing voice and sharp-edged tongue enlivened such* CBC TV series as Up At Ours, and The Wonderful Grand Band. *Jones has co-produced and performed in many local shows and actively participates in annual International Women's Day celebrations. In 1986 she wrote and performed her one-woman show—A* Wedding in Texas and Other Stories. *She lives in St. John's where she charges the stage with her energy, while being continually recharged by her Scorpio daughter, Mara.*

🍎　🍎　🍎

I love to entertain and laugh with people. I don't like to write funny things; I prefer the funny things to write themselves. I believe that if I tried to write *feminist* comedy it would turn out very grim and unfunny. Yet I am a woman, writing from my experiences in this female jacket I seem to be wearing. As a place from which to write comedy, it is a decent sex.

My sex is, to me, an important tool in my learning process, and in my work. So much comedy, like so much feminism, takes itself too seriously, presuming some sort of exclusivity. Recently a "feminist" was offended that a character of mine, who was a lesbian, died, implying I suppose, that she should have been treated with kid gloves because she was a lesbian.

What??? Lesbians don't die??? I have always found the key to life is to face it dead on.

And the key to comedy is reality. Reality with a twist. They say that in curing cancer, attitude is of the utmost importance, I say, why wait for cancer? In my comedy I keep a bravado attitude that makes women (and men) laugh. I act as if I've got the whole thing under control. Like I've won the battle of the sexes. My character, Vave Gladney, hostess of "Fudgeos and Feminism" says: "It's great to be a woman ... especially considering the alternative! Because, things are looking up for women! These days, we burn up more old calories just *making choices*! Whether to make cookies or teach up to the university."

Vave subtly hits on the inconvenience of bearing the birth control burden, and the hideous possibility of sudden unwanted pregnancy. "That old birth control is not fixed yet! I had my IUD out and I had someone else's period last month, not my own! So if anyone missed their period, don't worry ... I had it!" Vave says flippant, sexist things like, "My husband Bob thought that sex was like doing the dishes ... if you did it badly enough you wouldn't be asked to do it again!" Vave has it all figured out, she says that "Men are like a box of chocolates ... and I know what you're thinking ... they're fattening and its hard to stop at one ... but you've got to learn to pick the nougats! It's no good fooling with the world of men if you're going to end up eating a load of vanilla creams! Get the guide and go for the cherries! I'm publishing a new book, *Vave's Guide to the Chocolate Box of Life*. Read it! If you've got a bordeaux, and you want something harder, like a brazil, you might have to go to the bottom layer. What of it??? The main thing is stay on top, don't get under it! Stop putting yourself down. Everybody's bum gets dimply! Don't watch the twenty minute workout, it's depressing. Don't pick up men, they're too heavy and you'll put your back out. And if some kleptomaniac wants to lift your man, take a good look at what she's getting ... you might want to say "Thank you very much, Miss!" And remember the old Vave Gladney motto: Ask not what you can do for buddy ... but what buddy can do for you!!!"

And of course in my real life, off stage, I have often lived the hideous realities of my characters in their domestic fights, and I have put my back (and spirit) out picking up men. I have been the girl who drives away and never sees her mother again. I have freaked along the way with the best of them at the conditioned fear of becoming the *wife*. Yeah, yeah. But to me life is bittersweet, and the pain intensifies the joy. I love the strength required to handle it all. It rains on the males as well as the females, though, and I feel we are heading towards a more spiritual era, when sexuality will be less relevant and marked. Yes, there is much work for women alone, but life is so much bigger than sex. If I learn to accept myself and other people, to relax and have faith, to be true to myself and you ... I don't know that it will matter that in this life I was a woman.

Martha Joshua

1987 Profile. Martha tells her own story.
Transcribed by Fran Williams.
Martha Joshua was born at Killinek,
Labrador on July 27, 1911. Her family
moved to Okak when she was still a baby;
however, the remainder of the family moved
to Nain after the Spanish flu. This flu is
said to have arrived aboard the last mail
steamer in the late summer of 1918. The flu
spread from areas such as Mud Lake,
Rigolet and further northward to Okak.
Hundreds of people died as settlement after
settlement was stricken with the deadly flu.

Martha was married to Titus Joshua for fifty years. Only two of seven children
survived. As a young woman she did a lot of native handicrafts, such as
embroidery and making boots and clothing from seal skins. She continues to
contribute to the community in this fashion, but failing eyesight prevents her
from making boots and other clothing. For Martha Joshua, a survivor of the
Spanish Flu, being outdoors, taking in the fresh air, and visiting friends is her
most pleasing pastime. In 1985 Anne Budgell and Nigel Markham directed a
film, The Last Days of Okak based on her experience and that of the mis-
sionaries and other Spanish Flu survivors.

ぷ　ぷ　ぷ

I was around seven years old when the Spanish flu hit my family's camp.
We were hunting and fishing on an island off Okak. There were five of us
there. My grandfather was chopping wood in the fall. He had his dickey
on, his hood up and an armload of wood when he collapsed there and then
and died. That same night while I was sleeping in my bed, I woke suddenly
when something heavy fell on me; that was my grandmother. She also
died. That left my father's sister-in-law, her daughter and Emelia
Merkuratsuk's son. The old lady was making ready to row the remaining
children back to Okak when she collapsed and died.

The family had made lots of *pepsi** and *nipko,** and that's what the
young girl fed us for awhile. One day when the sea got calm the young girl
dressed me up and got ready to pull the rowboat to sea. I was sitting and
waiting for her until she had the boat pulled out. She told me to go into
the house and wait for her until the boat was pulled out because, she said,
it was cold outside. I obeyed and waited inside. After a while I got tired of
waiting and went out to check on her. When I looked down the river I saw
her half way to Okak. I sat down where I was and bawled and cried.

I don't remember a lot after that except that I cried and hollered for my grandparents every night. In the shock of all this, I even forgot about the baby. One day I was so cold that I had to find more blankets. I found the baby in the bed clothes. He lived for awhile, but I guess he starved to death since I didn't really know how to feed him or what to feed him or how to care for him.

I don't remember being very hungry, thirsty or sleepy after everyone died. The house we lived in was a small *illusuak*.* The husky dogs we had for work used to fight all the time. One day they broke a sack of hard bread. I somehow managed to save a little for myself. I lived on this and a handful of snow now and again for three months or so. I remember I could only sleep sitting up. That winter many dogs came to the island. They had shiny fur and were very wild. However, there was one dog who used to guard me from the other dogs.

I later found out that the young girl had left us because she thought she might die in the middle of the ocean and leave us to drown in the boat. She managed to get to Okak and told the minister Leoni that she had left me and the baby on the island. The minister tried to row over but the fall winds prevented him from reaching the island. After a while everyone figured us dead.

One day hunters came to the island. The first people I saw were Gustave Sillit and another man whose name I forget. They were shooting all the wild dogs and also shot the dog who protected me. The men did not know I was there, but when they killed the dog who protected me from the others I started to cry for the dog. I called out *"anaanak"** because I thought this dog was my mother. The dogs had made a terrible mess of the house with flour and everything else thrown about. I, too, was covered in flour and dirt. When these men saw me they thought they had seen a ghost. After a while they brought me back to Okak.

My hair was stuck straight up with grime and dirt. It was full of lice, but at that time it didn't bother me at all. I had no boots and was using my grandfather's longjohns. I don't remember much of returning to Okak except that I could not eat or drink for a long while. The only food I could keep down was *pepsi* and drink water.

When I left the island the only thing I took with me was my grandfather's gramophone because this was rare at the time. The minister Leoni took a thick yellow story book which belonged to my family. I was supposed to get a sum of money for that, the minister said, but I don't know what he's done with it. All I know is that I lived to tell the tale.

Pepsi—dried fish or dried caribou meat.
Nipko—dried seal meat.
Illusuak—a house made from animal skin.
Anaanak—Inuit word for mother.

Kathleen Knowling

1991 Profile
Original interview by Susan Hart
Born in St. John's in 1927 into the Ayre family, Kathleen or "Muffet" was educated at Bishop Spencer College in St. John's, Netherwood Boarding School in New Brunswick, and Barnard College in New York. She then spent two years in Paris and returned to St. John's to work in a few local businesses, before marrying William Knowling, an insurance agent, with whom she parented three children (Sarah, Susan, and Ronald).

She combined work as mother with studying art and now is a fulltime professional artist, well known and respected for her paintings in watercolours and oils. Knowling has had solo exhibits at Eastern Edge Gallery and MUN Art Gallery, as well her work has adorned the cover of Waterlily, *a feminist newspaper and was also used on the cover of* Each Small Step: Breaking the Chains of Abuse and Addiction *published by Gynergy Press in Prince Edward Island.*

❧ ❧ ❧

I never had any connection with art until I was in my late twenties, and just as a matter of interest I took drawing and painting at the Sheppard's Academy of Art and found that I loved doing this absolutely fabulous thing, which is drawing a bit of drapery and making it look three dimensional. Back in about 1975 I decided that in ten years I wanted to turn myself into a professional artist, and I have, even though I don't make much money in my profession.

Before I built my studio I did the typical thing that women do, kind of work here and work there, and shift around, with no space that was my own space. I don't think this sort of problem adds to people's creativity, I think that certainly women of my generation are very much in a certain kind of mould, which takes an incredible amount of effort to break. You can feel resentful, you can feel unpaid and exploited, but you still feel that you shouldn't dirty the living room and you shouldn't make a mess in the kitchen and that you should clear up everything in time to get supper. This just goes on all the time, and how you train yourself not to have that feeling is our life's challenge.

It took quite awhile for me to really feel that the studio was mine, but I've got it nice and dirty, the floor isn't spanking clean anymore, it's much more me. It's enabled me to go larger, and by providing a place to store my media and paper, it encourages me to go ahead and try something new.

My family is a very important inspiration for my art. I think on a small scale the history of a family is the history of all of us, and you can see the way society's changed, and the way ideas and attitudes change, by just looking at changes within your own family. I guess I've always liked family stories and remembered them, and I wish I remembered more. Living in Newfoundland and being part of its history, and having my family roots go back a long way gives me a particular feeling. I don't think it's something you should really be proud of, because it's something you can't help; no point in being proud of your ancestors, you just hope your ancestors can be proud of you.

I like to wonder about my feelings, and whether my ancestors had similar feelings. What was my grandmother's reaction to the fire of 1892 that destroyed the city? She had two little girls and she was burnt out. What kind of life did my great-grandmother live? One of her children died in a cholera epidemic in the 1840s. How did she feel about that, what kind of life did she live?

The work I'm doing now is based on a very traditional art form, the hooked rug. I'm doing drawings in colour pencil and oil stick, with a border all around, depicting scenery and figures and so on, but simplified very much as a traditional hooked mat would be. I could be with this for the rest of my life, because there's so much scope: abstract patterning, colour relationships, landscape, figures. Women made hooked rugs out of a combination of necessity (as a covering for the floor) and the desire to create a kind of memory book. They had all these scraps of material; father's shirt, mother's dress, all went into the hooked mat. The rugs were worn out of course, had hard lives, they were used roughly. But for many women this was a form of artistic expression, and they reduced the chaos in their scrap bags into a kind of formal shape. And that's one of the things that art is about, bringing order to chaos. I think we can justifiably claim hooked rugs as an art form.

I'm very interested in colour, which relates me to the Fauve movement, a French post-impressionist movement. They were interested in colour. Another school was the Symbolists, who saw colour as symbolizing certain things. For me green symbolizes new life, rebirth, spring; blue is spiritual values, inner strength; purple is pride, regal, royal spirit; orange is fire, movement, quickness.

There's a real flowering of women's art going on in Newfoundland and Labrador. To my eye, the artists who are doing the most innovative work are women. They do work that is personal but they're not hyping their own egos. They really show a sensitivity and a sensibility to the world, and to what's going on around them. I feel very close to a lot of women artists. We talk the same language.

Young people and people who know about art relate to mine quite well, but many people don't see the point of it. Motorcars or law or money doesn't particularly interest me. I don't think that making art is necessarily more creative than making money, except making money is much more popular. You go to a party and people say "You're an artist, how interesting, I've always loved art." But no-one ever goes to a party and says "Oh, you're a banker, how interesting, I've always loved money!" Somebody should say that some day, "I just love money, I wish I knew more about it." People who make art work very hard, and they don't get paid very much. And if you do something a little off-beat people are very uncomfortable with it, "That doesn't look like a human being!"

As an artist, you don't always express exactly what you set out to express. But you have to believe in your work because you can't create art if you aren't motivated by it.

ROSE-MARIE KENNEDY

Millicent Loder

1992 Profile
Interview by Marian Frances White
Millicent Loder was born in Rigolet, Labrador on February 23, 1915 and first went to Muddy Bay School in Cartwright and later to St. Anthony to finish up to ninth grade. At age fourteen Loder returned to North West River in Labrador to work for the Grenfell Mission. In 1968 she returned home to North West River after living in Newfoundland for almost twenty years. She served for nine years on the Board of Directors of the Grenfell Regional Health Services and was director of nursing at the Northwest River Hospital before retiring. She has been recognized for her efforts with an honourary degree from Memorial University and an honourary membership in the Association of Registered Nurses of this Province. In November 1989 Millicent Loder published her book of memoirs, Daughter of Labrador.

ã   ã   ã

*W*hen my grandchildren were small they were always asking me to tell them about the olden times, but even then I was busy nursing so I told them that when I retired I would write my stories down. My grandchildren have been brought up elsewhere and I wanted them to know about their heritage. It took me ten years to write because I'm not a writer but I really wanted the young people to know what it was like for us. The satisfaction of reaching a goal I set for myself was great. I wrote the book for all the children in Labrador because the times now are so different.

The health services and education today have much improved; now, children can stay in their own community and get up to their grade twelve. It sounds so simple today to say I want to be a nurse, but when I went to school I couldn't even get grade nine up here. With regards to health care we still have a long way to go. The only proper hospital for acute care is the Melville Hospital and that is always full.

My mother gave birth to eleven children; three died years before I was born and later on in life when she had no more children, she adopted a baby. She made all the clothing and boots for the family and she was a midwife. Seeing her work, I wanted to do the same. Nursing took up most of my life. I nursed from age fourteen to when I retired when I was sixty-five. When I began nursing I made fifty cents a month, but I was able to support myself because the mission fed me.

Once I had a very scary experience when I was sent from St. Anthony up into a bay because a midwife was in trouble with a delivery. I remember it took a long time to go up by dog team and when I arrived and examined her, I knew I would never be able to deliver that baby up there. So it was a very scary trip with her in labour riding in a Komatik box pulled by a dog team and I was on another team. Every twenty minutes I'd stop to check her. I kept saying to myself "we'll never make it," but we got there and she was alive but her child was already dead. It's very scary when suddenly you're responsible for somebody's life and have no one to turn to.

Later when I had four children of my own I volunteered as a nurse in the night time and when they grew old enough for school, I nursed in the daytime. I don't like how so many children are being raised in daycare services, I wish there was a way for the children to be closer to their parents when they work.

I had a very happy childhood although we were considered to be poor and underprivileged, we never felt poor because we were happy at home. I have so many fond memories of my childhood in Rigolet. We children would have to go away in the winter to school and stay at a boarding house and when I came back those were the happy times to see your friends and family again.

I don't think children are any happier today even though they have much more than we had. It seems to take much more to make and keep them happy. I think most children are happy if they have good parents, that's what counts the most.

North West River is home to me. My husband and I always planned to return here when we retired but he died young. I thought it would be better if I came back here and got busy. I don't think I would have survived otherwise. Since I returned here I worked on the town council and I really enjoyed that because I was doing something for the community and for the last ten years I've been the president of the seniors group called Helping Hands. My very best pastimes are skidooing and fishing through the ice from March on. My brother and I usually take a trip by skidoo up into Doublemare which was our family's old hunting grounds. This is the ideal spot to retire and the closest place to heaven because you find peace and contentment here. I say to myself where else can you sit in a chair in your living room and look over at the Mealy Mountains and in the summer see the boats come in and feel complete peace and freedom and know that you're safe?

I'm a person who is hoping that NATO won't come here any more than it has because there are some things that you see now in the country that you wish wasn't happening. People who lived there felt that it was their place and that nobody should hunt their ground. It really irritates me if I go up in the country and want to walk about and there's a sign that says "NO ADMISSION." Well, that's my country and when I find out that maybe through that path there's a club belonging to the military, I get mad. I'm not against progress and people here want jobs but I'd like to see it done in a sensible manner so that lands and people's way of life is protected and respected. I don't think we have to have people making ready to go to war when we could develop our country's natural resources like tourism and forestry.

I feel that if it was just up to Newfoundland, we wouldn't be developed yet. It was the Grenfell Mission who came here years ago and paid their way and made schools and nursing stations. Even Northern Newfoundland, up around St. Anthony is much different than the Avalon Peninsula and the money goes where the population warrants it. Communities like Rigolet haven't got water and sewer yet. Even though I'm Canadian, I think of myself first as a Labradorian and I believe that most Labrador people do because the people who owns us, that is New-foundland, are remote from us. We're divided by water and we can't even get there unless we fly and that is just too expensive for most people. We've wanted a trans-Labrador road connecting to the ferries so people could have access to the Island, but there's never been any effort to make it easier for Newfoundland and Labrador to be together.

I have a story I want to tell about a five dollar gold piece I had won as a child for getting best marks in school. We had this little office within the Muddy Bay school where I put the gold piece when I went home for the summer. I thought I was rich and imagined when I came back next fall I'd be able to go over to the store in Cartwright and buy treats. That year the school burned down and my five dollar gold piece, which was like a fortune to me, must have melted in the fire. Often I'd go there with a stick and shuffle through the ashes but I never did find it. A short time ago some of my good friends had a dinner for me and announced that they had a presentation to make. There on a plaque were five loonies to replace the money I had lost. I was really moved by that.

Economics has always played a large part in everyone's life. When you were a fisherwoman, you had to be out working on the fish flakes. Both parents had to work together. Other women make baskets and skin boots. Women are just as brilliant as men, they can do the job just as well, but I hope they remember that they can still be themselves.

Sheila Lynch

1991 Profile
Interview by Marian Frances White
Sheila Lynch was born in St. John's, the second of five children, spent her early childhood there and moved to Carbonear with her family. She attended Memorial University where she studied pre-nursing, pre-med and then completed a science degree with a biology major. She worked in a variety of occupations and travelled in Europe. She did research with Dr. E.R. Seary on Newfoundland Family Names and Place Names. In 1979 she completed her medical degree, sub-specialized in psychiatry and completed her psychiatry fel-
lowship in 1984. At the present time she is in private practice psychiatry with Dr. John Angel in St. John's.

🍁   🍁   🍁

When I was a young child, my sister and I spent summer holidays with our relatives in Carbonear. My uncle kept cows and horses, there was lots of farmland and places to explore. We were thrilled when mom and dad told us we were moving there to live.

To me as a child of ten, life seemed much more exciting in Carbonear than in St. John's. The school had potbellied stoves and boys in your classroom. There seemed to be more freedom of movement and you got to know more people. In the spring many families moved to coastal Labrador to fish for the summer. We would go to the public wharf to watch the hustle and bustle of loading on small boats, supplies and people for the first trip north. In the fall many students would miss some days at school to harvest their potatoes for winter. In the early spring the sealing boats—the Kyle and the Terra Nova would leave with flags waving and families of the sealers watching from the last vantage point on Harbour Rock Hill.

There were many eccentric characters amongst the grown-ups in Carbonear and I realize now in retrospect that Carbonear was very tolerant of eccentricity and perhaps there was something about the place that attracted it.

My early years as a student at Memorial University were exciting and enjoyable. The university was much smaller then and allowed for an opportunity to know both students and faculty to a degree not possible with the size of the university today. For me those years were formative years—the exposure to spirituality, family, relationships etc. There were many hours spent in debate of what we then considered crucial issues, often at the expense of our formal studies. However, at that time we did not feel the great pressure of finding a job at the end of it. When I returned to University in the mid seventies, I was aware of the great level of concern of present day students with economic security.

In the late sixties, gender inequality issues were of paramount importance in the budding feminist movement. In professional school in the mid-seventies the increase in numbers of female students was evident and gratifying. It was interesting to realize that many of these students did not have a conscious awareness of the struggle to affect this change in attitude and opportunity.

When I entered medical school I did not plan to specialize and had not considered psychiatry as an area of special interest to me. My interest in psychiatry developed in my clinical years. I found the work challenging. It's an area of medicine in which much research remains to be done. The knowledge of brain biochemistry is expanding at a rapid rate and many disorders previously felt to be mental or psychological are being reassessed in view of these new discoveries. Psychiatric illness often affects all areas of physical and psychological health of the individual. As an issue of women's health, the reported high incidence of depressive illness in women as well as the biochemical changes through childbirth and menopause are all presently being researched more thoroughly with current technologies.

In the Newfoundland context there has always been a scarcity of psychiatrists and mental health professionals. Beginning in the early 1980s, attention in the media to issues such as battered spouses, child physical and sexual abuse, dysfunctional families, and relationship conflicts have raised the awareness in the community for the need of skilled professionals. The increased public awareness of the degree of alcohol abuse and other substance addiction problems has helped to bring many individuals thus affected to seek help. In the past there was stigmatization of individuals in the Newfoundland community who were known to suffer from psychiatric illness and this stigmatization added further stress to individuals and their families.

Newfoundland does not yet have the degree of street drug addiction as other North American centres. The small size of communities and the extended network of family and friends can offer support and caring not often found in other parts of North America. However we are rapidly catching up.

There has been over the last ten years an increased awareness of nutrition and lifestyle assessment to promote health and longevity. I encourage yoga, tai chi, walking, relaxation, massage and eliminating a lot of stress. Overall I see the physical and psychological health of individuals as inseparable from other factors in our lives. These factors are a sense of individual self-worth and self-reliance in relationships at home, in the workplace and in the political and economic institutions of this province.

My clinical experience has given me great respect for the power of the individual to grow, make changes and heal, despite obstacles. I enjoy the challenges of psychiatry because I believe in the evolution of the individual.

Emily MacDougall

1990 Profile
Original interview by June Hiscock
Born Emily Moore on October 31,
1911 in Jersey Harbour on
Newfoundland's southwest coast,
she left home at age twelve to work
as a domestic in Ramea. After
three years she moved to Port-aux-
Basques and worked as a
housekeeper until she married and
settled in Wreckhouse. Emily has been diagnosed as having Alzheimer's Dis-
ease and has been living in Port-aux-Basques for the past fifteen years with her
son, Lochie, who cares for her.

ﾟ   ﾟ   ﾟ

*W*reckhouse is known for having the worst winters anywhere. The ferocious winds played havoc to the Canadian National Railway; many trains were literally swept off the rail attempting to butt the hurricane-force winds.

"I'm the woman what looked after the wind in Wreckhouse"

I was born in Jersey Harbour but I lived in St. Andrews which was a good place to grow up. Everyone had big families and a lot of people lived there. My brothers and sisters and I would walk the four miles to school, carrying our dinner with us and we would all take turns bringing kindling to light the fire. I only went as far as Book Four.

When I was twelve years old I went up the coast to Ramea and worked as a domestic for three years. Then I took the coastal boat up to Port-aux-Basques where I worked as a housekeeper for Mrs. Wilfred Gillam. I met my husband, Lochie MacDougall, in Port-aux-Basques and after we were married we moved to Wreckhouse, the place where he was born. It was all woods up there at one time until they cut it all out. It was a really pretty place, beautiful in the summer but no good in winter. It was lonely up there at first and I done lots of crying when I first moved up there from being lonesome.

Now Lochie, my dear, he was some worker. He looked after the wind back then. He'd use his hand (Emily holds her arm straight up), go outdoors and come in, tell you right where the wind was. Smart my dear, he was some smart. We had the dairy farm and he'd be in the woods either cutting wood or trapping. I tell you, he'd get his foxes and his rabbits. He was a wonderful worker and he was good as a woman when it come to raising our family. We had nine boys and three girls. All my crowd was good, well, we learned 'em to be good.

I raised the twelve children while I tended the farm. It wasn't an easy life, that's for sure. The children had to walk eleven miles to get to and from the St. Andrews school. They all got good learning, though. All except for young Lochie, he was hurted with the wind. Gale of wind took him and blowed him, broke his little back. He was only small then. But still for all, he'd keep going.

We had ten and twelve head of cattle, twelve sheep, three pigs and so many hens and ducks. You'd have to make hay and put it in the barn for winter. And I made pounds and pounds of butter. We used to sell it for sixty-five cents a pound. We sold fresh milk, too, and people would come from miles around to get it. Come right to your door and take it and go on. One time I had fifty-five pounds of butter put away just for eating. I misses it. When I goes to Codroy Valley with my daughter Kay, I gets it from the people who got farms up there.

You'd have to get up at five o'clock in the morning and to get water from the pond in winter you had to cut the ice, and then melt it on the stove to get your breakfast. I went through some there, I tell you.

Everybody loved the house at Wreckhouse. There'd be flowers up in the windows and on the table. I had a garden, you know. We had it all, my dear. And we always had a house full. Crowd from Port-aux-Basques would come up here berry picking; it was a wonderful place for berries.

You'd see them coming in the morning, probably one of the men would bring a bottle of rum for Lochie and they'd stay well into the night.

The trains would run every day. You'd hear the phone ringing, "Is that you, Mrs. MacDougall, what's the wind like today?" I'd say, "Tis good now but there's a big storm coming up." I lost two trains. Blowed off the tracks, but it wouldn't my fault, a big storm come on. Thank God nobody got hurted. I don't know what they got done with the trains now dear. They used to close them down when there was a gale on. There's not so much wind as there used to be, see. The wind goes down in the spring of the year. In the fall is the worse.

A good many times we put people up for the night. We had to, blowing hard, see. You'd see them bringing their baskets of stuff. I must say, they were good to us. We used to hear from them afterwards. I'd get postcards and letters from people from all over. I had them all put away somewhere but I can't remember where I put them. And you know, we never used to miss a dance. I was right full of life back then. We'd go up to St. Andrews to the dances and go down to Cape Ray to parties. I loved it, dearly loved it.

It was a hard life, dear. When the poor old man was living, it wasn't so bad. God bless him, he'd dead and gone but I really misses him. And I loved it up to Wreckhouse. I'd go back today if it wasn't so lonely.

CP Photo, courtesy *The Evening Telegram*

Joanne McDonald

1987 Profile
Interview by Marian Frances White
Joanne McDonald was born in St. John's on August 16, 1952 and grew up in St. Mary's, St. Mary's Bay. Because she was born with Spina Bifida she spent much of her childhood in various hospitals and rehabilitation centres. Nonetheless, she graduated from Dunne Memorial High School in St. Mary's at the age of seventeen.

At twenty-two she won her first gold medal in slalom at a national competition in Manitoba. She continues to hold the provincial, national and North American slalom record.

McDonald worked as a medical secretary and later as secretary of the Provincial Recreation Advisory Council for Special Groups. She also worked with the Canadian Paraplegic Association for six years and currently works with Secretary of State as a Social Development Officer.

ෙ   ෙ   ෙ

I became involved in wheelchair sports in 1973. Although sports for persons with disabilities had been organized in Canada in 1967, it was only introduced to Newfoundland in 1972. No one here had ever heard of persons with disabilities taking part in sports, outside of just being spectators. This situation changed dramatically after a few people travelled to a national competition in Calgary to observe athletes with disabilities competing in a host of events. Observers to this competition returned to Newfoundland and organized clinics demonstrating the 100 metre sprint, shot put, javelin, table tennis and various other events. I was invited to travel with the Newfoundland team in 1973 to compete in the National games being held in Vancouver. That first year I must have tried every event! Although I very much enjoyed sports as a spectator, it had never really occurred to me that I, as a women with a disability, could be a competitive athlete. This national competition was my spring board to the competitive world of sports. I realized that I had found something I truly enjoyed and wanted to continue with for as long as possible.

My 1974 gold medal win in slalom was a complete surprise to me. I had never imagined that I would win a gold medal, and certainly not in only my second year of competition. Training for this event had consisted of setting up an obstacle course with the tables and chairs in the cafeteria of the Children's Rehabilitation Centre. As my sporting career evolved, training techniques for this event became much more sophisticated. Unfortunately, at that time there was virtually no training information, no coaches and no equipment. The formation of the Wheelchair Sports Association for Newfoundland and Labrador in 1973 provided significant support to those of us who wanted to be involved in competitive sports. With the formation of this Association we now had greater opportunities to access training facilities, equipment and, to a lesser extent, expertise in coaching.

There were many other events that I was interested in and following my second year of competition I decided to develop my techniques and skill level, especially in the area of track and field. I analyzed the equipment I was using, the equipment other athletes were using across the country, and various methods of training. I was very impressed with the calibre of athletes throughout Canada and although I started sports relatively late in life, I felt very comfortable with what I was doing and where I was going. When I was chosen for the national team and started competing internationally, I began to realize the impact sports was having on my life and how important it was becoming to me. At the international level I saw and met athletes from all over the world who were outstanding competitors and very dedicated to achieving their dreams of being the best in the world. Their skill level, techniques and equipment far exceeded what I had experienced in Canada. Competition at the international level proved to be a very positive experience for me and one that reinforced my desire to achieve the level of success many of my teammates and opponents had attained.

During my early years of competition, both nationally and internationally, I wasn't considered a threat to anyone but the more they saw me coming back, the more they watched out for me. The competitions are very intense; every trick in the book is used to try to upset the opponent psychologically. At the international level this was much more noticeable and initially quite disconcerting to me, however, you do get used to it and learn tricks of your own.

As a member of the Canadian Women's Basketball Team I travelled to many international basketball tournaments and enjoyed these competitions immensely. It was really the only opportunity I had to be a part of an all female basketball team. At the provincial level we had a mixed basketball team as there were not enough women involved to form a separate team. I know there are many, many women with disabilities in this province and this country capable of competing athletically. I believe, however, there would be more women with disabilities, and indeed non-disabled women, involved in sports if there was a fairer system of support given to athletes. There is a serious imbalance in the financial and human support given to male versus female athletes. Male athletes often receive a much higher profile and greater financial incentive for their sporting endeavours while female athletes often receive token appreciation. If this inequity was addressed, I believe there would be many more women with disabilities involved in competitive sports. When you take a look at the major world competitions, like the one I went to in England in '84, and see only eight women's teams compared to the men's thirty-five, it is hard not to get a little annoyed. Considering that there are statistically more women with disabilities than men it would seem that there should be at least an equal number involved.

Wheelchair sports has had a major impact on my life. When you are involved in sports, you gain self discipline. Developing my athletic abilities and competing in sports was a very positive experience for me. I gradually became very comfortable with myself, my self confidence increased dramatically, and I became more involved in the community. It meant, of course, that if I wanted to, I had to go out and talk to people about my involvement in sports. I found this very difficult for a while since I had always been a fairly shy person. The first time I spoke at a sports banquet was nerve wracking. I had a ten-page speech that I'd spent hours writing and I never took my eyes off the paper and read it in warp speed! I doubt if anyone knew what I was saying. Through sports I quickly learned that I had found a place where I was on an equal basis with others. This gave me added confidence and, I believe, contributed significantly to my personal growth and development.

I believe that it is important for people who are disabled to accept who they are and strive for the goals that they themselves want to attain. I hope that some of the things I have accomplished make the statement to both women and men with disabilities that we can achieve our goals. It is not productive to try and live up to someone else's expectations.

Unfortunately, too many people automatically prejudge persons with disabilities. I find this extremely frustrating because this judgement is based on the disability, not the individual. These attitudinal barriers create a form of discrimination that is obviously unfair and limiting. The judgements we place on individuals can be destructive and cause a great deal of personal pain.

I ask the larger community not to make judgements based on a person's disability. If you must judge, then do so based on character, caring, humanity, friendship, etc., and other personal attributes, but not on any disability that a person may have. Remember, an individual who has a disability is a person first and foremost!

LAURA JACKSON

Mary McDonald

1987 Profile
Interview (through letters)
by Marian Frances White
Self-taught fisherwoman from the age of fifteen, Mary McDonald continues to be outstanding in her chosen career. Born in West St. Modeste on May 14, 1940 into a family of eight sisters, she often took on roles that were considered only for men. Her father, reluctant to let his daughter follow his footsteps in the boats, soon gave up trying to persuade her otherwise when he recognized her capabilities. For the following twenty-five years McDonald and her sister, Josephine, fished for a living. She acquired her own gear for salmon fishing and continued to fish for salmon, and cod until her license was cut. McDonald now works in the fish plant on the stages as a 'layer' and 'salter' during the fishing season. She lives close to her environment, cutting wood, planting potatoes, cabbage and other vegetables that last throughout the winter. In 1978 the CBC-TV programme Land and Sea produced a show on her while she fished. Although her speciality in fishing is salmon, she catches a variety of fish and ice fishes in winter.

ẽ   ẽ   ẽ

I suppose I was thirteen when I started fishing. That was just for fun back then. I would go out in the boats with my father jiggin' fish. It was very exciting. It wasn't long before I realized I could make a living by fishing so I started to take it more seriously. There were no boys in a family of nine girls so we often found ourselves doing things that normally only men did. My father didn't want me to go fishing all the time, but I wanted to do it, so I did.

I had very little education, just up to grade seven, so I had to think of a way to make a living. Fishing seemed fine to me. The men then didn't seem to mind me in the boats even though it was unusual. It was only when I got me own gear that they started making something of it. I guess they thought I had no business doing what they thought was men's work. As the years rolled on their attitude got a bit better. I fished in the boats for twenty-five years. I've caught a lot of salmon and cod in that time. One year I sold fish to a buyer with nineteen different grades of cod. That's quite a variety for any one to have. I had West Indian (the kind that is sun burnt); I had tom cods, choice and many more. It's all in the way you cut it and put it up and lay it out to dry. It's cut for different grades. I think a woman can do anything a man can do and even sometimes do it better.

Most often I'm treated fairly with the federal government but sometimes the inspectors give me a hard time. Once I wasn't quite so lucky. I had twenty-five barrels of herring that usually sell for $28 a barrel. The herring inspector turned them down, said they weren't good. What he said was, he couldn't tell if they were bad, so he figured they were no good. He tore them abroad and heaved them away. I had to dump them because the inspector couldn't tell if they were good or bad.

In the time I've been fishing I haven't seen many women in the boats. I think that's changing a bit nowadays. Some think you got to be different to do this work, but I think it's all a matter of putting your mind to one thing and doing it because you want to. My sister, Josephine, fishes with me. She can use a compass as good as any man. One winter me and Josephine hauled one hundred and twelve loads of wood out on the skidoo. That kept us busy right up until Christmas. When we aren't fishing or hauling wood in the summer and fall, we're picking berries. The bakeapples around here are right plentiful. A few years ago I bought an old fashioned wood stove for $450 out of bakeapple money alone. Whatever I do I enjoys it. I wouldn't rather be anywhere but here in West St. Modeste.

In 1982 a few things changed around here concerning me and fishing. I left me boat and started working as a layer and salter in the fish plant here. There were lots of salmon and I caught lots, but there were no buyers, so I couldn't get enough money for me work. If you don't work during the salmon season, June and July, you don't get stamps to tie you over with unemployment insurance during the winter. The problem was after I took a job in the fish plant me salmon license was cut from two hundred permitted to catch to one hundred I could catch. They called me a part-time 'fisherman' which I don't understand since I only work in the plant for about ten weeks. I don't know why the federal people got to make it so hard. If I want a full-time license again I have to fish two years to qualify. I don't like that (their rules) too much. If they don't expect me to fish salmon and cod, I don't know what they think I can do with me gear I've bought over the years, the nets and rope and anchor. I'd get about $200 for it, but what I really want is to be able to fish when the season comes around. I'm the only woman who fished in the boats around here for a living, but that seems to make it more difficult rather than easier. There's poor communication in Ottawa and I know a lot of the problem is because I'm a fisherwoman.

The first year I applied for unemployment as a woman fishing for a living I had me unemployment insurance cut off in March. I thought this strange since none of the men around me had theirs cut off, so I inquired as to why. The taxation people told me directly that they figured I'd used me father's stamps. Somehow I managed to convince them I did the fishing and I got me money rolling in again, got all the back pay too. It wasn't that long ago that the wife of fishermen couldn't get UIC.

In most ways I learned what I know from being out on the water here in Labrador. One winter, though, an instructor came up here from the College of Fisheries in St. John's and taught a four-week course on mending gear and the like. I enjoyed that. I always mended me own gear. I was the only woman in the class. Me and Josephine have done a lot of fishing, so has me mother when she had the chance. There's equal pay for both men and women in the fishing industry now, but before the '80s that wasn't the case. The way I sees it, fish is fish, no matter who catches them!

Ella Manuel

1989 Profile
Compiled by Marian Frances White
Ella Manuel was born in Lewisporte in 1911, a seventh-generation New-foundlander. As a child she spent most of her time outdoors or reading and at age fifteen she shipped out to Boston to go to High School for a year. Manuel completed a Bachelor of Science in Chemistry at Boston University in 1930, but with the Depression starting she returned to Lewisporte and worked in her parent's store. She also taught piano to earn enough money to go to England in 1933—the cargo boat fare was $25.00. Manuel remained in England for seven years and worked for Marks and Spencer as a 'social worker' helping the mostly female staff organize for benefits that included canteens, free uniforms, mostly free medical and dental attention, paid vacations and a raise every birthday!

Manuel, who married a Marks and Spencer worker, moved to Connecticut before World War II where she had her second son. With the deterioration of her marriage, she brought her sons back to Newfoundland and started her broadcasting career in Corner Brook. In '58 she moved to Halifax to work with CBC public affairs and became involved with the Voice of Women, a peace group which actively opposed the Vietnam War. Manuel wrote many of the children's stories she read on air, published That Fine Summer in '79, and is included in From This Place.

In 1968 she was the only individual to present a brief to the Royal Commission on the Status of Women in Canada. Manuel lobbied for the creation of Gros Morne National Park; was a member of the advisory board of Grenfell College in Corner Brook and was on the Board of Regents of MUN in the '70s. In 1980 she received the Person's Award for promoting the cause of women in Canada and for attempting to make children aware of social issues. Ella Manuel died in Halifax on Nov. 24, 1985.

❦   ❦   ❦

Although Ella Manuel was taught no sciences in Newfoundland she said after getting her degree in chemistry: "That seems to me the most ludicrous thing I ever did in my whole life ... I graduated during the worst part of the Depression and there just weren't any jobs (laboratories were closing down) ... I returned to Lewisporte since the idea of going to Toronto then sounded "too boring for words."

After working with The Voice of Women in Halifax, she wrote: "... I really came to myself ... I realized with a tape recorder and some tapes I could live anywhere. So I moved to Woody Point..and had a house built there in '68 ... I sat on the hill in Woody Point and read feminist literature and said 'Oh my God ... the world is full of people like me.' That is when I began to look back without a sense of failure."

Manuel, who among many other things, helped to persuade the British government to allow into Britain 3,000 Basque children who were not orphans, but living "under bombing," was often watched by the FBI and was quoted as saying: "I would have been insulted if I hadn't been watched in those days."

Newfoundland Herald, March 21 '79

105

Excerpt from Ella Manuel's brief presented to the Royal Commission on the Status of Women in Canada, July 1968:

The situation of women in Nfld. is that of inferior beings in a society of underprivileged citizens ... Government has recognized change in industrial techniques as it relates to the economy of Nfld. and has given massive aid to fishermen, loggers and farmers so that they might understand and cope with change. It has not recognized the fundamental change in the domestic and social life of women.

Women have been left to deal as best they can with the plethora of problems arising from change in their traditional way of life ... In order to improve the quality of life for all, it is necessary to institute a great education program for human beings—in all respects equal to the one offered the male edition ... To break the vicious circle binding Nfld. women, education is both the means and the end.

In view of this, here are (my) recommendations:

1. Opportunities should be offered women, even in the most remote settlements for education ... child care and health ... Such training would necessitate the participation of both Federal and Provincial Governments ... to the same extent that they now underwrite financing technical colleges and schools, travelling schools for fishermen and special informational programs for male workers.

2. To this end, Memorial University should ... furnish teachers to travelling schools, institute programs of information, study and make recommendations for the solution of problems peculiar to rural Nfld. women.

3. ... Particularly should efforts be made to educate women in the processes of government, from federal politics down to local community councils, so that they would be able to participate on every level.

Justice demands that the female editions should have the same chance as the male editions to realize their potential as human beings. It is only just that government invest proportionate amounts of money and planning to that end.

While asserting that education is the only means to improving the inferior status of women in Nfld., I wish to point out two important matters that could be considered immediately; the machinery for implementing them already functions, but inadequately and without imagination:

1. Family planning clinics should be within reach of all women through the present Dept. of Public Health facilities. Access to information should not depend, as it now appears to do, on the convictions or the compassion of those staffing nursing stations, clinics or cottage hospitals, but should be freely available and freely advertised.

2. Television and radio programs dealing specifically with health, child care and consumer information should be available on the basis of the real situation of rural women in Nfld. ...

Program planners and producers display a complete lack of comprehension of the needs of rural women and the conditions in which they live ... Valuable changes could be made in a short time (if an intelligent, informed effort was shown) for in areas where newspapers and magazines are non-existent, radio listening is an important part of daily life.

The world has changed, for women as well as for men, and as long as the community relies on only half its members for meaningful participation in public life, so long will the community suffer. As the preamble to the United Nations Declaration on the Elimination of Discrimination against Women states, "The full and complete development of a country, the welfare of the world and the cause of peace require the maximum participation of women, as well as men, in all fields."

Margo Meyer

1990 Profile
Interview by Marian Frances White
Born 1929, into a family of five in Greffern, Germany, Margo Meyer studied as an apprentice potter in Baden-Baden and later with a ceramics master in Landshut, Germany. In 1956 she came to Toronto, Canada, and later travelled the country before coming to Newfoundland from Winnipeg in 1960. Meyer lived for fifteen years in Corner Brook where she taught full time craft courses at The Fisher Institute. In 1975 she moved to St. John's with her two teenage children and together with three other craftspeople, opened The Salt Box, a retail craft shop. Meyer was one of the founding members of the Newfoundland and Labrador Craft Development Association (NLCDA). She has also served as director of the Canadian Craft Cooperation. "I was the token woman on the executive," she says. Her pottery is distinguished by its unique shape and floral or fish decorations. Her home and studio is on Bell Island—a tiny island, five miles long and some two and a half nautical miles by ferry from St. Phillips.

❦   ❦   ❦

*M*y first idea to be a potter was really only a joke because amongst my brothers and sisters we would go to movies and many of these little films were culturally uplifting. One of these shorts was on pottery and I was so fascinated by the way a pot grows that I kept talking about it amongst my

107

siblings. I would give everyone a role; I was making the pots, my sister was going to sell them and my brother was going to make the clay.

It was an unusual trade for a girl at that time because most potters in Germany were men and to be a potter you have to be pretty strong and hefty. It's hard work lifting the clay and slapping it about but I find it great psychologically.

My father was a French prisoner of war until two years after the war ended and my mother wasn't so pleased that I chose to be a potter. I guess she would have rather seen me go to university and be something where you don't get your hands dirty and you make a good bit of money. She capitulated when she saw that she couldn't change my mind. I'm a very energetic person and I couldn't see myself sit in an office all day. While I was an apprentice I did a great deal of painting and sometimes I would have to sit for days painting tiles for custom designs and every once in a while I would have to get up and run up and down the winding stairs that went from the studio down to the kiln area, then I could sit down again. I need something that will charge my intellect and my manual skills.

My family lived in the country on the Swiss border. My father was a professor at an agricultural college and we had a lovely life roaming about freely. It was a small place and everyone knew us. If we wanted to climb the mountains we did; that for us was the important thing. From my early childhood I was surrounded by struggle because of the war, but when you are young and in the middle of it, you see more the adventure than the hurt. I was ten when the war started. There was shelling across the Rhine and the front of our house was hit. My parents were heartbroken because they lost everything that was dear to them. We slept in the night with everything we owned; food was rare and rationed and we didn't have clothes unless it could be made from a suit that our dead grandfather owned. My mother sewed very well and that was a great asset. There was great disruption for the family, but also disruption in schooling; for a year and a half we didn't have school. As a girl you weren't safe unless you were accompanied, because you had to go through small woods on your bicycle. There were no cars at that time except military vehicles. Then as soon as I finished school I decided to be a potter.

I like best to make pots; the actual making of it before glazing it. This just seems like the most natural thing to do. When it comes right down to brass tacks, when I make a pot I never see that pot coloured. I am interested in shape, the silhouette and the texture, that is what is important to me—the glazing and decoration is really secondary. What strikes your eye is the decoration and the finish but I think subconsciously people like the whole pot, not just the surface. Yet in my surroundings I like colour, but not a lot of bright colour. You cannot be a successful potter or craftsperson in general if you are not organized. I'm not good at self promotion but I am confident in my work. If I like what I have created I don't need anyone else's approval to feel good about it. In my life I am glad I make useful, practical things that people can also admire. I couldn't make things that are just to look at. I like things that are functional but every now and again I like to goof off and make wildly improbable things just for the fun of it.

I married late by many peoples standard; I was twenty-six. We had a good marriage but things started falling apart when I decided not to be a doormat anymore. I didn't have children for several years, so my husband was my main focus, but then when they came along, I didn't have so much time to tend on him. I love children but when they are very small, they can play tricks on your mind after awhile. Making pots really kept me going. For some women, they want to be home and take care of the house, but I must have some other work. I think my children never suffered because the time I spent with them, I was really with them. My parents were a very volatile couple and loved one another madly and that's why they often fought and made up and fought again, but as a child these fights were troublesome to me and I swore to myself that I wasn't going to have a marriage like that. Now when I look back I think that the way I handled it was bad too because I would never argue.

I chose to live on Bell Island because there is something utterly romantic about an island and that island doesn't need to be in the tropics. After all these years I am still a European and most Europeans are fascinated by islands. I love the sea. I grew up inland and I was twenty-four years old before I saw the sea; since then I would not want to live anywhere else—a lake, even a large lake wouldn't do. There is something wonderful and changeable about the sea, you know, everything else seems static to me. While I lived in St. John's I had a studio downstairs in my house and even though the windows were large there was never enough sunlight. My children and I would take little excursions by boat and one weekend we found ourselves on Bell Island. It looks so forbidding when you approach it from the sea, like a microcosm in itself. I never see things as they are, but as they could be. I bought an old house there and had to replace all twenty-two windows, but now I have lots of sunshine while I work.

Bell Islanders are used to being put-down, especially after the mine closed and many were forced to go on welfare. But that is not what Bell Island is. The people who have get up and go, really have get up and go. The citizens demonstrated this when they protested using the mines as a waste disposal site for chemicals from Europe. Women were the force behind that, there were some men but the ones who were most organized were the women. They have more sense and are bound to earth more when it comes right down to it. When they asked questions, the vague answers they received were not good enough. The worst was that we depend on ground water for our water supply and the reservoir where the ground water collects is below the level of the mines! The general climate in

Canada and the world is against inorganic waste so I am thrilled that Bell Island is no exception.

I consider myself a quiet feminist because I don't like to be dictated to and I don't like to dictate to others. My parents believed both sexes should have equal opportunity, so I've always felt equal and capable of doing anything. My daughter says I am one of those lucky ones who have been able to do what I want to do, but I always say it is not luck, it is attitude and hard work.

SANDY POTTLE

Lorraine Michael

1987 Profile
Interview by Marian Frances White
Lorraine Michael was born in St. John's on 27 March 1943; her parents are Fred G. Michael and Ann M. Rockwood. After graduating from Holy Heart of Mary Regional High School, she entered the Congregation of the Sisters of Mercy in 1960. She graduated with her Bachelor of Education from Memorial University of Newfoundland in 1970 and received her Masters of Divinity from the University of Toronto in 1979. She taught French and music at high school and has been principal of two junior high schools: Belvedere Junior High and St. Joseph's Junior High. From 1978 to 1979 she was a member of the Social Action team of the Archdiocese in Toronto.

Lorraine Michael has been active in the Newfoundland Teachers' Association (NTA) and has served on two ministerial advisory committees to two different ministers of education. After graduating from the Canadian Urban Training Project for Christian Service, she became Social action Coordinator for the Archdiocese of St. John's; she resigned this position in 1990. Michael has been involved in many social issues, ranging from nuclear disarmament to the social impact of oil exploration on Newfoundland. After the tragic Ocean Ranger disaster, in which eighty-two men lost their lives, she became chairperson of the Ocean Ranger Families Foundation in 1982. Michael sang with the MUN Festival Choir, sews, and cares for numerous house plants. In September, 1991 she left the Congregation of the Sisters of Mercy and presently lives in Toronto where she is writing a book of her impressions and experiences. At present Lorraine works as co-ordinator of the women and economic justice programme of the Ecumenical Coalition for Economic Justice in Toronto.

❦ ❦ ❦

110

As a woman my struggle for liberation on both a personal and social level is a freeing, exciting experience that opens me to humanity in a way that could not happen otherwise. I am grateful that in a world based on an imbalance of power that creates oppression, I am a woman. If I were not a woman I would not have the same opportunity to have my heart and eyes opened to the reality of the evil of paternalism.

I know what it is to be at the bottom of the heap. I know what it is to be told by male clergy that I would be more credible if I dressed less fashionably—i.e. more like a *nun*. I know what it feels like to read minutes of meetings of men where I and my work are discussed, pulled apart, and decided upon in my absence. I know the anger of rejection upon being informed by a male superintendent that I was no longer needed as principal in a school system because I wasn't *the average sister* (to which I can only respond "Thank God!").

For many years I acknowledged that I was oppressed as a woman within the Roman Catholic Church and yet at the same time was able to continue to struggle for social justice in the name of the church, believing that women like me could change that system. In 1989 the revelations of abuse of young boys in the diocese by members of the clergy changed everything for me. As I worked with others to analyze what sexual abuse was all about I came to a very clear understanding that the abuse wasn't about sexuality, it was about power. I began to name clearly for myself my own psychological and emotional plan because of the abuse of power that I experienced at the hands of the clergy. I lost all hope that a system that was based on patriarchy could even identify the victims in its midst. I came to know that there could never be a place of equality for me as a woman within the Roman Catholic Church.

But it is not enough for me as a woman to know my oppression within a paternalistic society. I have to reflect upon and analyze the extent of paternalism. Is it based merely on sexism, or are there other dimensions? Reflection and sharing with others' experience has proven to me that paternalism is based at least on sexism, racism and economics. The system that oppresses women also oppresses those who are not white and it creates an economic structure that causes suffering to a majority while keeping the white male on top of the heap.

My experience of oppression as a woman puts me in solidarity, then, with all other women who struggle for equality, dignity and a recognition of rights. It also puts me in solidarity with my sisters and brothers who suffer from apartheid in South Africa; with my sisters and brothers struggling for revolution from an oppressive, capitalistic system in Latin America; with my sisters and brothers, native peoples of Canada, who struggle to regain what is rightfully theirs after hundreds of years of oppression; with my sisters and brothers who ask for dignity in their

111

struggle to live their lives according to the sexual orientation they are aware of in themselves.

But recognizing solidarity with all others who suffer in this society is not enough. I have to look at political implications of this awareness. The system that controls and oppresses is not just economic—it is political. The economics that create inequality require a political will that supports it.

My sisters with whom I most find solidarity then are those who align themselves with all other groups suffering oppression. But they are also women who reject our political-economic system as it is and are searching for political structures that by their very nature can create equality.

I find it very difficult to understand how women who are feminists can belong to political parties that support the status quo socially and economically. True liberation leads to a politicization that is based on a total social analysis. I have to say to every woman who asks me to stand in solidarity.

> ... Please do not ask me to stand with you if you do not want to stand in solidarity with the hungry both in our country as well as elsewhere, with blacks, with native peoples, with gay women and men, with peoples struggling for liberation in developing countries.

This is a hard thing to write because I often come across those who call themselves feminists but who cannot accept the implications of being involved in some of these struggles.

The exciting thing is that as women experiencing liberation we can use our imaginations to create new systems that are life-giving rather than destructive. The structures our hearts are crying out for will bring new life not just to us but to all who are suffering in this world that has been created—both oppressor and oppressed. This is the exciting challenge that is mine—that is ours.

Elsie Miles

1988 Profile
Interview by Marian Frances White
Elsie Miles was born in Boxey, a small community situated on the remote south coast of Newfoundland, on June 16, 1909. She attended a one-room school with about fifty other children. Marrying at twenty-two, Miles worked for over thirty-five years at a general store in Boxey.

In 1975, together with Marget Davis from MUN Extension Service, Miles started a craft production group called Yarn Point Crafts. Like most rural production groups, Yarn Point Crafts is community-based in the immediate area of Belleoram. However, the eighty-five hand knitters and sixteen machine knitters currently producing come from many coastal communities, as far away as St. Anthony. Originally, while their products were marked up a hundred per cent of wholesale prices by various retailers, the knitters only saw about 20 per cent of the products' selling prices. Today they are paid by piecework, with established rates for the various items.

Miles received a commemorative plaque for her services in developing Yarn Point Crafts in 1978. It is due to her work, and that of Marget Davis and a few other women, that women in the more isolated areas of this province have a source of income, and that in itself is an accomplishment worth supporting.

❧ ❧ ❧

I learned to knit when I was about six years old. My older sister, Margaret taught me the basic stitches and later how to knit lace. My grandmother used to knit a lot, but my mother never had much time to sit down and knit. Years ago, most everyone knit for their own family. I don't think I've done anything much different than anyone else. I just started earlier and kept it up longer.

Today I don't find the younger ones are that interested just yet in knitting and that's okay too. There's a time for everything. I can see things have changed a lot since I was a little girl, especially the way children are brought up. They don't learn to knit very young nowadays. But then, I think you've got to want to do it to be good at it. I couldn't wait till I knew how to hold the needles properly, but then I didn't have as many other interests as children these days have. Of course, back then we had our own sheep and we carded their wool. We got to see the whole process from beginning to end; that made it all the more interesting. We made everything from long wool stockings for the girls and women, underwear and longjohns for the men, to crocheted blankets. Then we'd dye what we made with whatever colour dye we could find and years later when the garment wore out, we'd ravel it out and put several parts together to hook rugs. Nothing went to waste, that's for sure.

After many years of knitting I started making my own designs. Marget Davis had a lot to do with that, though the first time she suggested it I thought she was crazy. But when I started looking at variations of the designs I had been doing all my life, I began to see how I could rearrange patterns and create my own. We then came up with the idea of getting a bunch of knitters together. A lot of women on the coast needed the income, so before we knew it we were in business. The one thing that is very appealing to women about knitting is being able to do it on their own

113

time—in their own home, while they chat with neighbours, or attend community functions.

Women from many points along the south coast got involved, so that's why we called it Yarn Point Crafts. If it's changed from the original intention, it's only been for the better. The intention was to give women a little extra money and now it's become a part of their lives. I think knitting is a good outlet for women on the coast. If they didn't have that to look forward to once their children are in school and the men out in the boats, they'd get tired looking at the same coastline and the same four walls. Knitting means they are getting paid for their work and if they don't, they call Jean Sheppard, our manager, and she puts it all right.

There were lots of problems in the beginning because everyone had their own way of knitting, whether it was right or wrong. I remember one day I came home with thirty pairs of mittens to repair—the thumbs as long as the mitt. I wanted the work to be quality looking so I didn't mind putting in the extra hours, but I soon realized I was losing and Yarn Point Crafts was losing because the time I spent repairing others' mistakes I could have used knitting a sweater. I realized that reading patterns and knitting was like learning another language, so Marget and I went to different communities and gave workshops.

We're lucky here on the coast when it comes to getting the wool and the knitting from around community to community. Often a neighbour knows someone travelling further up the coast or even into town who doesn't mind taking a package along—this cuts down on our costs. You know, there are knitters for Yarn Point Crafts that I haven't even met. Sometimes we hear by word of mouth of a woman who knits and we get her phone number, if she has one, and call her up. She usually sends a sample of her work and we decide from there if she can do the work well enough. She usually can, I find.

Right now I like figuring out the pattern and let other women do the knitting. For me figuring out the pattern is the most challenging part. These days, if I don't feel like knitting I'll go out in the garden. I like outside work, so if someone comes by and wants me to help her with some project, I throw down my needles and help her the best I can. It might mean I'll have to work twice as hard tomorrow, but I like the freedom of choice this gives me.

When I worked in the general store in Boxey I never had any choice about my working hours. Even if I didn't feel up to it, I'd have to open the store because other people depended on it. I eventually had the store hauled up to my house because it was hard getting down to the shop in a snowstorm. This meant I was working all the time; when I wasn't in the store I was making meals or keeping house. Still, years later when I sold the store, I missed the social contact. Knitting has changed that for me.

I've always thought of myself as a country girl. All of my family went to the United States, but I didn't want to go. I've visited there several times, but life there is too fast for me to want to stay. I don't think I would want to get into the swing of things there, if you know what I mean. What I find is that it's always nice to go away, but it's better still to come home.

So this is how I spend my days, and I love it. Sometimes I think my knitting days are over because everybody changes in their lifetime, but today I finished off another sweater and something tells me it's not my last. One thing I've found, it's good to look forward to your day's work. When I look back on my life, I don't look back to say I should have done this or that differently. We usually don't make the same mistakes twice anyway, but for the most part, if I had my life to live over again, I would live it exactly the same way as I've lived to the present.

Joan Morrissey

1989 Profile – (A special thanks to Mr. Tom Cahill, a professional and personal friend of Ms. Morrissey and to her daughters Beverly Thistle and Debbie Stafford for their interviews.) This story is told by her daughter, Debbie, through interviews with Marian. Joan Morrissey, one of ten children, was born in St. John's on January 23, 1935 to Kathleen and Charles Learning. She made her singing debut on a CJON Variety Show when she was nine which led to any number of engagements, but it was not until 1959 that she took up a career as a professional country and western singer. It has been said that she took to the stage like a duck to water. In 1952, age seventeen, she married Tom Morrissey. They had six children; Debbie, Beverly, Colleen, Linda, Sherry and Tommy.

Morrissey gained a great deal of popularity on numerous VOCM programs and by her performance in such shows as the CBC Variety Showcase *and* All Around The Circle. *She hosted prime-time CJON* Talent Showcase *and co-hosted CBC Radio's* Jamboree. *Morrissey performed live at the Admiral's Keg, Hotel Newfoundland on an eighteen month contract, six nights a week. She also toured the Province and sang at the Newfoundland Club in Nova Scotia and Toronto. As well as others, she sang with a group called The Dipsy Doodlers.*

In '69 Morrissey starred in the broadway musical Annie Get Your Gun, *with a cast of seventy and a twenty-five piece orchestra. Staged at the Arts and Cul-*

115

ture Centre and produced by Tom Cahill, the show was a smash hit. Later she played the role of Gypsy Rose Lee in the musical Gypsy.

Morrissey, who was nominated for a Juno award in the late '60s, recorded three albums. In her early forties she suffered from a heart condition and died tragically on January 10, 1978.

> There has never been a Joan Morrissey since Joan Morrissey. In context if she were around today she would be the grand lady of show business because she put Newfoundland on the map long before the Newf-cult revolution began.   Tom Cahill

In our eyes, mom was basically the same person at home as she was on television. Of course, the one we saw in the daytime didn't look as good as the one at night because usually when we came home from school she had rollers in her hair. I don't think she started out to make singing her career, but eventually she saw it as a way to survive and to raise her family—and it worked for her. Mom loved to do parodies of popular songs she heard on the radio with lyrics pertaining to local situations or politics. Tom Cahill often wrote songs for her to sing. We'd come home from school and there she'd be sitting down with her guitar scribbling out lyrics and then putting new ones in. Sometimes we'd help her, or at least listen to her while she tried them out. For the most part she was her own manager doing her business dealings during the day while we were in school. Although when I look back, it seems she was always on the phone trying to straighten out some contract.

Mom didn't read music. She learned it all from listening and watching. For her engagements she developed her own repertoire of songs, and clever monologue routines. Even during the years when her career was at its peak, she made time to sing with us. We'd get out the guitar and jam in front of the fireplace. She always made sure she was home at special times, like our birthdays, that meant a lot to us kids. Mom had job offers in other provinces, but she wanted to stay here because she said she could never feel at home anywhere else. I can still see her and Helen McNiven driving off in her little volkswagen. The two of them would pile into it, luggage, equipment and all and go off on a tour to such places as Kelligrews, Carbonear, Ochre Pit Cove, the West coast or the Southern Shore. We were sixteen and seventeen then, so we could pretty well take care of ourselves. Her hectic schedule didn't mean a row of beans to me then, but now I honestly don't know where she got her energy to do the two jobs of mothering us and singing all the time as her career.

Mom was so organized. If she worked on a show during the day, there would be a gigantic note on the refrigerator when we got home explaining where she was and who should do what in the house. When we were real young we lived in a big house on a pond beside Pippy Park.

The pond is still there, but the house isn't. In the summertime we'd go down to the pond and mom would wash clothes on a board, singing while she washed. I was only seven or eight but I remember her with the big board under one arm, the laundry under the other arm and the sunlight soap in her hand. We'd go swimming in the other end while she washed and watched us. We have a picture of our dog loose while Bev is tied to a tree! The garden was so big mom was always afraid she'd lose her ... we have lots of fun memories from there even though we didn't have conveniences like running water.

Mom was constantly striving to get recognition for herself and for other Newfoundlanders because she could see the business she was in was a tough one and she often said she hoped it would get easier for the next generation behind her. She didn't push us to follow her footsteps because she knew it was a hard road to follow. She wanted us to do what we wanted to do, just as she had, I guess. I sang with her a bit, especially at benefits, she never turned one down and was given an award as Newfoundland's Good Will Ambassador. Her work was very time consuming and pressuring and together with the pressures of raising six kids, I think she wanted an easier life for us.

When mom was alive I really enjoyed working with her, but afterwards I had no inclination whatsoever to continue. The tribute I did with friends of hers at the Arts and Culture Centre after she died was something I felt I had to do because she often talked about us doing a show there together. If she was alive, perhaps I would have gone on, but it was a hectic life and on times a rough lifestyle. She wanted to expand her career and do more musicals, so the *Annie Get Your Gun* show was a real thrill for her and for us. Three weeks before the show opened she slipped on ice and broke her ankle. The cast on her ankle wasn't removed until the day of the opening, yet few people knew that in her cowgirl boot there was a thick bandage. The show was a smash hit and ran for six nights to packed houses. Mom would talk of doing more shows at the A & C because she wanted to get out of the bars and enjoy herself more as a stage performer.

She worked very hard, needless to say, but often her hard work did not pay off as was the case when she produced an album with Marathon Music Incorporation. The album sold over 50,000 copies but she received few royalties. She spoke her mind in the media, as she was very capable of doing, and Marathon tried to sue her for libel; however, their suit was thrown out of court. The company folded so she never did receive any amount of money.

Even though mom seemed to work constantly, every now and again she'd take time off and go to the cabin in Paddy's Pond. The best thing for her about that place was the absence of a phone. She loved the outdoors and would walk in the woods for hours or just go fishing. When she came back she would be rejuvenated. Everyone knew her as a very outgoing personality, but she could be shy and even though she had a tremendous get up and go when it came to showtime, she really liked to sit back and listen to others once she was off stage. My mother brought me up to be a good, honest hard-working person. She always said if you worked hard enough for something you would get it. My own greatest wish, even after all these years since her death, is that people not forget her and when they do remember her, it would be with a smile.

SHONA ROSSEL

Marion Murphy

1987 Profile
Interview by Marian Frances White
Called Aunt Murphy because of her sense of one-ness with those around her, Marion Murphy was a midwife most of her life. Her living room walls are arrayed with plaques from the Royal Canadian Legion, and the town of Carbonear ex-pressing appreciation for her dedication and work. She was born into a family of thirteen in Salmon Cove, Conception Bay on January 23, 1903. Murphy did not receive much formal education because it was often too windy and stormy during the winter for a teacher to get to Salmon Cove. As soon as the warmer days of sum-mer permitted travel a teacher came to Blow Me Down. "We got there by Shank's Mare, meanin' my own legs," she explains. Marion Murphy left home at an early age to make her way as a domestic and became a midwife at the age of thirty. For the next thirty-five years Murphy worked under extreme condi-tions to attend to women giving birth. Her story is typical of hundreds of other midwives in the province. An old timer has said of her, "If she needed water from the well for a woman, she would get it supposin' she'd have to carry it in her mouth and spit it into a cup!" Her second husband, David, died April 23, 1989; however, at eighty-nine she continues to live at home.

❧ ❧ ❧

I began working as a midwife when I was thirty years old and had a family of me own. I went with a neighbour who was an old midwife around here. Since she was getting old and she could see I liked the work, she and the doctor who sometimes came around asked if I would consider becoming one. Yes, I loved the work, so I said yes. I felt it was a calling to serve the community and to do what I could to help them out. I got a lot of respect in return, but very little money. In them days no one had much, least of all money, so that was not why I agreed to do it. Sometimes I got five dollars and sometimes I got nothing except a thank you, and really that's all I wanted from them. Everybody was poor, so we was all alike.

I guess I attended to at least a hundred births over the next thirty years. I never thought of keeping count or writing down any of their names, although even today I sees many of them on the road and there's nothing none of them wouldn't do for me. Sometimes I says to them, "You don't know, do you, that I put the first shirt on your back!" Thanks be to God they were all healthy babies. There was never any tearing and none of the babies were stillborn. No woman saw a doctor in them days throughout the entire pregnancy. They would get in touch with me a month or two before the baby was due and I would make sure I was ready when they were. The one thing I made sure was that they stayed in bed for nine days after the birth. I would tend to the woman for those nine days doing everything from cleaning and cooking to taking care of her children. I often took a bit of bread out of this house in the morning and a few buns to carry to the little children 'cause that was the nature of me to help them along the way.

I'll tell you a story now that'll make you laugh. I got the call from two women whose time had come the same day, one during the day and one during the night. One woman lived in Freshwater and the other woman lived in Carbonear. Well, it was a starmy, starmy night St. Patrick's Day, March 17, when those two children were born into this world. Two men came for me on their horse and sled. They had two shovels with them, and a good thing they did. We barely made it to Freshwater, some seven miles from where I lived in Carbonear. It was some dark too, no pole lights like there are nowadays. I told meself I was on a good-will mission as we shovelled our way through the snow. The baby was born not long after I arrived. That girl grew up and became a nurse. I got a picture of her in the living room on the mantle piece. Anyway, like I said, these were poor times. I had to make a piece of string out 'a sewing cotton to tie the baby's cord. I had me own bag with clean scissors and an apron I made meself out of flour sack. I put this on and then boiled water on the wood stove to sterilize the string and the scissors. I took a lot of pride in me work. When the baby was born I'd wrap the child up like a little chick.

Once the woman and her baby was cleaned and comfortable, I'd burn the afterbirth in the wood stove. I'd take a little flour and put that right on top of the stove. Then, when it was a little brown, I would put it around the cord. That would keep any infection away.

Well, for nine days I went to one woman's home in Freshwater by horse and sled and then when I returned to Carbonear I'd go to tend the other woman. I had nine children of me own then to look after. I did that too, although some of them were old enough to help with the younger ones. I would take all the sheets and blankets off the bed from each house and bring them home here to wash by hand in this kitchen sink. There was a lot of wood choppin' and water luggin' going on in them days, I can tell you. I'll tell you another thing we did, if there was a real problem with a crying baby. We'd make a sugar teat. You did this by putting a little soaked bread with sugar or molasses in a cloth and you'd tie this with a piece of parcel twine for the baby to suck. There were wet nurses too if the mother didn't have enough milk or too many children to tend to. As poor as everyone was, someone always seemed to have a cow or goat to milk. Everyone worked hard in them days. The women worked baking and in the garden diggin' potatoes and caring for their children right up to the day they delivered. There was no buying clothes then. You'd get a bit of clothes ready bit by bit, making a shirt one month out of flour sack and collecting pieces of flannelette for diapers. Somehow ya managed and if there wasn't enough someone would give it to you. Each woman made their own bands at that time, there were no sanitary pads to buy even if you had the money.

This was all a midwife's work. The husband never helped with the birthing. He done nothing in that regard, never saw a baby being born or most often never heard a woman cry in labour. He went next door and waited until he was told the child was in the world. Perhaps if he had to see a child being born, the families would not have been so big!

Eventually the hospital opened up here and I was put out of business, so to speak. I didn't like that much, but I had to accept it. I worked at the hospital doing what I could until they pensioned me off, until they told me I couldn't work any more. I wasn't a midwife there, I wasn't allowed, but I was serving the public. Just because *they* told me I was too old to work there, didn't mean I couldn't serve in other ways. I'm eighty-nine now and I think I did a good job, but there's something else I plan to do before me time's up. That's a surprise though, but you just might hear about it someday. Now that's me story!

Baptiste Neis

1992 Profile
Interview by Rhonda Pelley

ROSE-MARIE KENNEDY

I was born in Toronto and I moved to St. John's when I was five months old. I moved back to Toronto for junior kindergarten and kindergarten. In one of the houses I lived in there, I lived with a friend who was the same age as me. My family had the bottom two floors of the house and her family had the top two floors. It was great for me because we were in the same grade and in the same class. My mother was writing, so my father took care of us most of the time. My friends mother and my dad switched a lot.

My father died seven years ago. That kind of thing makes you think about how precious life is and how easy it is to lose it. It's hard for me to say how it affected me because I don't know what I would be like if he was around, I would probably be a different person. I'm a very careful person because of it, it's only been the past couple of years that I am able to take the risks that I take and I don't take a lot.

I have a good relationship with my mother, I have a lot of freedom that I wouldn't normally have. I'm a very logical person and sometimes I claim a lot more independence than I probably should but I have a lot more independence than most people my age. Between my mother and I, it's a mutual respect and I look at her as a person, not only as a mother. She's a woman, she's a great woman. We are both very independent and have strong personalities. Our relationship has just developed over the past couple of years.

I remember going to peace marches since I was a baby. I was nine or ten when I joined Youth Acting Against Apartheid. I attended every meeting just 'cause that's how I am. When I say I will do something, I usually do it unless I'm sick or tied up in something else. There is so much out there and not enough people doing it. I go out and look for something to do. People who do that are sometimes accused of looking for a cause but there are so many causes out there that you can't look for a cause, they are facing you everyday.

I have a really low threshold for pain. If I were taken hostage, what would I do? I wouldn't live through it. I've become more sensitive, I never used to cry. The reality for example, of hostage taking happens every day. When the Gulf War started, it was the day before my exams, I had my worst exam the next morning. I had the most horrible vision before I went to bed. It was of a woman and her child and a bomb being dropped near them. The Gulf was far away but it was so close for me. When life is hurting, that's when I get angry. I could offer an alternative to that war because there's always another way other than hurting the world. How can we make them understand that? Saddam isn't the only mad man here.

One thing I have been looking into is all this Goddess worship. I'm not into worshipping anybody or anything but what happened before the white male god with white hair and a long beard came along and told us everything to do and when to do it? We lost all respect for our sense of the world and ourselves. We have to take care of ourselves and so many people aren't taking care of themselves because they are trying to fit an ideal that they can't reach.

I went to Grindstone, it's an alternative summer camp in Ontario on an island. I went there for two years in a row while my mother was writing. They had counsellors from all over the world. I learned canoeing, massage and drama. It was co-operatively owned and the whole island would take ten minutes to walk across. The camp could only fit fifty students so it was very small, like a community in itself.

The Youth For Social Justice camp that I participate in is very similar. The St. John's Youth for Social Justice group came about from this and a lot of different groups getting together; Ploughshares Youth, Youth Against Apartheid, The Peace - a - Chord. It got really confusing because the same group of people became involved in everything.

I have always believed in other forms of education besides school. It's too controlled, too structured. I had a lot of problems in third year junior high. It was my third year in that school and I was discovering all these rules I had never known about. I would go in, sign out and leave to go to a demonstration or a forum. I still didn't know the rules and I was getting in trouble for it. The rules were never made clear to me. I get really frustrated when there is a person who is in administration, who is much higher up then me, who is a man, who is twice the size of me and is telling me that I can't do this. I would try to leave, the secretary would get the principal and the principal wouldn't let me leave unless he could get a hold of my mother. I felt so powerless and I get pissed off with myself because I get so upset. It's a power thing, you feel so oppressed by it. Respect is a two way street and I can't respect someone who doesn't respect me.

School teaches you what to learn, when to learn it and how to learn it. A lot of it you forget, but one of the things you don't forget is when not to talk. I was picked on, I was suspected of things that I had never been suspected of before. I learned to speak out less. You would think that speaking out would help, it does at first. Then people just tune you out. I learned to listen to other people more and not speak out so loudly. People will generally take you more seriously.

One of my teachers said that the school wasn't big enough for me, that I didn't fit in this space, I didn't fit within the lines. This is true but all students are different, I should be accommodated, all the other students are accommodated. A total overhaul of the education system would be a total overhaul of society which needs to be done.

Ageism is the most important thing to me right now, the biggest problem I have. When your fifteen, fourteen or eighteen, there is a stereotype for that age and it is constantly pushed on you. If you don't feel you fit into those stereotypes it causes people a lot of insecurities because you are challenging their assumptions.

In the past year I have played the role of ages from twelve to twenty-two. I wasn't researching people, I was studying myself. This way I am not stuck in a bracket, there are no boundaries put on me because I am one age. I know how to manipulate the system. I will cross over that line of youth and adulthood that everyone crosses over whether they want to or not. I hope I don't get all the way over. I don't want to grow up, I want to be able to be any age I want for the rest of my life.

Joyce O'Doherty

1990 Profile
Interview by Marian Frances White
Joyce O'Doherty was born in Harbour
Grace, Newfoundland on November 9,
1942 and was raised and educated in
Gander. She graduated with a Bachelor
of Education and a Bachelor of Physical
Education from Memorial University of
Newfoundland (MUN) and taught for
two years with the Physical Education
Department at MUN. O'Doherty, is the
Vice-President of the International
Sound Foundation Society, a non-profit
organization working in developing countries. She travels extensively to learn
and exchange her knowledge of the healing arts. In 1977 she took up residence
in British Columbia, where she still lives. Between 1987 and 1989 O'Doherty
travelled to Mexico, Japan and India. On a November 1988 trip, she worked
with a medical team who were doing lens implants for cataract patients. She
also took a thousand pounds of vitamins and clothing that were distributed to
the villages. O'Doherty, who studied at the Canadian Institute of Reflexology,
works with a cancer group called HOPE and gives seminars at the Arthritis
Centre in Vancouver as well as workshops when she is in Newfoundland.

🐛　🐛　🐛

Although I live most of the year in Vancouver, I love returning to Newfoundland where my mother still lives. From travelling back and forth I
can see a real shift in attitude towards the medical profession. More and
more people are taking responsibility for their health and are learning to
become their own doctors.

People often change because there is a need in their life to take a
different path. In the late seventies my husband of nine years died from a
terminal illness. My own physical health, because of the stress that I went
through for a large number of years, was deteriorating. In fact, I was on
crutches because of my arthritis that had affected eighteen joints in my
extremities. I went the straight medical route for about two years and
wasn't getting any better. I decided to explore alternative, non-convention-
al techniques.

Self-hypnosis was the first technique I learned to control pain and to
reduce medication. I think for many years I put myself in a victim state,
like, why is this happening to me! It was important for me to shift that way
of thinking and take some responsibility for my own wellness. Through

self-hypnosis I discovered a lot of pent up anger that I didn't even know existed within me. For three years, people on the outside could see this but I wasn't aware of it. Unless you can recognize the areas you need to change, you don't realize you have a problem. That was my first volcanic eruption to facilitate health.

Reflexology is a great help. On the feet and hands there are a variety of reflexes that affect the energy going to certain body parts and when you massage this with the finger tips it eliminates some of the energy blocks that the body accumulates. I found chiropractic work, iridology, reflexology, massage, yoga, medication and outdoor exercise immensely helpful. There came a point when I wanted to get off medication and instead I took massive doses of herbs and vitamins. Within three days I was able to reduce my medication and eventually I cut it out entirely. For about ten days I had withdrawal symptoms and then I got gradually better and better. I do not have arthritis today.

From all this pain came a philosophy of living that centred around a holistic lifestyle. I needed to change my belief system that I had lived with all my life and I definitely needed to change my diet. I've found death to be one of the biggest catalysts to take a look at where you are and where you want to be. When my husband died and then my father eleven months later, I found myself asking where do I go after I die, why did my husband die at thirty-five? These are questions I didn'd deal with until I was placed in that situation.

In our culture, we are taught particular belief systems that we live under even when they are no longer viable in our lives. Often it takes a major shock to re-examine ourselves. Otherwise, we go on our merry way and stay in a rut. We also live in a society which holds a great deal of stress. In itself stress is neither good nor bad, it's how we deal with it, how we keep our head when all around us people are losing theirs. We're not taught to do this in our society; we get it by trial and error.

Oftentimes when things are not going right, we blame everybody but ourselves. We say, if only they'd change, I'd be all right. And this means it's time to look at *self*. This self-examination was one of the major areas that helped me heal. First one has to say I'm not happy with some aspect of my being or life before it can be changed.

When we get sick, our body is attempting to tell us that something in our existence is out of ease, it is *diseased*. Instead of popping an aspirin or Tylenol for a headache, we could try massage, deep breathing and relaxation. Technology has created a lot of this disease. We want our mashed potatoes *right now!* We do not want to take the time to peel the potatoes, boil and mash them. If we're sick, we want to get well *right now!* We fail to recognize that a headache is our friend because our headache is telling us that something is out of order. The headache is the symptom; not the cause. Maybe it is because we have an improper diet, we're overworked and we need to take it easy. We don't give ourselves permission to relax so we get sick in order to get what we need. We learn at an early age that we get more attention when we are sick. This belief system stays with us as adults.

I'm a vegetarian ninety-five percent of the time, but I don't think it's as much the type of food we eat as the quality of the food we eat. Fresh organic food with natural fertilizers is the best. Being a Newfoundlander I can say that the types of foods we often eat are not the best. We tend to over-cook our food and then salt or sweeten it to death! I read recently that there are more potato chips and coke consumed in Newfoundland than in any other province of Canada! We don't have to live that way. We are like a Third World country in how malnourished we are becoming and it is not from the lack of food, but from the quality of the food.

My quest in life is to find out how I can get in touch with all aspects of myself. That takes energy, commitment and an understanding that each situation I find myself in is a learning situation. I don't put things in black and white anymore. This is not right and this is not wrong, the situation dictates what is appropriate behaviour.

I think women view a situation from a feeling point of view. Our role has mainly been defined as nurturer and I know for myself I needed to find a balance between that and teacher. Part of this conscious awakening for women forces us to explore our sexuality. It's an issue that we keep in our emotional garbage can because it is so charged. Coming from Newfoundland I can only say that the culture wasn't open to that, and even today it's a taboo subject. Our sexuality is being defined behind closed doors and it is not discussed. I think women are finally saying, "let's explore this aspect of ourselves because it is a major part of me." Many times when people are going through change, it's painful. Accepting the fact that other people may have a different route to go than you and that there is strength in diversity is a very powerful lesson. If we can make the choice of accepting ourselves for what we are, we have already begun the healing process.

Julie Olivier

1989 Profile
Interview by Marian Frances White
Born in Cape St. George on Groundhog Day, 1959 Julie Olivier was raised and educated there. Situated on the farthest edge of the Port au Port Peninsula where several French communities survived the English influence, Olivier graduated from Notre Dame du Cap High School and obtained a Business Education Course at Bay St. George Community College. In 1985 she became the first coordinator of L'Association Francophone de l'ile Rouge in Mainland where she now lives. She continues to hold this position. Olivier has worked on a variety of projects from setting up a museum to designating and organizing special events to celebrate their heritage. In 1986, when Julie Olivier's daughter, Brandise, would enter grade three, she put her back in Grade One to begin a French program that was being offered for the first time.

ë   ë   ë

*Y*es, it was a difficult decision to put Brandise back in Grade One so she could begin school in French, but my husband and I and a few others in the town felt it was the only course of action to take if our language was going to survive outside of our homes. It bothered Brandise at first to repeat two grades with younger children, but after two years in the French program she's adjusted well and I know that as she gets older she will realize even more the importance of keeping her language. Socially it has been a little difficult because it's hard for her to see her peers go ahead to higher grades while she remains behind. The other problem arises because she is much more advanced than the rest of the kids in the class and consequently the teachers do not need to spend as much time with her. Some days she comes home frustrated because she feels rejected when what she really needs is somebody to take more time with her. There are special education teachers in school for people who need extra help, but we also need more people working with kids who are in similar situations to hers.

French has been the way of life for my family since the first settlers came over here, so I wanted to make sure our culture was passed on to our children. I grew up with French as my language and so did my husband. We could see that our language was being lost in the school system and that if we let that happen it would be like saying that what they were learning in school was better than our own culture. Even though our community is ninety-five percent French it was in danger of being lost with the younger generation—and that was the fault of the school system, not the children. Now we are in the process of building a French school, we have our own association and community television station, all of which help create a better attitude. Once people were ashamed to be called French, now they are proud of their language and culture.

It is always a shock to realize how many Newfoundlanders do not know we exist, let alone the rest of Canada. Of course, we cannot celebrate our culture if we do not recognize it ourselves. That is why we have begun to celebrate such days as Chandelieur, Candlemas Day, on the second of February. We involve the children in this as well, so that they can see our traditions. In this celebration we go from house to house to collect food and then we cook a huge meal that the whole community shares. By having celebrations like this there is communication with the older and younger generations. We also have a festival each summer, Une Journee dans l'Passe (a day in the past), when all the local people sing, play the accordion or violin and display their crafts, spin and card wool, make homemade butter and things like soap. We have set up a museum so that the hand-made tools and artifacts from our past are preserved in a place of impor-tance. It will still take a long while before we can develop the way we want simply because our hands are tied because of lack of funding. Francophone associations cannot function on a day to day basis when we are not sure where the next money to support us will come from. Gradually under official languages programmes we are gaining strength, but all that takes a lot of time and energy. Our affiliation with La Federation des Fran-cophones in St. John's and our exchanges with resource people from Quebec and with La Societe Nationale Des Acadiens makes us feel a little less isolated.

More and more younger people are staying here to find work and even those who go away to places like Toronto find their way back when they can. They are also acting on our incentive and encouragement to take advantage of programs and bursaries offered. We try to keep in contact with the students who are leaving the area for the first time, but we are doing much more than simply promoting French in our community, we are encouraging community development both french-wise and economy-wise—one cannot survive without the other. I have a strong belief in the importance of not only keeping my culture but doing my share to see that it thrives against all odds.

Rae Perlin

1987 Profile
Compiled by Marian Frances White
Rae Perlin says of herself, "I did not choose art, art chose me. When I discovered my passion for art I tore around New York sketching to appease that passion. That's when I can honestly say I had strength because I wanted to sketch and paint so bad. That's where passion and the physical work together."
Born in St. John's in 1910, Perlin was strong-willed enough to make her way to New York before she was twenty. After acquiring a nursing degree, she used the small salary from her work to study art. Throughout the '40s she studied with Samuel Brecher and Hans Hofmann. Perlin moved to Europe for five years, studying at Academie Grande Chaumiere and Academie Ranson, Paris. Her sketches illustrate Spindrift and Morning Light, poetry by Paul O'Neill. Although she is best known for her one-woman exhibitions at Memorial University Art Gallery in 1982, at the Pollyanna Gallery in 1985, and at the Christina Parker Fine Art Gallery in 1991, she is also a respected art critic.

Deriving much of her spiritual strength from the Baha'i faith, Perlin says, "If my thoughts drift to discovering the secret of art, I find that there is no secret, just the urge that is so strong you cannot ignore it." In 1991 Killick Press released Not A Still Life, The Art and Writings of Rae Perlin, a book of her commentaries, sketches and drawings, compiled and edited by Marian Frances White.

❦   ❦   ❦

Newfoundland has a culture drawn from its proximity to nature. The farmer and the fishers in their closeness to the soil and the sea have absorbed this culture. They deal in fundamentals; art also deals in fundamentals.

In the city the drabness of the surroundings has shut out the natural absorption of nature's culture and has offered nothing in its place. Our love of art makes us want to see the creative life more completely; that is, people growing spiritually and physically towards a life which means happiness for all. When we come to desire happiness for all, we will be on our way to creating true civilization.

A Sketchbook Extract
Weekend in Placentia, Placentia Bay, 1942

Half a day in Placentia and already one feels one has had many adventures. To arrive at any time would be interesting but on such a day everything is superb. It seems only when I commenced to *try* to paint did my sensations really take form. After a swim we went out to fling some paint around by way of exercise before supper. We walked into a meadow without a fence and set up our paints and easel. I had wanted to dash off one of the white-washed houses with the sun shining on it, but instead I was intrigued with the formation of pointed roofs. These were made up of a group of houses and a convent in front with the slanted roof of the church beyond. Besides the formation of the roofs, the colour appealed to me strongly. Hazy against the sun with the mauve colour of the convent and the worn pinkish red of the church, the sky a lovely blue and a light thin dash of cloud, I felt the whole a study in itself. A week here will scarcely be enough.

The interruptions however are numerous and senseless; a policeman (who at least questioned us civilly) and dozens of children. One felt kindly towards them, but concentrating is difficult. Imagine the scene ... this glorious colour ahead and behind me stretches a still body of water while beyond me lie the wooden hills.

Back for supper; feeling all things are possible—fish cakes ... and numerous flies! Off again for a walk along the waterfront. There is beauty in the greyish sheen on the water and in the rocky cliffs topped by spruce that rose out of it. We took time to make a sketch of a winding lane while an elderly man, closing up his shed for the night, sat on a boat and asked us if we were sketching for Hitler.

Impressions

The beauty of a giant schooner sailing beside a cliff.

At a hot dog stand a small, grubby boy was lifted on the counter of the stand and was asked to fish out what he would like to eat. He chose an orange and was given a chocolate bar as well. It seemed someone had left thirty dollars to give all the children a free treat! A bit of information like that could make one happy a whole day, just thinking about it.

The night closing in—the light of the moon behind the clouds—the soft slopes and rising shoulders of the hills around this town—the lovely velvet shine on the water—a light from a store falling across the lane—the putt, putt of a motor boat going back and forth across the bay as it ferried people across...

Rae's comments after rereading this excerpt some years later

Funny how this writing can give such an impression of tranquility and I suppose for that moment I was at peace with myself, but that period in my life was a turbulent one. I had recently returned from New York and didn't know what direction my life would take next. Of well, no one is content all the time.

Helen Porter

1989 Profile—At that time an excerpt of her short story, **One Saturday,** *was published in the* **Almanac.**
For this book it seems appropriate to take a closer, more personal look at the writer.

Helen Porter was born on the south side of St. John's on May 8, 1930, the first child of Robert W. and Evelyn (Horwood) Fogwill. Following graduation from Prince of Wales College and a business course, she worked as a shorthand-typist with the Dept. of Justice. She married John Porter in 1953 and lived in Corner Brook and Fortune until they moved back to St. John's in 1959 with their three children: Kathy, Anne and John. Their youngest child, Stephen, was born in 1960.

Porter began to write seriously in 1962, but it wasn't until 1973 when she resigned from her work at the Arts and Culture Centre Provincial Reference Library, that she devoted her full time to writing. She has had short stories, articles, poetry and reviews published in most major Canadian magazines and overseas, as well as plays produced on radio and stage. In 1977 she collaborated with Bernice Morgan and Geraldine Rubia to produce, From This Place, an anthology of Newfoundland and Labrador women writers. Her memoir-history, Below The Bridge, was published in 1980 and her first novel, January, February, June or July, released in 1988, won the Canadian Library Association's Young Adult Canadian Book Award in 1989. In 1991 Porter published A Long and Lonely Ride. She also enjoys writing songs; one of them, (The Southside Hills), has been recorded by Phyllis Morrissey on her compact disc Where I Live.

Helen Porter's keen interest in politics led her to run for the New Democratic Party in Mount Pearl. Her lifelong frustration with inequality of opportunity also led her to the women's movement. Porter's husband died suddenly in 1983 and after twenty-six years in Mount Pearl, she now lives in the centre of St. John's.

ଔ   ଔ   ଔ

Written on February 2, 1992

It's cold and white today, lots of snow around. The sun was shining earlier, when I walked down to Duckworth Street from my house on Franklyn Avenue. When the sun shines I have to get out of the house, no matter how cold it is. I've heard a lot recently about the fragility of the ozone layer, but I don't think the sun will damage me on a day like this.

Now I'm sitting in a cafe booth, having just finished a bowl of turkey soup and several cups of tea. I spend a good deal of time in restaurants these days, even do a fair number of first drafts sitting at restaurant tables. I don't mind living alone, but there's something about being alone in a house that's not conducive to writing, at least for me. I like this feeling of being in a warm place, alone but surrounded by people having quiet conversations that don't require anything form me. Also, there's the sense of rewarding myself for housework, exercise, the occasional babysitting I do, my journalistic writing, my writing-class work, my self-imposed obligations. There's something freeing about not having to cook supper for anyone, to come and go as I please. It's lonely sometimes but I'm not willing to give up my independence for an intimate relationship.

I was married for nearly thirty years to a man I'd known for seven years before that. Our marriage was, I think, as happy as it's possible for a marriage to be. Marriage can be a difficult way of life; it's not called an institution for nothing. But there were joys. My husband, John, and I had many interests in common, and a mutual attraction that never waned. We communicated well with each other most of the time; although we certainly didn't always agree, there was something solid there. When John died suddenly in 1983 I felt I had lost part of myself. I have no interest in beginning again with someone else. We had four children, two girls and two boys. They're all in their thirties now but we're still close. My grandchildren give me great pleasure but I wouldn't want to be totally responsible for them. Bringing up children is difficult and demanding work.

I began to write when I was young, as soon as I could hold a pencil, in fact. In Grade One I wrote:

> I have a dog
> His name is Laddie
> He's a very nice dog
> But he barks at Daddy.

When I look back on those four lines written when I was six, I realize that they foreshadowed the writing that was to come. Nothing was ever totally good, or totally bad either. I've always been blessed—or cursed— with seeing two sides of a story; my present day writing still reflects this. Not for me the happy endings found in Harlequins and other romances. Yet I hope that most of my stories end with the possibility of happiness even if only temporary, as all happiness is. One of the many things I admire about the work of Margaret Lawrence is that in spite of the sorrow, the unfairness, the despair contained within her stories, there is always at least a flicker of hope at the end.

131

At times throughout my life, however, I've identified more with Franz Kafka; everything is hopeless when I feel that way. I was fifty-one before I discovered that the awful blackness that had been descending on me periodically since I was nine was the result of clinical depression. With the help of anti-depressive medication, sympathetic doctors and nurses and the support of family and friends, I have learned to deal with those dark episodes. I'm sad that some others who suffer from depression have not been helped as I have been.

After my Aunt Jenny read my most recent book, a collection of short stories, *A Long and Lonely Ride*, she said, "I've got some advice for you: Lighten up. Your stories are too dark." I explained that the stories had been written over a period of fifteen years. The writing of most of them coincided with sombre periods in my life. One story, *The Plan*, grew out of the deep fear of old age and separation I experienced when I was in my forties. Often during those fifteen years I was happy, hopeful and positive; at such times I'm rarely compelled to write a short story.

I've published a number of humorous pieces in which I laugh at myself and the world around me. I can't force the mood of a piece; most of my writing reflects the way I feel at any given time. I identify strongly with writers like Woody Allen, Ray Guy and the CODCO people and I love the way my friend Gerry Rubia blends the sublime with the ridiculous. Perhaps most humorists have a dark side to their nature.

Today, at sixty-one, my life is fairly serene and busy enough to keep me out of trouble. My friends and my family mean a great deal to me. I still shiver when I contemplate the lives some people have to live, people in my own city as well as those far away. But when I compare women's lives now with women's lives in the past, I'm convinced that, with all its problems, life for women today is better that it was a hundred years ago.

I seem to be growing lazier as I grow older; perhaps that's just a natural part of aging. When I recall how much I did in a day years ago, compared with what I do now, I'm filled with admiration for the young woman I used to be, and for today's young mothers whose days are so very full. My writing is important but not the be-all and end-all of my existence. I continue to enjoy Writers' Guild workshops, discussing my work with students, playing with my grandchildren, gabbing with my siblings and other family members, reading Alice Munro, the Manchester Guardian Weekly and People Magazine. And lots of other things, like listening to music, singing, walking, eating alone in restaurants and watching certain television shows.

Old age doesn't frighten me nearly as much as it used to. I don't trust the pop-magazine kind of stories that describe people, especially women, as being "happy at last" but I can say that at the moment I am reasonably content.

Nancy Riche

1987 Profile

Born in St. John's in 1944, Nancy Riche went to the University of New Brunswick and Memorial University of Newfoundland. She first taught business education in the province's vocational school system and is a member of the Newfoundland Association of Public Employees (NAPE). By 1976 Riche was the second woman elected to her union's negotiating team. The leadership of the union did not want her actively involved because she was considered a "trouble-maker and because I was a woman ... in whatever order. But, I just pushed on." By 1981 she was on staff with NAPE as its Director of Education, Research and Communication, a position she held until her election as Secretary-Treasurer for the National Union of Provincial Government Employees's (NUPGE) in 1984. In this position with Canada's second largest union, Riche is one of the country's foremost labour leaders.

Nancy Riche is also a board member of the Canadian Centre for Policy Alternatives and an executive member of the New Democratic Party of Canada. She has paid special attention to the concerns of women in the workplace, in unions, and in society as a whole. Presently, Riche is Executive Vice-President of the Canadian Labour Congress and President of the Federal New Democratic Party. Internationally, she is the CLC member of the International Confederation of Free Trade Unions Women's Committee.

ℰ   ℰ   ℰ

I am a trade unionist and a feminist—I believe the two terms are synonymous. When I first got involved in the trade union movement there were very few women active in leadership positions. In my own union, The Newfoundland Association of Public Employees, I was the only woman on the Board of Directors in 1977. The former leader of the union was not what could be described as 'supportive.' It seems that for every ten steps taken forward, twenty were taken back. To be fair, that leader was only reflecting the views of the membership. In the early '70s there was in Newfoundland a definite attitude problem; in fact, women's *liberation* was viewed by many (not only the labour movement) as being an extremely radical view.

Knowing all of this, I believed, and still do, that improvements for women in the workforce could best come through their unions. A review of NAPE collective agreements over the past ten years will show clearly the progress we have made. We now have sexual harassment protection clauses, outstanding articles on technological change, and major improvements in maternity leave provisions. In addition, the union must be given credit for removing the blatant discrimination in Newfoundland's pension legislation.

Having gone from a Provincial to National position in the labour movement, I am even more convinced that there's still much to be done. As we begin another year, I feel we are entering the "eye of the storm" of the Women's Movement. It appears that the backlash is greater (and nastier), and our young women are not convinced that feminism is an honourable label. The Women's Movement itself has been criticized by visible minority women for our apparent exclusivity; I think they are right!

Sometimes I get tired. But most of the time I get angry. This anger and my manifestation of it doesn't always help me politically. But so what! I'll continue to struggle on—if I am to be criticized for being a "one issue" person, I'm proud that one issue is equality.

My view of affirmative action is much broader than to put women in place to provide a *balance*. Women need to be where decisions are being made so that they can have input into the decisions, not merely to report back on what the decisions were. My concern is that in creating extra seats we are merely providing lip service. The women I know (including myself) could be accomplishing a great deal more with their time than merely filling seats.

Am I sounding too negative? I don't believe so. We still have a long road to travel before we can say we have achieved equality. Until we get equal pay for work of equal value; until we get quality day care for all who need and want it; until all training programs are open to women; until the public starts writing female newscasters about their opinions rather than the length of their hair—we will not have true equality.

I still believe the way I chose to work on the concerns of women is the best way for me. As a committed trade unionist who has worked at the local and provincial levels, and now nationally, I think the labour movement can and will lead the way in achieving equality in the workplace and in society.

Margo Meyer
Pottery –
Linda Boddie
Photo

134

Phoebe Rich

1990 Profile
Original interview by Laura Jackson

Born at Kennamish, Labrador "down the bay" on Lake Melville, February 17, 1904, Phoebe Rich was orphaned early. She grew up in the Grenfell Mission in St. Anthony and returned to Red Bay, Labrador to teach when she was twenty. Phoebe Rich started sewing grass in 1926, and is one of few grassworkers continuing this disappearing Labrador craft. She has two foster children in Colombia and Senegal through the Foster Parents' Plan.

🍎 🍎 🍎

*M*y parents died when I was a child, so after I lived at the orphanage in St. Anthony the Grenfell Mission sent me to Brookline High School in Boston for a year to prepare me for teaching. The only thing I got out of my school is to learn to read and write. I forgot everything else but I never forgot how to read. I guess I wasn't cut out to be a teacher because I felt young and inexperienced and I didn't feel I had a lot to teach the children. I used to be wonderful for reading in the olden days but since I started sewing grass work, I've had to give up most of my reading.

My grandparents were Scots and my parents were from the Rigolet area. They went to Kennamish to work in the lumber mill; that's where I was born. They had their own money, some kind of aluminum that you could only use in the town. I remember my mother giving me a dollar and a fifty-cent piece but I gave it away to someone who admired it. My mother was Helen Shoogal and she married old Arthur Rich, an old man. She was his fourth wife and he had a grown up family already. There was one grown up son left and that's the one I married so she married the father and I married the son. Seems like I married my brother but he was really nothing to me, not no way blood related. I got married to Arthur Rich in 1926, two days before I turned twenty-two. We were married seven years before our daughter was born in 1933 and our son Gus (Arthur Rich III) was born in 1937 and that was it!

Back then we'd go from winter house to summer house and you had to take everything from one house to the other. We used to go down in motorboat them days, dogs and everything. Where there's a long bar you can only go in so far, and when we would get to that bar, we would throw the dogs overboard and let them swim or run ashore. Then you'd get the motorboat, poke it in as far as you could and then get out in the little rowboat to go ashore. Happened I was pregnant twice while we were moving from one house to the other. I had to stay in the boat and they had to drag the boat in with me in it, that's what I didn't like, see. My mother was a midwife that borne babies north and south and up and down everywhere. There was no hospital them days, only up the bay in Northwest River so wherever she was needed they'd come and pick her up and she'd stay until the baby was born. She and two other women helped borne my first baby. Ann was born bum first; it's a wonder I ever got over it. I'm smarter today every way than when Ann was born and that's over fifty years ago because for a long while afterwards I was like an old crippled woman. I think I was crumped over, doubled over more then than I am now.

We used to live in Rocky Cove in the wintertime. All the women were sewing grass and cleaning sealskins and I thought I might as well try, too. They'd sew mats, big baskets to put clothes in, barrels with hoops on it, hats with rims, the children would have tea pots and cups to play with and dolls cradles; there'd be shoes made out of grass and a mattress of fine grass with a cover made from big flour sacks. I had never seen any grass work being done before I was twenty-two years old and I had never even seen a seal before, but whatever the other women did, I had to try to do, too.

Once I started sewing grass work, I found it to be real therapy. I'd work at it in the daytime, in the night after supper, have tea and go to bed. It's really restful and I never get bored with it because you got a chance just to think the kind of thoughts you wants. Grasswork is a wonderful, wonderful pastime and I sew all the time even though I'm a slow sewer. If I was knitting, I'd be sleepy and tired but grass work, I could sew and sew. I enjoy every minute of it and love every stitch of it. But it's got to be something people take time to do—'tis no use to rush it, you got to concentrate. When the grass dries, you have to keep wetting it. White grass is picked and dried in the fall and green grass is picked and dried in the summer. To dye the grass some people use red berries. I like to do open-work and most of my work has a star pattern in it. That was my own idea but you can just put in there whatever you mind to. According you sews, something comes. I get enjoyment out of making things with grass because people really want it, you know. You wouldn't believe the places my grasswork has gone—California, Ontario, the Netherlands, Texas and Michigan. When I'm sewing grass, I don't want to do anything else, not go out of the house or anything—I even dread to hear the phone ring or someone at the door. With grasswork I could sew and sew and sew. I'm a contented women.

Maisie Rillie

1991 Profile
Original interview by Beverly Brown
Maisie Rillie was born in St. John's on December 24, 1947. She studied teaching at Memorial University under Joey Smallwood's free education program. Rillie's teaching career was short. In the mid seventies, while pregnant with her first child and with little theatre training, she began acting and has performed in numerous roles since then—to name a few: Frog Pond, Chickens, The Best Man, *as well she starred in such films as* Faustus Bidgood, Multiple Choice *and* Boat In The Grass. *She lives in St. John's with her husband, Jim, and their two children, Claire and Andrew.*

❧ ❧ ❧

I was the second last kid in a line of six, so I escaped the strict discipline, which was wonderful! I had free rein to explore my childhood interests; however, it wasn't until I met a kindred spirit when I was twelve that life became really exciting.

I came alive when I met Janet Michael at a party. She was the most exotic looking creature I'd ever seen with big brown eyes, dark skin and dark curly hair. I was white and pasty and skinny and we started clowning around. We recognized something in each other that kept us good friends for years; life got better and better from then onward; laughter makes all the difference.

I have no real vision of myself. At first that worried me. I didn't know what it meant to say I believe this and I am this. I'm sure my values and my personality will continue to change over the years; I certainly hope so. I don't want to be the same person at twenty that I am at thirty, as I am at forty and so on. I don't aspire to become a great actress, but I love acting because I love being on stage with other people who are in this fantasy with me. I love the absurd.

As a child I often playacted in my room doing everything imaginable; putting on a hat and pieces of shower curtain and prance about. When people don't allow little girls to act like grownups if they want to pretend they're models or actresses, I get upset. It doesn't mean they're going to grow up and be vacuous, it just means they're role playing.

Acting gives me a jolt and I think my self-confidence needs a jolt ever so often—feeling on top of it all the time is dangerous! Writing, on the other hand, continues to mystify me. It's like trying to write a letter to a friend when my mind is going one way and my hand another. Collectives don't work well for me because I can't say what I feel in writing scripts. Collective writing works well for groups like CODCO, but I prefer to be given a challenging script and good direction, then I'm in my forte.

Having had my daughter, Claire, made a big difference to me because I figured if she was safe at home, healthy, and tucked into her bed that's all that really mattered. Friends and family are most important, so when there's nothing wrong there, I can go on stage and give it everything. What the hell difference if I make a fool of myself. It only matters to **me** if I make a fool of myself, and if it doesn't matter to me, then it doesn't matter. For this reason, reviewers never bother me.

I'd like to see more roles written about mothers. The mothers that you see, especially in Hollywood films, are suburban mothers. I'd like to see her character and values explored more than the fact that she can cook a good breakfast and drive the kids to school.

I think it's really difficult for men to write for women. They just don't know the territory. They can write for a woman as a sex object or woman as bitch, but they just don't know enough about women to capture our personality. Good women's roles are difficult to come by. If you're going to play a character who props up one of the male characters, it's not challenging; you don't feel inspired playing somebody's mother or girlfriend. Women have the responsibility to write for women. It takes a very sensitive person to be able to write, so if you have a point of view to express, then get to it.

I loved being in *Chickens* by Janice Spence because I love her sense of stage. It's marvellous to be out on stage with language I haven't had to struggle with to find an interpretation and nail down. Her language meant something to me so I could play with it and still have fun.

More and more women writers are coming up with good plays. I like doing original works written by local people. I know they've got flaws, but I'd rather do them because Newfoundland theatre speaks **OF** its culture. I don't mean talks about it, but it comes out of the culture; not that you cannot speak effectively from imagination too; but in that case the creativity of the writer is at work. I think people have to experience Newfoundland theatre because it is good acting, not because it is from here.

One of our biggest problems locally, besides the small audiences for great works, is the amount of work that goes into staging something that will be mounted for two weeks and then dismantled. That isn't fair. Our Provincial Government simply does not support the arts and with Canada Council and Secretary of State cut backs all the time, there is less money to produce good works. Everyone likes to be entertained. We have to laugh and cry; it's part of what makes us human, but because the government is not supportive, artists live in abominable living conditions just to pursue their art.

We're saved by the fact that we are an island. It does make a difference, we don't escape that easily, we don't bring in as many "cfa's" and there are not that many people who leave as would happen if we were on the mainland. We are constantly battling the elements and reacting to the immediate world around us. That's why there's no end to the exciting theatre that's staged here.

Bobbie Robertson

M.F. WHITE

From the 1989 Profile
Interview by Marian Frances White
Born Bobbie Pirie at Birkhill, Scotland on April 29, 1892, Bobbie Robertson immigrated to Newfoundland in 1923. Considered a smooth running dynamo, Robertson has had tributes written to her by Michael A. Butler and Paul O'Neil; Jack Fitzgerald wrote poems about her, Calvin Coish called her indefatigable, while—as she said—she was just doing her job right. Yet there are not many of us who can boast a working career into our nineties.

Bobbie Robertson was a first for many things, not only in Newfoundland but in the world. From 1935-41 she worked at the Dept. of Rural Reconstruction during Commission Government, and dealt with their Land Settlement Scheme. For the next five years she worked as secretary to five different companies and in 1942 she was secretary to the first Canadian Government Trade Commissioner, R.P. Power. In July, 1942 she became the first female executive in Newfoundland and the first female trade commissioner in the world. For the next twenty-three years she was Ottawa's trade commissioner for Canada and the only woman commissioner among one hundred and sixty-four men. In 1967, age seventy-five, she retired from civil service and became the office secretary of the Newfoundland Historical Society. After six years of service she gained the title of Archivist and Teacher rather than secretary. In 1976 she was honoured with the first ever Heritage Award and in 1984 she received the honorary degree of Doctor of Laws from Memorial University. On Saturday, August 8, 1992—just three and one-half months after celebrating her one hundredth birthday—Bobbie Robertson passed away at St. Luke's Home, a senior citizens home in St. John's.

❦   ❦   ❦

I came here with my husband, Alan, when he was given the choice to come to Newfoundland or Bermuda to expand a distillery company he had been working with. We came on the old Sachen Steamer in the spring. The trip took longer than scheduled because with the ice breakup and bad weather we got stuck on the ocean for days. I knew nothing about Newfoundland when I came except the name of the place. I've certainly gotten to know it over the years and have loved it ever since I first put foot here. My earliest memories are of the catamarans from outside St. John's lined up along Duckworth St. to sell their products. That was a wonderful sight.

My husband died forty years ago. I've lived alone every since but I've never been lonely or bored. It's been a thrilling and exciting life working as trade commissioner and trying to formulate Canadian foreign policy and trade policy between Newfoundland and other parts of the world. Every year on my Remington typewriter I wrote hundreds of letters to straighten out passports and to promote Newfoundland enterprise. I've bargained to sell or exchange everything from fish to apples and leather goods to blueberries. After studying the economic needs of Newfoundland and trying to get new markets for our products, to this day I firmly believe Newfoundland could be a 'have' province if we used our resources wisely. I always thought Labrador would be Newfoundland's salvation, but it has been neglected like so many of our natural resources. There should be no poverty here, if we could work independently as an exporter. We've got fish, live stock, we can grow everything from corn to potatoes and asparagus, we have hills full of berries. There isn't sufficient work for the population but we could made work by using more of our resources. I think resettlement was a mistake and by making that mistake we destroyed much of our potential to be self-sufficient.

One year I was in Glenwood in the partridge berry season, a town I still love to visit, and around Alexander Bay there were so many berries I had a pillowcase full in no time at all. The sad part about it, there was nobody picking but me. Another year when there was an awful crop of blueberries there was one man picking in the field. He had a great big pail full to the brim. He was living on the Gander base and he didn't know what he was going to do with them, but later that week we had a supper with his company and the berries were made into pies. I think there were sixty people that night. We ate caribou meat stew, vegetables and blueberry pies. The entire meal came to $2.50 each.

In my career I was always treated as an equal, just like it should be. I can't see what gender has to do with being capable of doing the job right. I felt comfortable in my position and only once in my twenty-three years as trade commissioner was I insulted. That was at Rideau Hall in Ottawa where all the commissioners were gathering after their meetings. A young fellow came up to me and bluntly said, "You have to leave. Women are not allowed here." I pointed to my badge (that identified me as a trade commissioner) and almost knocked him down with surprise! He felt stupid and so he should.

Women's lib has freed us from many obstacles that we had before encountered, but I worry about the small children who are growing up not knowing their parents. When women were on the flakes, spreading fish, that was a good idea. Everyone shared every type of work and everyone benefited. I think the children are suffering today but I'm not putting the blame on the woman. It's the way (society) has set it up. Some women have to work to make ends meet and others want to. I'd like to see a system set up where the children could grow up closer to their mothers. In the olden days Newfoundlanders had a good home life. They all got together and helped each other and celebrated together but that doesn't exist anymore. Today people think money is their friend, more than their neighbour. When I came here and started working most women around me were working in the home, but I think to this day they viewed me with a great deal of good will because they could see my work was of benefit and an asset to the present as well as the future generations. They took pride in their work too, and I think that is one of our problems today, women's work in the home is underrated.

I only hope people will go to the Colonial Building and use the material I have gathered on every community in this Province. I knew Margot Davis and Cassie Brown who came in often to do research. I knew Margaret Duley and loved her writing and read all her books. I kept files on them and anyone I thought important. Now that I've retired for good I like to keep up on what is going on. I gave up my apartment a few years ago after I retired and now live in a senior citizen home. I've never had to think too much about how I would occupy my time, so I'm a little lost because I'm no good at small talk. You see, I've always talked fish! Here in Newfoundland, there are many things that could be done to make life more pleasant for the elderly. In some senior homes, the elderly are almost forgotten by the people who are supposed to be taking care of them. With all the wonderful entertainment that goes on in Newfoundland, I'd like to see more of it. Many elderly people are forgotten even before they are gone, but I would have to say that my life here is well spent.

The one thing I really enjoy is looking at art. I get frustrated lately because my legs are not what they used to be, so I can't get around to the wonderful galleries like I used to, but I can still read so I spend lots of time doing that. I'm thinking I'd like to live at least till the year 2000 because I have the feeling something fantastic is going to happen then, and I don't want to miss it. I have all these ideas about what I think life will be like then and I'd like to experience it to see if my ideas are crazy or not. Somehow I still don't feel that I've accomplished all I set out to do. If there is a secret to longevity I think it must be to enjoy the work you are doing. I don't believe in procrastination but I believe my motto, *God Guard Thee*

Newfoundland, has helped me help Newfoundland prosper, and I hope that will continue even more so in the future.

LINDA BODDIE

Gail Rogers

1990 Profile
Interview by Marian Frances White
with help from Cathy Young
Gail Rogers was born in St. John's on December 29, 1953, at the Grace Hospital and grew up in Mount Pearl. She received her high school education from Bishops College and graduated from there in 1971. Rogers is a graduate of the General Hospital School of Nursing and holds a Baccalaureate degree from Memorial University of Newfoundland (MUN) School of Nursing. She also has a diploma in nurse-midwifery from MUN. Since 1987 Rogers has worked as Regional Program coordinator for the Gander and District Continuing Care program. She has a broad range of nursing experience both in Newfoundland and outside the province.

In November, 1987, Rogers and Linda Ross, a staff member of Oxfam, joined representatives from the Canadian Postal Workers, United Steelworkers of America and Oxfam for a two-week tour to Chile. Rogers was chosen when she responded to an ad which was placed in the Nurses Union Newsletter. She was chosen because of her keen interest in community health. Rogers, a human rights activist, is also a member of Amnesty International. She has travelled extensively throughout the Province giving slide shows on her experiences in Chile.

🐛 🐛 🐛

*U*p until 1973 Chile had a long history of democracy which ended tragically when the elected Marxist government was overthrown in a bloody military coup headed by Augusto Pinochet. Thousands of people lost their lives. Up until the coup, under President Salvador Allende, Chile had a universal health care program making it accessible to the poorest. Since the coup, Chile has experienced a dismantling of its social programs due to privatization. It is a country whose people live under tremendous repression and violence against those who dare to speak out.

I welcomed the opportunity to see what was happening with health care in another country such as Chile. I was so overwhelmed the first week with what I saw, that I thought we were just being shown the negative side of Chile, however then I began to realize that there is very little positive about a dictatorship.

The most striking thing about Chile was the repression, it was astounding to realize that for most Chileans every time they walked down the street there is a possibility that they could be arrested. There are police everywhere; the military is very obvious and along with that there are approximately fifty thousand secret police. Our tour lasted two weeks and we were taken to many regions in Chile to see the health facilities and hopefully set up a health care linkage with the Nurses Union in Newfoundland and nurses in Chile.

Since the Pinochet dictatorship seized power, health care is only available to those who can afford to pay. Disparity between rich and poor is very extreme with about twenty percent of the people having most of the money—which means these are the only people who have access to the privatized modern hospitals and specialists. The other eighty percent, even if they are lucky enough to be able to see a doctor, face long line-ups and have to make do with badly equipped clinics which rely mostly on volunteers.

We visited an infant feeding clinic which was originally designed to help poor children; today however the scale used to decide if a child is nutritionally sound is far lower than similar scales used in North America. When these babies go home there is very little in the way of social programs to maintain their health, so you knew these babies would end up in being just as sick. We visited a city dump in Santiago where people lived around the dump. Children spend all day rummaging through for food and clothing while the garbage was constantly burning.

We not only met with nurses but we met people from all walks of life. We met union people and political leaders who told us how difficult it is for them to unionize. All of these meetings had to be organized almost on a clandestine basis because if you oppose the government and speak out against it you run the risk of being arrested, tortured or worse. We heard terrible stories of imprisonment and disappearance.

While in Chile we met with "The families of the disappeared." It was so difficult to meet with them and hear the stories about what happened to their children. One woman told me how her pregnant daughter, who spoke out against the government, disappeared. She doesn't know what happened to her or the baby. She did hear that the baby was born in prison. There seems to be some evidence that it was sold on the black market. These families keep up their protest in demanding information about their children. It is not uncommon for the Chilean police and military to arrest people walking home from work and not have to account for them. This particular woman told me when she asked the authorities about her daughter, they told her she must have walked over the Andes. Anyone familiar with the Andes knows a woman five months pregnant can't possibly walk over the Andes.

The women in Chile are the real movers and shakers. While there, we were able to go to a rally. It was amazing to experience so many women from so many different political groups and organizations who could put aside their differences to form a common front of opposition against the government. Chile is still a macho society and the men are not involved in these types of rallies. The men are finally trying to put aside their political differences, and join the women in opposing the government.

The government in Chile is trying to privatize everything, from post offices to hospitals and universities and combined with the freedom of the multinationals, the end result today is extreme poverty. I experienced this poverty first hand when I visited a soup kitchen and saw everyone bring together what little food they had and cook it. The two pots on the stove had to feed one hundred people.

Despite all this, I think there is hope. I feel that since the plebescite to see if the Chileans wanted Pinochet to continue, came back with a resounding NO to the vote, that this has given renewed hope to an impoverished country.

We in Canada should all take a lesson from Chile with its mass privatization and its disastrous effects on their social programs. I am trying to inform people about conditions in Chile with talks and slide shows and continuing my involvement with the Newfoundland Nurses Union and Oxfam. It was very encouraging when a resolution was passed at the Annual General Meeting of the Newfoundland and Labrador Nurses Union in 1988, to support one of Oxfam's projects in Chile which involves the nurses college of Chile.

There is a lot we can do as individuals; I learned that. Already through my talks people will discuss with me what they have heard in the news or read about the country. This has made me feel that I am doing my part and I'm not just letting someone else do all the work and accept all that responsibility. I think that my visit to Chile has made me more aware of the struggles that people in other countries experience and the importance of being involved where possible, to help prevent these struggles from escalating.

Laura Jackson photo

Gerry Rogers

1992 Profile
Interview by Marian Frances White

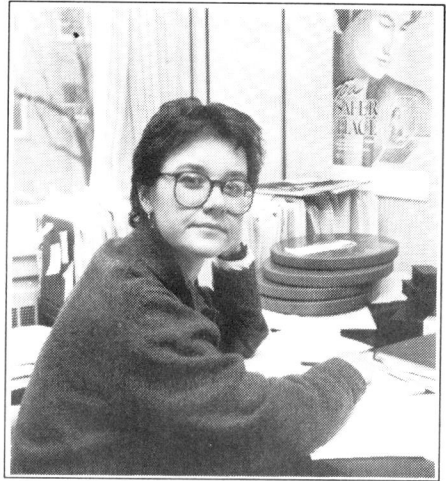

ANN PEARSON

Gerry Rogers was born on August 17, 1956 in Corner Brook. Before she was a year old her family moved to Montreal where her father was stationed in the army. Besides Montreal, throughout her school years she lived in Toronto, Germany and Winnipeg where she completed her high school education. Rogers then entered the convent in Edmonton. In 1977 she left the convent and returned to Winnipeg where she worked in a juvenile group home for girls. In 1978 she returned to Newfoundland with her family and shared co-ordination of the Women's Centre in St. John's with Barbara Doran. In 1984 Rogers moved to Montreal to work with the National Film Board of Canada. Since then she has produced seventeen films, most notably "To A Safer Place" and directed the film "After The Montreal Massacre." Rogers continues to live in Montreal; a film about body image, "The Fitting Room" is in her vision.

ɤ   ɤ   ɤ

$\mathcal{M}$y experience of Newfoundland has always been with me because wherever my family lived, we identified as Newfoundlanders. Our family wasn't a closed system. We were like tumble weeds, transplanting our Newfoundland culture in the communities where we lived. I think this is why I can be at home where ever I am because I have a sense of bringing my home with me.

I'm a survivor of the Catholic school system and I'm a recovering Catholic, but when I look back in my life, some of the strongest role models I had were nuns that were my teachers. I was a sponge growing up, absorbing whatever was around me. I knew I wanted to learn things and travel and work with people and I didn't want to be owned. Because of my parent's influence and encouragement, I learned I had a right to be happy and to fully participate in the world as I wanted to.

I entered the convent thinking I was taking a step toward freedom, but I certainly didn't find what I was looking for there. I was not a religious person, but I was spiritual. I loved communal prayer and meditation and on those occasions I was able to go places spiritually that I couldn't on my own. There I was able to get in touch with the deep respect for life that I always felt and my intense curiosity that pushed me beyond borders.

However, my eyes were like layers of onion skins being peeled away to reveal the inherent sexism in the Church. The religious life I experienced within the Church was not so much a process of discernment and spiritual reflection as one of the value of obedience to the point where you cannot interpret your own feelings and your own spiritual movements. I was being taught to be suspicious of what my mind was saying, and I saw that this was distancing me from my own experience. At that point I began to tell myself this is not spirituality and liberation, and this is not where I want to be. This is a box and this is destructive. When I left, I felt like I had been wearing a pair of super tight shoes and I had taken my shoes off and wiggled my toes. My decision fit into the hypothalamus of my soul and for the first time I felt I had truly done something that was life giving for myself.

I went back to Winnipeg with the three hundred dollars they gave me after three and a half years and I got work in a juvenile home for girls. Everything was so different. I had come from a place where my environment was so controlled; the convent not only defines who you are, but what you're wearing, and it also defined how others react to you. So all of a sudden I didn't have that any more and I felt like I had entered a new world of music and sound.

If anyone had told me then that I would eventually leave the Church, I would not have believed them. There were pockets of the Church that I really liked, the social activism and the community action, so I imagined I would continue to be involved. As I looked closer I had no choice but reject it as one of the most serious patriarchal, misogynist institutions on the face of the earth. This was the mid seventies, long before the Mount Cashel revelations, but then I was always aware that there was violence within the Church. My father quit school in grade nine because he couldn't stand the violence of the Christian Brothers in the classroom.

Indirectly because of the fundamental formative message of the Church, which was that pain and sin and evil are brought into this world through a woman, I became a feminist. To not become a feminist you would have to actively decide to close your eyes, deny reality and experience.

One of the last times I was in a Church was at midnight Mass with my parents. Here was this old man, supposedly celibate, saying that the epitome of womanhood was to be like the Virgin Mary, a woman who could give birth and still be a virgin, and all I could see in front of me was this sea of tired women who could never be virginal mothers, but who had given and given of themselves all their lives. I had to leave because I saw this as the ultimate abuse.

When I returned to Newfoundland, I felt I was where I belonged and stayed for five years, but I had to reconnect with the Rock in a physical way and that was exciting for me. To reconnect with the ocean, the rocks, the forest and the woods happened with my family and also with women like Sandy Pottle who is a strong feminist activist. To go out to the ocean at night and watch the breakers and feel the wind and taste the salt on my lips is something that will never leave me and it's something that I'll have to constantly return to.

My involvement in the women's community coincided with this return to my roots. I finished my social work degree at Memorial and became involved with the Women's Centre, which was one of the best things that ever happened to me and marked the beginning of my formalized initiation into the women's movement. I remember having to do an impact evaluation of unified family court and I'd sit in on court proceedings and watch the many battered women that passed through the court system. I observed how women were treated in court and I watched the fear on the faces of these women as they were not protected from the men who were hurting them. My life was radically transformed by these observations as I began to see women's reality through their eyes. Women like Barbara Doran and Bonnie Janes helped push me into things that I never thought I would be able to do. I ended up representing NAC (the National Action Committee on the Status of Women) and being a spokesperson in Regina and Ottawa for women in the Province of Newfoundland and Labrador. I never felt more alive in all my life!

I grew up not wanting to be like regular girls, and began to see that my most profound connections were with women. It's funny because I also went through a period in my life where I didn't like women a whole lot; I didn't like who we were supposed to be in this society. I always envied lesbians and felt they were so lucky to have found each other. Although there is no closet big enough to contain me, it took awhile for me to find my identity, but when I did, that was a true celebration of self discovery. It was another life giving decision I made for myself.

My work with film gives me a deep connection with the grassroots struggles I had experienced with women in Newfoundland. I remember saying to Kathleen Shannon who had been to Newfoundland to launch "Not A Love Story," that the strength and power of women's voices are not being heard. We needed films about the experience of being a Newfoundland woman, not films that someone from the outside will make about us; we need to speak to ourselves, our experiences and our dreams. So I came to Montreal in 1982 for six weeks to try to express some of these ideas and I've lived here ever since.

As Newfoundlanders coming from that God forsaken Rock, we always feel marginal and as an anglophone in Quebec and as a lesbian and a radical feminist activist I could be quite marginalized, but I feel like I'm in the centre of where I want to be. I think that political activism and community building and identity is all about creating your own space in the world. Although I speak French more now and I understand the

147

struggle of the Quebecois, I feel very much like a guest in Quebec, not a formal guest but a cousin hanging out with the family. Alors, je suis chez ma cousine. A few years ago I almost left here because my French wasn't so great. It was during the Chantal Daigle case and I wanted to express my activism on the pro-choice issue. We worked entirely in French and I felt that I finally had found a feminist activist community that I had a commonality with.

Working on "To A Safer Place" with Shirley Turcott changed my life. I had wanted to do a film about incest that would reach out to women and say you're not crazy or alone and I wanted to work on a film that would be healing, but I could never have dreamed that it would have the impact that it's had. Filmically it's won awards all over the world, but more importantly is how it has touched so many lives.

Producing the international women's film festival in Nairobi was such an empowering experience because it taught me so much about racism and imperialism. One of the biggest payoffs in filmmaking is seeing your film with an audience because I am not a separate, objective expert. I am often accused of being subjective and I ask since when has this come to be an accusation, when to be subjective means to do work about something that you are passionate about and know about. I believe this journalistic standard of objectivity is a myth that will keep us separate from each other. Filmmaking is a communication of many voices so that we can speak to one another and break silences and empower one another.

Woman-talk excites me because women are such wonderful storytellers. I want to produce a film that will look closer at women and body image; not just as a critique of the media and the "male stream" portrayal of women, but I want to look at how we take our space and our power, and I want to use music and poetry and dance and I want this work to be an explosion of the celebration of our lives, despite all the restraints and contemporary efforts to make women smaller and smaller until we barely exist. Somehow, we're breaking through and I want to show these survival mechanisms and give each other permission to explode and to take our place in celebrating our survival.

I've learned that it's so important to be in touch with your gut and to trust your gut feeling and follow those rhythms even though sometimes you don't know where that is going to lead. When I look at the existing structures and systems that exist today, they're not working so well, so to me to fit into those systems and structures is not a sign of success. Things can be really tough financially, but that should not get in our way of daring to dream. To dare to dream is not being naive or stupid. I think it's one of the most courageous things we can get in touch with.

I have a sense of myself and Newfoundland as rocks that float; not fighting or being tossed around in the wind. I go home and I hear the music and we dance and pick blueberries and sit by the ocean, that's home. And yet I feel that it is within me where ever I go, so I have a sense of living in a transmutable home. The uncertainty of my life is not frightening. I feel I am like a kid in a candy store in terms of how much there is to learn, but I do not have the same sense of urgency because I know all the changes are not going to happen today, but I have the time and energy to help them happen for our continued struggle.

Geraldine Rubia

1991 Profile
Interview by Marian Frances White
Geraldine Rubia was born in 1929 in Brooklyn, New York of Newfoundland parents and since the age of three has lived in the St. John's area. Hospitalized as a teenager with osteomyelitis Rubia had her leg amputated at the age of twenty-one. She is the founder of The 'Longside Club, providing opportunity in the performing arts, employment and recreation for persons with disabilities. Rubia is the recipient of many writing awards; the author of A Poem In My Soup, *published by Jesperson Press in 1988 and in 1991 Killick Press published a book of her poems,* Skating Among the Graves.

M. F. WHITE

❦ ❦ ❦

*A*ssuming that I live to be 90, I have just entered the third trimester of my life. In 1984, age 55, I retired from my job in vocational rehabilitation with the provincial government. My intention was to devote a substantial part of my time to writing. Prior to retiring I could only write short pieces of work in my spare time and I looked forward to writing novels, full-length plays, or perhaps an autobiography.

Since retiring I realize that I need to be in a challenging situation— that's when I feel better emotionally and physically, as long as things remain just challenging and not overwhelming.

I think this applied to my marriage as well. I went into marriage rather late, age 38, knowing that there were going to be problems, but quite confident and determined that I could handle them. The difficulties turned out to be far greater than I had imagined, but I was committed and I guess for about sixteen years it never entered my head to think about leaving my spouse. When I could no longer hide from myself the fact that I was in an intolerable situation, I still didn't see how I could break up the marriage. We had two children, Rene and Devin, (in their teens by then) and the biggest of all, I was afraid that my spouse would feel rejected and unloved. Also, as a strict Catholic I felt I was married "till death do us part" and I even looked askance at annulments.

Finally, in 1986 after nineteen years of marriage and after much soul-searching, pondering and prayers, I surprised myself and everybody else by leaving. It turned out to be the best thing for all concerned; though my husband seemed to have mixed feelings about it, I think the predominant one turned out to be relief. He is now very content in his own apartment, the boys live with me, and we are all on friendly terms.

No matter how I have imagined things happening in my life, the actual events turned out to be stranger. In 1989, I sold our bungalow in Mount Pearl and bought a big two-storey house in St. John's, taking in boarders to help pay the mortgage. The renovations it required provided me enough challenge to keep my mind occupied for years!

I have always had more trouble making small decisions than making really big ones, though I don't think there is any big decision in my life that I ever regretted. But given this experience I would never again marry anyone if I had any indication of deep-seated emotional or psychological problems, no matter how attracted I might be. I have had to cope with some difficult situations in my life. I was probably born with an anxiety neurosis; add to this the serious illness of osteomyelitis and subsequent physical limitations, a stressful marriage, coping and helping Rene deal with his Tourette Syndrome, having a challenging job working with disabled persons and my involvement with the *Longside Club*—not to mention having the writing bug which gives me no let-up.

No doubt I take on too much; it's hard to strike a happy medium, but if I have to err I think it's better to err on the side of having too much to do rather than not enough. My anxiety is worse when I don't have concrete problems to deal with. Of course, there's hardly been a time when I don't have concrete problems to deal with.

I might be described as an instant sook but a long-term survivor. I'm sometimes over-sensitive. I'm a perfectionist, but I'm learning that a thing worth doing is worth doing badly. When I was young I tended to be rather prim and proper and there may be those who would say I still am. But I did start to loosen up when I struck fifty. It was also only then that I stopped being ashamed about the imperfections of my body, and became a little freer in talking to my friends about my feelings and personal problems. I have been blessed with faithful and supportive friends. Prayer has sustained me all my life.

I get a tremendous amount of joy out of life. I'd hate to imagine what my life would be without music and poetry and books and talk and the ocean and ducks and grass and rocks and trees and pictures and crocheting and fun and foolishness. Even when I'm feeling depressed and tragic, I soon start making fun of myself or making up a poem about it so I don't wallow very long.

The big thing I have to face right now is the strong likelihood of being on my own for the rest of my days. To a certain extent, I enjoy being on my own. I have always been independent and I can do with quite a lot of solitude. On the other hand, I have always had this dream of finding the man who would be my kindred spirit and living with him happily ever after. But who is happy ever after on this earth? I'm happy most of the time. My sense of humour hasn't deserted me yet and I hope I live to be a hundred.

I still plan to write a novel, some children's books, more poems, songs, and plays. And I have an idea for a new club—The Best Medicine Club—just for laughs.

Sarabande

1988 Profile

Sarabande, A St. John's-based all-women's singing group, made its debut March 8, 1985 performing for an International Women's Day concert. Over the next few years they performed at many other benefit concerts, at local pubs, and on a CBC Radio Special. Sarabande (the name of an ancient Spanish dance once popular throughout Europe) had ten members whose characters and expectations of their music were as diverse as they were in their chosen careers. They all share their love of life through their singing, and their material ranges from Italian and Spanish madrigals, gospel, country and western music to traditional songs.

While Sarabande generally shared the tasks required of any large group, Paul Steffler and Kathy Phippard did the musical arrangements. The group as a whole had a strong, shared empathy toward their music; a belief in the need for peace, laughter and song that was deepened by each individual's unique and separate viewpoint. While reading, bear in mind that the "we" in the story represented the group's consensus while the quotes represented the individuals. Although the group stopped singing together in 1990, this story is important because it offers a glimpse into the various opinions of these women, and might inspire other women to form such a singing ensemble.

❦   ❦   ❦

*W*omen's voices have a particular quality and feeling; a quality that gives us a lot of strength just by singing. The impetus for Sarabande came in waves just like our inspiration to perform does.

(left to right) Debbie McGee, film maker; Allison Dyer, NFB and peace worker; Kathy Phippard, music teacher; Joy Tillotson, librarian; Isabella St. John, potter; Antonia McGrath, photographer; Ester Squires, horticulturalist; Jane Robinson, university studies; Eleanor Dawson, psychiatric nurse; and Susan Williams, social and economic researcher.   SAND NORTHRUP Photo

*After the Battery Big Band folded, there was a hiatus that I needed to fill; Sarabande does that. It's a good, warm feeling to be with a group of people who enjoy making music together. Everyone can, it's instinctive, but too often we're spectators or rely on others for some 'mass produced' sound.—*Alison

There's no hierarchy in terms of who's the boss in Sarabande. We do everything by consensus. It's more a situation where you're concentrating on the immediate note—this note right here—it's that involving.

To me, Sarabande is a small miracle—that ten feisty, busy women should want to plug away at practising, often two nights a week, that, in itself, is a considerable statement. I love the songs we sing, like Il Bel Humour, an Italian madrigal, because it is such a tongue-in-cheek mockery of love, and the message of women's struggle and solidarity in the songs.—Jane

152

We never actually stated any particular political focus, but we like liberation songs and songs that focus on women and that are from women's groups or that express positive energy. We wouldn't choose a song that had lyrics we didn't agree with even if the harmonies were good. That's why we dropped some of the madrigals.

> *I wonder if the people who are afraid of feminists are as afraid of them as I am of R.E.A.L. women*—Antonia

Yet we are searching for traditional Newfoundland songs that express women's experience and because part of women's experience is their living situation, we aren't looking to change historical statements made through music.

> *For myself, Sarabande gives me the opportunity to indulge in musical forms other than traditional. Singing has always been a source of great joy to me and the friendship and closeness of the group provides a sharing of the celebration of music.*—Eleanor

> *I think The Roches have a lot to do with our choice to be an all women's band. We feel complete, as a band, without men so there hasn't been any need to have men join us. Most music, like most professions, are dominated by men and to break free of that and make all the decisions ourselves is a whole new area to explore.*—Susan

Most of our performances are done for benefits and we love doing them, but with the mothers in the group we recognize the need to have a babysitting fund—it can get quite expensive to come to practice a few nights each week—so when we receive money for performances we use it for that.

> *I've played with lots of groups since I started playing flute twenty-five years ago. What makes Sarabande special for me is the variety of music we play and the performances and response from the audience.*—Joy

People in the community are a great support to us. We're only one of many combinations of people trying new things in St. John's and it's great to be a part of that process of exploration and discovery. It's also a social event that brings its own rewards in being just that.

> *Being a piano teacher is very enjoyable, but I need to fulfil the 'performance' aspect of music as well. It's a change from classical music which is my main interest.*—Kathy

There's been a definite musical progression over the past years in terms of becoming familiar with reading the music and the great challenge of learning to control rhythm. The practice is paying off; we sound better and enjoy how we sound more. Women in general have a problem with sometimes undermining their abilities, and when you get ten women together the potential for either extreme is always possible.

Band practices are very dynamic. The most exciting moments are when we've been working on a song and it finally comes together and we capture the feeling of that song.—Ester

Joining the group has greatly affected my direction in my present life. I came here from Vancouver and intended to only stay until after our first IWD concert, but by the time that concert ended I had already decided to stay indefinitely. Now I'm pregnant and I love to think of the baby absorbing all that musical female energy.—Debbie

Sarabande embodies qualities that mean a lot to me. I like to speak my mind; I prefer creativity to passivity, and I love being involved in this long, continuous learning process; I like the immediacy, the intensity and the pleasure of singing. I treasure the friendships that are growing amongst us. I fantasize about us still doing this when we're in our nineties.—Isabella

ROSE-MARIE KENNEDY

Doris Saunders

1991 Profile
Interview by Marian Frances White
Doris Saunders, the second in a family of six, was born in Cartwright, Labrador, on June 6, 1941 to Harriet and Don Martin. She attended school in this remote community located in Sandwich Bay until age fifteen when she won a scholarship to go to Happy Valley. Cartwright, a tiny community of about three hundred, was settled in the mid seventeenth century by Capt. George Cartwright. Saunders, a driving force behind the successful Them Days magazine, was awarded the Order of Canada in 1986. She has three children.

❦ ❦ ❦

*W*hen you come into Cartwright Harbour, you are struck by the sharp contrast to the virtually treeless coastline which brings you to it. There are families on either side of the harbour now, which were once identified by the Grenfell Mission on one side, and the Hudson Bay Company on the other.

As a child, my entire diet consisted of wild sea birds, partridges, rabbits, salt fish, fresh salmon, red berries, bakeapples and blueberries. I was very content there. I loved to read and knew about the outside world, but didn't feel I was missing anything by living where I was—it seemed like we had the best situation in the world. I came from one of the poorer families in terms of material things, though I certainly didn't feel poor. My dad and I built our second house, just about everything in it was homemade like the kitchen table and bunks; even the beds at our summer house was just boards nailed on with a feather mattress laid over them. Being second in a family of five girls and one boy, I grew up as the oldest son. Every Labrador family had to have sons. It was okay to have a girl first, but the second one better be a boy! We were taught to do chores indoors and outdoors. I hated indoor work. I married a wonderful guy who did all the cooking, so I never ever had to learn to cook until he died two and half years ago.

I grew up without grandparents on either side of my family. I think I spent my childhood yearning for grandparents and spent a lot of time with the older people. I'd listen to stories from the elders until I'd get sent home. Cartwright in them days was the perfect atmosphere for ghost stories. We didn't have electricity or telephones. My mother spent a lot of time in hospital and I can remember, especially in the fall, Rose, my older sister, and I would light the fire and sit in front of it and tell the little ones stories about things that we could see in the fire. Dad would come in and remind us it was time to get supper cooked.

My scholarship to study in Happy Valley was fifty-nine dollars a month; I paid forty dollars a month for room and board and eight dollars for school tax, but I worked in a restaurant for a little extra. A month before final exams I got into an argument with my teacher and walked out. She was a very cold and insensitive woman.

Life in Happy Valley was different from Cartwright; I was painfully shy. Up to that point I had only been away from home for one week when I went to Cape Charles. We spent our summers on Dumplin Island; usually there'd be three families fishing. Sometimes we'd go to Pack's Harbour where we could buy groceries and salt. That was the highlight of the summer.

I think if I hadn't been a woman, *Them Days* would never have survived because I don't think there is any man who would have worked without a salary for the length of time I did. Since Frank died I can't work without a salary either; I need the income to survive.

I believe that men and women are equal. I was turned off the women's movement in the mid-seventies at a conference in Halifax where I heard so much hatred against men. I believe in equal pay for equal work and I believe women can do anything men can, but I don't want to be part of a movement that hates anyone. I believe everyone should be responsible for themselves and answer to their own conscience, because if you're responsible to yourself for yourself, we would have a different, better world.

I've always felt that Newfoundland looks at Labrador as a place to take things from and does not recognize the people. We're the poor cousins that don't count. But when you meet Newfoundland people, individually, they are very warm and supportive. White cultures generally feel superior to native cultures, but that is gradually changing.

We've had our share of problems in Labrador because of our culture and because of the development and proposed development that is going on around us. I'm involved in a citizens group that is trying to keep an eye on the PCB incinerator. I definitely don't want the NATO base. When you read the environmental impact statement, you realize the worst thing for Labrador would be to have a NATO base. We want progress but not at the expense of our environment.

I'm a native Labradorian who is proud of Labrador and proud of the fact that I make my own way; most of us feel the same way. We have pride in ourselves as independent people who maintain a positive way of survival. There has been much destruction of dignity of native people in Labrador. The only way to regain that dignity is for each person to take responsibility for himself or herself. No person or no government can **give** you back your dignity, you do it yourself.

I love my work of preserving the cultural heritage of Labrador; I love the crafts that have been handed down for generations and I love berrypicking in the summer and fall. I've never lived outside of Labrador. If I'm gone for more than a week I get antsy and feel cut off from the world. When I'm flying back over Labrador I say ok plane, you can crash now, if you have to, I'm home.

JEANETTE LAANING

Vicky Silk
1991 Profile
Original interview by Cathy Young
Vicky Silk was born in Picton County, Ontario in 1952. She lived in Vancouver and Toronto where she studied electric guitar at the University of Toronto Conservatory; drove a cab part-time and worked at a day-care centre. Silk came to Newfoundland in 1978 and has fished, was representative on a Federal Fishery Appeal

Board, New Democratic Party candidate in the April, 1989 provincial election and Deputy Mayor of Petty Harbour. For several years she ran a costume business, Thespians, however, her present focus is on university studies where she hopes to get a degree that will make her more functional in Central America.

❦ ❦ ❦

𝒜 year before I came to Newfoundland there had been a terrible murder of a child about ten blocks from where we lived in Toronto. I was a single mom with twin four year old girls. A couple of months after this murder my kids disappeared. I called the police, convinced they had gone the route of this Shoe Shine Boy murderer. Fortunately, they were fine, but I felt it was just too hard, I needed a better place for them. I spent the whole winter looking for a farm outside of Toronto and didn't find one. When I had a chance to take care of a place down here I took it. It was a totally different culture. I thought a lot about raising kids in Newfoundland and my family asked me to come back to beautiful B.C., but the powerful drive was to come here.

The very first time I came to Newfoundland I thought it was hilarious. I had been told two things about Newfoundland, that it was very rocky and the trees were short. We took the ferry to Port Aux Basques and all I could see was sheer granite cliffs, driving across the island the trees were short compared to the semi-tropical climate of British Columbia; even Ontario is lush compared to here. I have this theory that I'm a drowned Newfoundland sailor in a past life!

My fishing was a total fluke. It's just like I decided to go to the Ship Inn for a drink and chat with friends, I decided to fish. I was up the shore visiting a friend, who was the doctor there. I had my Fender electric guitar and he had a boat; he liked my guitar and I liked his boat, so we traded. I took this little eighteen and a half foot boat up to Petty Harbour and started fishing.

I was the first fisherwoman in Petty Harbour and the laughing stock of the whole community. The first three days I took my boat out about a quarter of a mile, to the harbour's mouth and looked around and heaved the anchor over and dropped this line. When I got in to the wharf the men were just absolutely bonkers with jokes.

The second day I couldn't get my anchor; I didn't want to lose it, so I tied my life jacket around the anchor and left it. When I got in to the wharf the men were once again jeering at me. No one had caught any fish in that area for years, they said, so why did I think the tide was turning around. On Monday I went out three miles. I made my way out to what seemed like a journey to the North Sea near England and I caught four hundred and twenty-five pounds of fish!

I had a good season fishing and that fall I filed for Unemployment Insurance. Some of my stamps had been from a job in town before fishing, so I was turned down because if you fish, all stamps have to be made between June and September and not within the fifty-two week period. I felt I had really been discriminated against. When I got the letter of refusal I was so upset I cried for three days. I called Ottawa and I would get on the phone and this flood of tears would start.

I couldn't find a lawyer to represent me and I didn't have any money. I was a single mother with two kids, with zero income and no prospects for the future. One lawyer laughed out loud, he thought I was crazy. After snivelling around for a few more days I got this brainstorm. Ah Ha! What I need is a lawyer who is interested in the law and in justice.

I called Memorial University. They don't teach law but they do have someone teaching criminology, George Cummings. He took my case. We had to take the case to the Federal Appeal with the Unemployment Commission. We won, they had to pay me thirty-two hundred dollars in benefits. That money was mine even if the court case went anywhere else and the case was lost.

The case then went to the Supreme Court of Canada. The Unemployment Commission had their best litigation lawyer and I still won. That was March 24, 1983—a total of three and a half years later. I felt really great because finally this crazy act was changed.

The depressing thing about this is that even though the law was recognized as unjust and thrown out by the Supreme Court of Canada, eighteen months later the policy and lawmakers in this country rewrote the regulation. I still maintain that the regulation doesn't have a leg to stand on and is unconstitutional. The only thing I can say is that during that year and a half, people really benefitted. I'm still glad I took them on.

When I go out in a boat these days, it's mainly for pleasure; I love my time on the water. The costume shop in St. John's kept me busy, and I have four children now, so my life is full. I felt I broke new ground when I started fishing because a few years later, three or four women started fishing a scattered time with their husbands or partners. A couple of women have said to me, "I'm dying to go in the boat but my husband won't take me." I'm glad to see these attitudes are going out with the tide.

There's a saying that it's bad luck to have a woman in a boat. I like to think the luck is turning around.

Right now I'm fed up with Canadian politics and am studying languages, French and Spanish, to better equip me for a long stay in Central America.

Lise Sorensen

1989 Profile
Interview by Marian Frances White

*Born in Jutland, Denmark, on April 25, 1941,
Lise Sorensen moved to Ontario with her parents
when she was ten, and first studied art at the Ontario College of Art. She left home for New York
at the age of eighteen and studied at the Arts Students League of New York. In 1961, Sorensen
moved to Montreal to study at the Montreal
Museum of Fine Arts and in 1965 she graduated
from there with Honours.*

*Best known for her landscape paintings, Soren-
sen also sculpts, draws and makes prints. As a painter, her art encompasses
many aspects of expressionism—there is an analysis shown in her painting,
whether that be of the underlying geography of the landscape that she is painting, or the human forms she is drawing or sculpting. Sorensen has a studio in
St. John's where she resides and teaches in the winter, and one in Woody Point,
Bonne Bay where she spends her summer.*

*Lise Sorensen has had solo exhibitions at MUN Art Gallery, and has taken part
in group exhibits such as Artists de Terre Neuve in Congnac, France; Living
Nature in Ottawa; and The Human Form in St. John's. She taught at MUN
Extension Art for ten years giving adult and children's classes in mixed media.*

*The recipient of several artist grants, Sorensen has given workshops on
Newfoundland's West Coast. Her work is included in the MUN Art Gallery
Permanent Collection, at Petro-Canada in Ottawa and in numerous private col-
lections. Her drawings were published in TickleAce 1977 and in 1979 illustrated That Fine Summer by Ella Manuel. Sorensen's work illustrated the
stories of the women profiled in the 1989 Almanac.*

❦   ❦   ❦

I chose to study in Canada as I was impressed with Canada's Group of
Seven and the landscape in general. I liked their direct approach to
painting, their strength, colour and solid forms. I came to Canada when I
was ten with my parents and have numerous memories in Denmark of
spending much time alone, always drawing. I think that since I was quite
small I had a solid sense of who I am.

I was inspired to come to Newfoundland after listening to descrip-
tions of its rugged and beautiful landscape by a friend of mine in Montreal.
I brought my two young children to Woody Point, where we remained for
a number of years. I taught art classes there and painted when I could. It
was an extremely difficult time as we had little money. Due to the outport

social conditions of the '70s, I found it difficult being a single parent and painter, with less time to devote to my artwork. At that time the welfare of my children took priority over my painting; therefore, I painted little for several years. Now that my children have grown up, I have more time to devote to my art and this time has helped me develop fully as an artist. My attraction to Woody Point was based more on the environment than on the people. The Gros Morne Region surrounding Woody Point contains probably the most intriguing and powerful landscape that I have yet to see.

I mostly like to paint outdoors. I am not a studio artist, I don't like to make a quick sketch and invent the rest in my studio. Although it is rough going in order to include the entire landscape; I have to climb many hills and mountains with large canvases. I want to paint Newfoundland itself, not a studio interpretation of it. I like to analyze the type of light and type of very raw environment that I see here. It reminds me of a moonscape or some alien environment with its lack of vegetation and unique rock formations. The area of the Tablelands that I've been painting was an ancient ocean once and you can see the very basic rock that is millions of years old. I have found a rare beauty here—the kind of beauty you find when you strip something bare of all the decorations and see the underlying form. I haven't found any place to paint that comes close in strength to this island and I've concentrated on a very small area to this date, so I have many more areas to explore yet. Hopefully I will soon be able to explore other parts of this island. I have, of course, seen other places of interest in Newfoundland but the unchanging weather and relative inaccessibility of many areas makes my type of study difficult. I think it will take many years to explore the entire island.

Teaching has also become very important to me. I feel there is a real need for a more serious attitude towards teaching the fine arts. The development of the individual and therefore their art seems to be decreasing as art becomes more political and/or business oriented. I find it depressing that art does not seem to be taken as seriously as it once was, with thousands of "artists" being graduated from second-rate art schools. Often these "artists" end up teaching art before they have experienced enough to have anything worthwhile to teach.

I do not readily conform to the public's demand for "conceptual" art, focusing more on my need for self-expression than "fashionable" art. I enjoy teaching new ways of looking at art, but I don't think you can ever *learn* to paint. To me, one's work comes from the environment and within. There are a lot of people who put a piece of plastic on a string and call it art. It can only be art if it really has meaning instead of simple shock value. When I visit galleries and see this type of trendy material, its novelty wears off quickly. I get bored with art that is in vogue at the moment and with

160

art that is superficial. To me an artist who has lived and now has something of value to say to people is stimulating and thought provoking.

I don't like to philosophize my work to people; it should explain itself and if it doesn't, there is either something wrong with the work I've created or the person's ability to perceive it. I like to think of my work as being like the subject material and somewhat stark, but with an underlying strength. I feel uncomfortable putting my thoughts into words; words are to me a very inaccurate form of expression. I can only hope people will understand what I'm doing through my painting and in that understanding I will have said all that is necessary.

Mabel Squires

1991 Profile
Mabel Squires was born in Gander Bay into a family of thirteen on September 9, 1898. Her mother died when she was seven, after which time she lived with her uncle on Fogo Island. When she was seventeen she joined the Salvation Army and travelled extensively as a corps missionary. The following is a journal excerpt her son, Gerry Squires, and grand-daughter Ester Squires, encouraged her to write before she died on October 11, 1988.

🐦 🐦 🐦

I am going to try to write the story of my life, but it's a big task. I am now over eighty-eight years old and I do not find it so easy to concentrate … When I turned seventeen, I told my father I wanted to become an officer of the Army. He was determined to hold me back. When I threatened to run away from home, father agreed to let me go but said he would not help me in any way.

St. John's Headquarters first sent me to Doting Cove, Musgrave Harbour to teach. I walked (there) every morning … I became Cadet Payne. (Several appointments later), I decided to apply for work in China. In St. John's I used to see the Chinese people and my heart went out to them. While waiting for an answer, I was sent to Bridgeport in charge of Corps and school. I conducted my first funeral there. I never went to sleep nor touched any food from the time I was told that there was a person dead until after the funeral.

November, 1922 I got the happy news from headquarters to come to St. John's and prepare to leave for China ... we arrived in Peking Christmas Eve, 1922. On January 3, 1923 I started going to school to learn the Chinese language ... In November the Army opened five food kitchens to feed the thousands of beggars who crowded the streets ... (One) summer I was the only white person stationed in a village called Taku.

While working in the food kitchens, a man fell down beside me and died right there ... When the police came I took hold of one of the man's arms to help (and) a louse from his head crawled on the back of my hand. I felt the bite but brushed it off ... A few days later I was taken down with Typhus Fever ... I became unconscious ... I lost all hearing and my fever became so high that the doctors said I would never survive, but I did.

When the city of Peking was captured by the Japanese in 1927, I was fortunate enough to be one of the missionaries put on a train to Tien-Sin ... After two months we were taken privately aboard a cattle ship that took us to Colombo. We were to cross the Bay of Bengal, the roughest sea in the world. We were not only seasick but almost unconscious; none of us cared if we lived or died ... From Colombo we were taken to Ceylon for one week, resting and enjoying the beauty of the Island ... fruit trees everywhere, flowers and monkeys climbing around ... the saddest sight of all was the Leper Colony.

When I got to India I was told to take off my Chinese uniform and put on an Indian Sari ... When I was not in the operating room, I was looking after the out-patients and saw many horrible cases; sores full of flies, ears that were sore with maggots eating the flesh ... yet the time I spent at that hospital was the best time I ever lived.

In 1930, I was given my homeland ticket and sometime in March month I arrived in St. John's ... The years were passing away, I was getting older and in my heart I wanted to be a mother, so I got married to a man within the Army who was two ranks below me. By marrying him, I had to go back two ranks; the rule being that the wife could not have higher rank than her husband. This is still the case today. We were blessed with three lovely sons but I am sorry to say my marriage was not a happy one. When World War II started my husband went overseas against Head-quarters permission and left me with three small children ... Still carrying on the work in the Army, I was sent to Exploits ... It was very hard with services to conduct and travelling long distances to collect for Self-Denial; it kept me away from caring for my children. They would cry when I would leave them with babysitters and the thought worried my mind and heart. I asked to be moved to a place where I could do my duty to both the corps and my children. I was sent to Green's Harbour for two years and then back to Exploits. While there, my husband came back from Scotland. I was told by Headquarters that I could carry on my work as an officer but they could not accept my husband because he had wandered away from God. I considered that I had three sons to be cared for and I felt that I could not face it alone any longer, so I had to resign.

My husband went to Bonavista to visit his parents … He then went to Corner Brook to look for work and I took the children to Bonavista intending to live there with my in-laws. Sam, my husband, wrote to tell me he would not be coming, my father-in-law became angry and laid the blame on me. I packed up again and moved to Summerside. I crossed over to Corner Brook to look for a house and I brought the children (there). My husband decided to leave home again to go to Toronto. In my heart I was glad he was going … After he was gone two years he wrote and asked me to bring the family to Toronto. I decided not to at this time but after another two years, I considered that the boys knew little of their father so I boarded up my home and moved to Toronto in 1949.

I had to work nursing to help pay for our home. My husband became unsatisfied and showed his temper many times. He often drank so life became very miserable … I told Sam he would have to move out and we were eventually divorced. After he left us he did not support us in any way. I took in elderly ladies as boarders. The rooming house was hard work but I was free and happy … at last.

SAND NORTHRUP

Janice Udell

1988 Profile
Interview by Marian Frances White
Born October 3, 1954, Janice Udell has led a life of constant discovery and change. After obtaining a Bachelor of Fine Arts from the Nova Scotia College of Art and Design in Halifax, she struggled to get away from the clinical way of expression to find her own medium in pencil drawings. Udell's work has much surrealistic imagery that uses spirals and gothic structures, often set in the background (or foreground) of the wild Atlantic. While exploring various planes and using illusion to create these images she forges into a spiritualism that is mythical and yet very much of herself.

In 1981 Udell had her first solo exhibition at the Elca London Gallery in Montreal. Since then she has had solo exhibitions at Memorial University of Newfoundland Art Gallery, Contemporary Graphics, and Christina Parker Fine Art Gallery. Udell also shared several group exhibitions, such as In Celebration of Women in 1983. She has won several awards for her pencil drawings including the Canada Council Art Bank Purchase Award.

For several years Udell lived in a renovated saltbox house in St. Michaels, a small community on the southern shore of the Avalon Peninsula. She challenges her pencils to explore and reveal mysteries that are timeless. Twelve of her sketches were reproduced in the 1988 A Woman's Almanac.

ぐ　ぐ　ぐ

I think that our most illuminating experiences are the ones when nothing is predictable and you're not quite secure; that's when the spirit can really move in and touch you because you're vulnerable. In one way that's troubling, but in another way it's fascinating because you really feel the effect of the forces around you. When I draw I sometimes have women falling off the edge; that's why it is disturbing to most who view it. Somebody once said that art lives by destroying itself. I believe that. In any sincere work you have to break down barriers to explore.

If you live in an insulated world, you live in a bubble and never experience that open dialogue with life and with people around you. When I look out the window at the ocean, I realize how much I am at the mercy of nature.

Today women enter into a history of art where we have never before been so active a force. For centuries we were subject under the brush of male painters and in a sense women were 'painted out,' not only from studios and exhibitions but by the false image of ourselves defined by men. We are now finally searching for our own visual statements. Look at the strong graffiti-like painting of Sue Cole, and then to the passive illumination from Pam Hall's *mother stone* constructions. As image makers we must create our own history that is central to our experience. I see our vision as more than dogma; our statements have the power to encompass and project not only our beliefs, but the humanity from which these beliefs flow, are charged and full of truth. Ancient women are speaking through us all the time, yet when we accept and live falsities like the dogma the church preaches of women's place in society, we insulate and debilitate ourselves. I think if we open ourselves up to spiritual experiences we recognize our hidden power.

There are systems in place in our society that move us away from this identity, this phenomena of how we connect with nature and other people. Sometimes in my work I try to find the source that wants to obliterate us and correct this in my drawings. I remember one night walking through the aspens with Kathleen Winter. It was about midnight, and the sound of the aspen leaves crackling made it a very metaphysical experience. It was like magic, so I went home and tried to draw that experience. In the drawing the people were organic like the trees, and in some ways were not very distinguishable from each other.

I use the sea as a metaphor for women to show their strength. An image of women looking out to sea recurs in my work to portray the longing for knowledge. In this sense Newfoundland is very important to my work. My ancestors are from here, and I like to think they speak through me. I find Newfoundland very gothic and Celtic and get this really ancient feeling from this island, as though I can block out the twentieth century if I wish. That's why there is seldom a car or a machine in my drawings because I believe people are timeless. I don't know a lot about the mythology of goddesses but I do know there is a woman's voice that speaks when I open myself up to it, but these are not conscious thoughts. I feel very strong in this female voice and try to focus on the strength I find there. But I don't care for my work to be edited or didactic. Art should never *serve* anything. Art should be what the person producing it is, and if that expression moves towards enlightening women, well, that will come out in the drawing. But to actually say that the drawing is going to have a message misses the whole point of artistic expression.

There are many stereotypes in my own life in a small community that I have to break down: that of the woman living alone and needing a man et cetera. I don't isolate myself from everyone here, because I don't see that as the answer either. There are lots of older women who live here alone long after their husbands pass on, so I empathize with them. I see them hanging out their clothes and chopping wood. In the daytime I love to sit and listen to their stories and in the evenings I draw.

I'm like this woman that recurs in my drawings, a woman who walks in open landscapes by herself but is not at all lonely. She's walking through many spaces; she's always been by herself, but the drawings are a celebration, they aren't at all sad. I also like drawings that have no beginning and no end like a Moebus Strip. This woman is caught in time. Depending on the way you look at it she could be entering or exiting, climbing walls, or on the horizon, but in whatever way you look at it, her path makes sense.

In some of my work I am very pagan and move from religion to ritual to become spirit; it takes away the material plane to be elevated to art and hopefully to truth. Unfortunately women's history has been largely a lie—once one lie was told or one piece of history misconstructed another lie had to be told to cover up the first. So in a sense our lives have been illusions of what others make us into.

Many people buy art like they buy stocks or gold. Artists need to break away from that system and find new ways to share our images; away from companies and institutions whose policies are threatening the dignity and survival of minorities and third world countries. By selling to them, by having our exhibitions served to them for their own publicity, is in essence supporting that oppression. We, as women, should question the ethics and politics in art and generate our own answers. It is us who must decide where our voice will go and how it will be used—that is ultimately our decision.

CÉCILE TRUFFAULT

Mary and her Aunt Mae

Mary Walsh

1989 Profile

Mary Walsh was born into a family of eight in St. John's on May 13, 1952. She was raised by her Aunts—Mary Waddleton and Josephine Walkins and her Uncle Jack Waddleton. Walsh came out of high school in 1969 'bloodied but not beaten.' Engaged to an American serviceman, she took a part-time job at the Arcade, but in 1970 left the Arcade and her fiancee and worked with CBC Radio and Here and Now *TV. Walsh performed and toured extensively with the Newfoundland Travelling Theatre Company where she met other members of CODCO. While studying Theatre Arts at Ryerson in Toronto she decided to perform with CODCO in their first show* Cod On A Stick. *This was the early seventies—a time that marked an era of irreverent and award winning work by that group and helped establish Newfoundland's reputation as a hotbed of theatrical activity.*

In '76 she performed in Newfoundland's first feature length film Faustus Bidgood. *In '78 she held the lead role in the TV show,* The Root Cellar *and performed in* Up At Ours. *In '79 she toured with Theatre Passe Muraille through England and Wales and 1980 marked Walsh's directorial work in* Terras de Bacalhua; *since then she has directed a string of successful shows such as* A Child Is Crying On The Stairs. *1982-83 Walsh was Programme Anamateur at the LSPU Hall and in '83 joined* The Wonderful Grand Band *who toured nationally and produced a series of TV shows. Since '86 she has been producing national TV shows with CODCO, as well as continuing to do projects at the LSPU Hall like* Ntesinan, *a play about the Innu of Labrador. In April '88 her play,* Hockey Wives, *premiered in Toronto.*

ॐ ॐ ॐ

once my mother gave me a red coat

once when i was eleven my mother and father came out
from around the bay where they'd moved that year and
brought me, on the fleetline bus, home with them

once my mother sent me a christmas card that said, in
her writing, merry christmas mary, love mom.

once when my sister was angry with me, when I was
fifteen and drunk and hurling insults my father took me
outside and walked me around the yard and told me that
i was his little girl

once when I was eighteen months old Aunt Mae and
uncle jack and aunt phine took me next door to live
with them because i was just out of the hospital with
pneumonia and my parents house was damp and theirs was
dry … and that was it, that's where I stayed and
grew up, from then on they were my parents

and the one person who has made me, who has influenced
the way i am, the way I fit in the world is Aunt Mae.

The overwhelming truth about the nature of this piece just struck me …
the fact that these almanacs are going to be hanging around in people's
pocketbooks on the table next to the phone … this is not disposable stuff
… this could haunt you … this could fall into your brother's hands
sometime and you could receive a series of late night drunken phone calls
from Alberta … see I'm in trouble already. Well no point worrying about
the future … on with bothering the past.

If you were to ask me what the major influences on my work were …
Do you wanna ask me that question? Do you care even a little tiny bit what
they are? Ah, go on, ask me just for a laugh … My reply would be my
family … Tho' I didn't really grow up with them, they've informed
everything I've written … them and Aunt Mae.

Sometimes I actually, and I'm blushing as I write this, steal the words
right out of their mouths but mostly its, but usually, it's an attitude I
borrow from them. My older characters, Mrs. Budgell, Mrs. Ball, Bette
Furlong, all seem to be different parts of Aunt Mae with a little of mom
thrown in and, of course, a bit of me.

In 1971 I was much more active in the women's movement than I've
ever been since..at that time I was involved in a fairly destructive personal
relationship..and I remember I went through a year in a consciousness

raising group and I never once told any of the women in the group what was happening in my life..of course, I was only nineteen at the time, but I just seem to have been plagued for years and years with that "catholic I grew up in downtown St. John's and I'm not as good as everyone else" syndrome ... I thought my problems to be so plebian in nature that they, of course, could be of no interest to this group of largely middle class women ... in truth I have no idea what class these women were, it was just an uninformed assumption on my part. One that, thank God, I'm getting out of the habit of making.

Everyone else in the world seemed to lead a much more "Leave It To Beaver, Father Knows Best" kind of life..with a white collar dad, a car, a house in around the back of town and sisters who were head of the student council ... we lived on Carter's Hill right in the centre of town. One year I waited at the bus stop in front of the Basilica ... I went to Mercy School ... pretending to be getting the bus to my well appointed home "in around the back of town" till everyone else had gotten on their buses and I could trip down over the hill to my well appointed home on Carter's Hill.

What is she getting at now, you ask. Are ya askin that? Are ya? Go ahead ask me just for amusement sake ... well, aside from family, matters of class distinctions between the haves and the have nots, between the upper class and the under class would seem to be the other theme that informs my work.

Well that's it. Except to say that I find getting older is better, a lot better. You just get so sick and tired of the upkeep and maintenance costs on the castle of hurts that you've been building brick by miserable brick since the first real or imagined rejection in your life ... you just get so weary of it. You're forced to start a demolition process..now, of course, you're not a fool, you don't bring in the huge wrecking ball ... it'd be too frightening ... God where would you live if not in the castle. Anyway you start dismantling the huge, costly west wing bit by bit and maybe you rip it all down or maybe you're left with a small manageable cottage of hurts by the end.

Abies balsamea (L.) Miller

Theresa Walsh

1989 Profile
Interview by
Marian Frances White

CÉCILE TRUFFAULT

Theresa Walsh calls herself 'a Downtown Street kid.' She was born on July 6, 1955 at St. Clare's Hospital in St. John's and grew up in the heart of the city. After attending Presentation School, Belvedere and Holy Heart consecutively she finished school and took a job at Parker and Monroe shoe store, until she began work with Canada Post in June '75.

Walsh's first job as mail handler was her introduction into the then male-dominated work force. After proving herself as good as 'one of the guys,' she was promoted to postal clerk in Sept '75. Within days the post office went on a forty-two day strike over the postal code. This strike marked Walsh's initiation into union work. She was elected Shop Steward in '84 and elected Vice-President of the local in Nov.'85. In April '86 she became President of her union and in December, '87, Walsh lead the local into one of the most bitter strikes to date. Although the Tory Government legislated them back to work under Bill C-86 after a two week rotating general strike, the unions work to stop privatization and the loss of thousands of jobs, continues. In 1990 Walsh took the public relations position for the St. John's Status of Women Council. As a committed feminist activist she continues to work for change within the women's community.

❦ ❦ ❦

I've lived a very provincial life, you might say, a very downtown St. John's life to be specific and know what it's like to have the city squat in around you. My grandmother's house, where I lived with my parents, was torn down with the urban renewal development. That was the earliest injustice I can recall experiencing. She had just finished fixing up her house after everybody had grown up and was looking forward to retirement. The money they gave her to move didn't even cover the cost of her renovations; she had a nervous breakdown over that, like you would. I thought I was too young to be influenced by these wrongs, but the image of the wrecking crew smashing her house has always remained with me. I've learned now that if you want to keep something you have to fight to keep it. Because the neighbourhood had been torn down, there was no place to play and sadly enough, I spent half my life playing on the post office parking lot! From my bedroom where I lived on Water St. I used to look right in at them processing the mail, *never dreaming* that I would someday work there. It was all men then, so the shell has cracked a little.

Working with the post office gave me a real sense of what union work and solidarity is all about. There's a lot of needless pressure in all areas of postal work like not being permitted to speak to the person next to you or sit on a stool when you're sorting mail. It's the old story of *always having to be busy* in the eyes of the hierarchy, which makes the work place much like a prison camp. I was always a solid union member and remember well the '75 strike to boycott the postal code. We were fighting against technological change that was doing away with jobs and introducing more noise into the workplace. What we didn't know then is the amount of dirt we inhale when they clean the machines and the injuries caused by the repetitive strain from working on those machines. Many have to wear braces and have had surgery on their wrists from repeated punching of keys for the postal code.

The turning point in union work came when I felt pressure from my employer who was trying to release me for absenteeism. I was a shit kicker and when my marriage broke up after a year I was depressed and lost work time. My employer sent me to a doctor for an assessment, but I refused to sign any papers that said this information could be released to Canada Post. This served to make me more vocal and active within the union.

CUPW fought for forty-two days on the street to win the right to refuse any unsafe work and to obtain paid maternity leave. The strike around the issues of cutbacks and privatization was as close to a war that I've ever felt. I'm deadly opposed to the erosion of accessible public services and the loss of good paying jobs. People talk about the great money that's made at the post office and suggest employees are overpaid. This stems from being indoctrinated into believing that living under or below the poverty line is a bowl of cherries. It's a women's issue as much or more than anything else since women compromise a large part of the post office labour force, but we will all suffer in the long run.

By December 1989, I decided to leave Canada Post having struggled with the decision for three years and having just returned from a trip to Nicaragua. I felt very strongly that I had something to give outside of Canada Post in the broader struggle for social justice. After several months of rest, reflection and a trip to the Michigan Women's Music Festival, which was as pivotal for me as seeing the destruction of my grandmother's house, I began to address issues in my personal life. At the festival I experienced first hand the possibility of living in an environment that is created from women's vision of the world. In the middle of no where, there is one square mile for one week a year where women have a place for peace, fun and equality regardless of sexual orientation, disability, race or spiritual beliefs. The challenge is to incorporate this into our every day lives.

I firmly believe that until the most vulnerable and oppressed women have their issues addressed, the entire women's movement will never achieve its goal of true equality. The game I'm trying to win in Canada today as a lesbian feminist is a lot more complicated than those I used to play as a kid on the Post Office parking lot.

Patricia Whelan

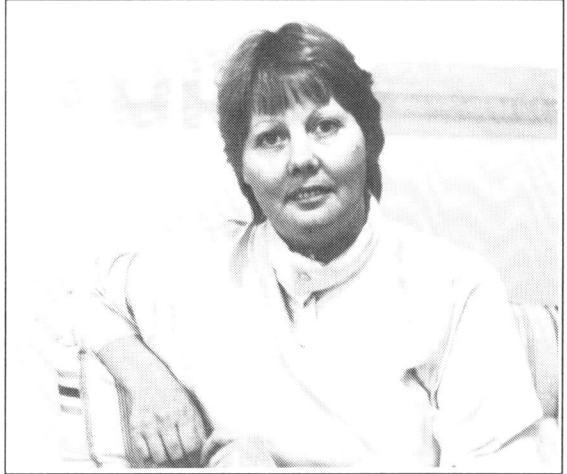

SAND NORTHRUP

1988 Profile
Interview by
Marian Frances White
Born in St. John's on March 14, 1947, Patricia Whelan was the youngest girl in a family of two girls and three boys. She describes her upbringing as traditional, though her father, Frank Power, realized the impact her mother, Evelyn, had on the family. She was educated by the Mercy Sisters at Holy Heart of Mary Regional High School, graduating in 1965. Whelan then took typing at the College of Trades and Technology and worked as a typist until she married at age eighteen. She had four children fairly quickly.

Once her children were in school Whelan entered Memorial University, completing two and a half years of a Social Work program before both financial concerns and the extra care required to raise a child with a birth defect demanded that she leave. She worked for the Child Care Division of the provincial Department of Social Services, as a childcare worker at Daybreak Centre where she helped establish a daycare program, and at Presentation House doing childcare and placements for foster children.

For the last thirteen years Pat Whelan has lived in Rabbittown—a neighbourhood of St. John's. In 1984 Whelan, who derives much of her desire to instigate change in social services from personal experience, acted as coordinator for the Single Parent Project for Rabbittown, has served on the Board of Directors for its Community Centre, and is an active volunteer organizer.

❧   ❧   ❧

I lived for a long time on a fixed income, which means that monies that should be available for kids to get involved in something constructive, like the arts, aren't available. Because of this these kids sometimes get in trouble with the law. That's why I started to help organize a group of parents so that we could voice our concerns and let the public know that just because we were poor didn't mean we didn't care about what happened in our kids' lives. As a result of this, a better relationship began between the Newfoundland and Labrador Housing Corporation and the tenants.

It was obvious the so-called outreach services, that is, community service groups, were not seeing the social life of teens as a priority, even though the mandate for many teenage organizations is to address problems from all income levels. The majority of the tenants in this area are Roman Catholic, yet up to that point we hadn't had an active outreach from the Church. I have a strong affinity with my faith but not with the Church per se. I've been involved in different church projects myself and have unfortunately found that the parish does more lip service to us than anything else. In fact, the only time I see the parish priest up here is when the parish dues are being collected. These days I'm glad to see that outreach services are slowly becoming more sensitive to our needs. Lorraine Michael and Francis Ennis helped by giving us a place at the Social Action Centre and showing us the best way to approach problems without taking from our individual methods.

I was a single parent when our first project got underway in 1985. The four of us on the steering committee were there for different reasons, yet all of them were valid reasons. Having gone through the social service system myself and seen the lack of options, I felt compelled to work on women's issues. The more I worked in that area, the more I could see that the problems women faced were because of their socialization (that is, being brought up to see a man as the head of the family) and their lack of education. What happens when the man cannot find work? In all too many cases there is a lifetime history of being on social services—those who were dependent upon the system often find their kids and their kids' kids are now on the system. It's easy to say that we should be helping ourselves and using our talents and time, but when you live in a system that goes against everything that helps you grow, it's very hard to do that. When that same system takes away your self-control, it takes away your will to want to change things.

I was caught in this vicious cycle once. When I was pregnant with my fourth child (actually the day before I was to go in hospital), I was evicted and put out on the street. The shack I was living in was insulting as it was—no plumbing so that meant no hot water—but I had no choice. I was a victim of my own circumstances. The social service system treated me almost as sub-human. Eventually I was put in a shabby hotel room with three children and an infant, and told I had to abide by the rules. I remember one day after breakfast I went to my parents' home, and when I returned that evening for supper the social worker told me I had the choice of either staying with my parents or staying at the hotel all day. I couldn't accept that so I was forced to go back with my parents until I could find another place to live.

My own awareness of what I wanted in life emerged through these trials. The situation hasn't changed much in the past decade, and single mothers are still given very few options. I wanted to get inside the system and help those trapped there. While at university I went through a great conflict with myself because I was brought up with the assumption that my life's happiness depended upon my husband. I think I can honestly say when I resolved to not follow prescribed notions that society thought was good for me, I went through a wonderful growth period; I began to realize what it meant to be an individual.

During the two summers I worked in the child welfare office I realized that my sacred mission wasn't a sacred mission after all; I realized that social workers are only carrying out their orders; they do not make policy. The ironic thing about that work experience was that I had to work with the same social worker who had told me I had to abide by their rules when I was staying in the hotel room.

The volunteer work I am doing now is an extension of what I envisioned doing then. I view life from the heart out, not necessarily from the head, but I think if there were a balance of the two we'd have a more effective system. What I envision is a system empowering women with monies to direct their lives differently. If a woman is suffering from a lack of education—the average grade level for people in Rabbittown area is grade seven—her chances of thriving and becoming self-sufficient are just about nil. Women have to realize that their lot in life should only be dictated by themselves.

I feel strongly that if we pooled our resources much would change. The present system doesn't work because it doesn't allow us to reach our own potential; it takes away our drive and motivation by dictating what's supposed to be good for us. We are tired of being told what to do. The only way things are going to change for the better is if we lobby; if we get mad enough to take matters into our own hands. Back in the 1930s people felt desperate; they had a riot here in St. John's. Sometimes I think this is what it will take to alter the existing structure for our benefit and the benefit of our children.

Planned Parenthood block of PAC Status of Women Quilt Project '91.

Minnie White

1990 Profile
Original interview by June Hiscock
Born as Mary Hoskins in St. Albans,
Bay D'Espoir on April 1, 1916, Minnie
White attended school until she was four-
teen years old. She then left school to
look for work and became a housekeeper
in the Codroy Valley. In 1937 she mar-
ried Richard Lewis White and settled
down in Tompkins where she still lives.
Minnie has always been known as
"Newfoundland's First Lady of the
Accordion" In 1991 she was the featur-
ed guest on the CBC TV show, On The
Road Again.

🍂 🍂 🍂

I first started playing the accordion when I was eight years old. I have a lot of my father's style of playing. He didn't sit down and teach me, but he gave me tips like not to shake the accordion and when he saw that I was interested, he bought me an old fashioned double-row accordion. The first tune I learned was "The Irish Washerwoman." I also fooled around with a mandolin that a sailor gave me, but I didn't get interested in the instrument until I got a real good one.

My home town was quiet and peaceful, everyone knew each other and helped anyone who needed help. If there was a strange visitor in the Bay, everyone knew it. We all mixed together, no matter what faith or church one belonged to. Across the Bay from where I lived, there is a settlement of Micmacs called Conne River. In winter, the young men and women our age would come over to St. Albans skating. We always had good ice to skate on; the Bay used to freeze up, and be frozen until the spring. The coastal boats could only get in five miles from St. Albans, a place called Rody Point. There was a lighthouse there at that time and we always looked forward to the Micmac boys coming to skate with us. In the summer we would have St. Ann's Day on the 26 of July. All of us would go to Conne River to church and after, there would be a dance in their hall.

I stayed home to help my mother until I was sixteen years old. Up until I left home, I was singing in the church choir, although I am not a singer. I prefer to play music anytime. I left home and came to the Codroy Valley to work as a housekeeper and after being there a while, I got to know the people, who were very nice to me. I stayed one winter with an old lady who taught me how to chord with the fiddle players or violin players. There were excellent players at that time. There were three McDonald fiddlers and three McIsaac fiddlers. I learned to play the piano while I was with this lady. She taught me how to do it, and believe me, I soon caught on and got interested. I started to play piano and organ with the fiddlers. Whenever they were called to play at a dance for the church, they wanted me to play along with them and I remember playing the organ or piano with five fiddlers playing at the same time. That's what I enjoyed.

I met my husband in the Codroy Valley and we were married three years after. We had a family of six children, five girls and one boy. While I was raising my family, I had my accordion put away, but after they were grown up, I decided to get back into playing it. The accordion that I use today was given to me by a close friend. After I had it a couple of years, I knew it would do what I wanted it to do.

In the early seventies Lew Skinner of the Ducats asked me to go to St. John's to record my first album by Audat Company, so I joined them after taking a few months to fill out the contract. My first album was recorded in 1973. After my record came out, it sold so fast that I was asked to go to a local club to play on Sunday afternoons from three to six o'clock. I tried it with just a guitar to accompany me and it went over very well. That's how it started for me to be at the Starlite Lounge for thirteen seasons playing every Sunday, unless I had a booking at the Halifax Newfie Club, or the Port au Port Peninsula, or St. John's. I finished playing at the Starlite in 1987. I enjoyed every Sunday, doing it for the hundreds of fans who used to come there. I got to meet so many people, people from Cape Breton and Nova Scotia that came to the Starlite every long weekend. I am going to miss them, but all good things come to an end; I will never forget them.

I played with a lot of different bands in those years. They were all good bands. If they were no good, I just would not have them. I have two LP records out and a forty-five. On my first album there's a jig called 'Sally's Jig.' It's name came from my grandmother who lived with us and she used to be humming that jig and it stuck to me. When I recorded, I put it on my album and called it after her. My second album, "Homestead Reels" has a number of my own tunes like "Saddle Mountain Jig," "Midnight Waltz" and "Starlite Afternoon" that I first played at the Starlite Lounge.

Although I've been on a few radio shows like "The Newfie Bullet," "Jigs Dinner" with Neil Murray was my favourite. He was very interested in Newfoundland music and did so much in helping me get on with my music. The TV show "The Root Cellar" with The Wonderful Grand Band was a lot of fun; we all got along and had a great time working together.

In the winter months I very seldom play. I enjoy crocheting and knitting and with this break from music it gives me time to do some of the hobbies I enjoy. It's during this break from public playing I practice my music and write new material. I am not giving up music until I have to. That's what I enjoy and I believe that's what keeps me going. Music is healthy for anyone, keeps one's mind active. So, musicians keep going; it sure would be a dull life without you. The key to all musicians is to like what you are doing and like doing it for others.

Fran Williams

1987 Profile
Interview by Marian Frances White
Frances (Fran) Williams, a native of Hopedale, Labrador was the first Inuit woman president of an Inuit Association in Canada. Born in Hopedale on March 17, 1944 she received her elementary education at Hopedale and her high school education at North West River. Williams studied nursing for three years at the Grace General Hospital, St. John's. Nursing took her to the coastal areas of Newfoundland and to Labrador.

A resident of Nain, Williams works as Program Director of Onikatet, the first Inuit radio and TV broadcast in that area. Working with the Okalakratiget Society, the communications network for northern Labrador, she is a translator, a negotiator with government for Inuit affairs, and a leading activist in protecting Inuit culture. Living on the northern coast of Labrador that is icebound several months of the year, she has become an expert survivor. While very progressive, Williams carries on the Inuit traditions and is intent on building upon these. This sensitivity and respect for the Inuit, and especially for the needs of Inuit women, brings about a new sense of awareness to those around her.

🍎 🍎 🍎

Inuit Broadcaster

*T*he Inuit culture is centred around its language and its lifestyle. Our language has made us unique even from Newfoundlanders. There are other Inuit in different regions of Canada who have their own way of doing things, but their language and basic lifestyle is the same. Therefore, there is a strong attachment to the mainland of Canada.

Perhaps the foremost aspect of the Inuit lifestyle that distinguishes it from others is that we have had a life of quietness. Since time immemorial we have depended on the land and on the animals and we've respected the land and the animals. Now we see outside influences coming in, like developers who don't give a damn about the resources of the land and the sea. This upsets the Inuit because they used the animals as clothing, as food, and as shelter. Today animals are still used as clothing and certainly as food, but not so much as shelter. You don't see many igloos or illusuaks today, not like back in the 1930s.

As a child I used to go back and forth by dog team with my grandparents to their fishing and hunting place during the summer and winter. As I grew up the Americans came to Hopedale and built a base there. What we couldn't understand was that they said Hopedale was a part of the United States. As far as we were concerned, it was Hopedale and no way was it a part of the United States. People just come into our world and say things like that without consulting us. They show a lack of respect for our culture.

In northern Labrador the language has almost been made extinct because we've only been taught in English through the educational system. It is only recently that the Inuktitut language is being brought back into the schools. One of the objectives of the Okalakatiget Society, our communications network, and of Onikatet, the Inuit radio and television programs, is to help retain this lifestyle by researching and airing stories from the older generation. These stories show us how our foremothers and forefathers hunted and survived here. They are broadcast half in Inuktitut and half in English, which we feel is a good beginning.

In my past position as president of the Inuit organization I began to see that women were becoming just as powerful as men. That is not to say that we ignore the tradition of looking to our elders for advice in decision-making that will have an impact on the way of life of the community. Sometimes I am the one who will give advice. Perhaps I have gained their trust because I speak English better than many of them and because I was the one who nursed many of them back to health.

I see a lot of changes in the role of women throughout Labrador over the past several years. Slowly there is a transition from the passive woman who accepted her job as caterer; the men hunted and brought home food, the women cleaned it, cooked it and did all the other jobs around the house. Sometimes she hunted too. Today you see the Inuit woman getting more away from the role of caretaker. They are becoming more aware of themselves as being an important part of a community and attending meetings. They are becoming more political. Many Inuit women now have full time jobs. This brings about a big change in the family, in some cases this creates a problem because traditionally an Inuit family is very close. However, with full time jobs they can no longer spend so much time with their children. Yet, they are becoming as powerful as men especially in politics. In the years to come we'll hopefully find the work load fairer for women.

In the course of my work with the Okalakatiget Society I have become more aware of various types of abuse on women. I see battered women, neglected children, alcohol abuse, government abuse and social services abuse. I've seen a lot of families that have had their children taken from them because they are labelled neglected children. I've asked some of these children, who have been placed in any number of foster homes in Labrador City or in St. John's, where they would rather be. They usually answer, "I always know, even if my mother and dad have been drinking, that they love me. At least I know they are there." I don't think this bond should be disturbed and destroyed by an outside agency. This separation is very difficult for an Inuit child if you consider the difference in environments. I think this is one reason why we have such an outburst of suicides today.

I think the answer to these types of problems is education. People have to be educated as to who the Inuit are, where they live and why they choose to live that way. The outside attitude towards us seems to be very distorted. The only thing most people know about our lifestyle is that we lived in igloos! It's difficult to understand us unless people come up here to live for a while. Experience is always the best education after all. Governments have spent years educating us in English, now we can go back in English and educate them.

I think it would be more effective for the Inuit in their present life and in the years to come to have women in a more active role. Women are beginning to realize they can change and they want to change, whereas the older generation are more set in their ways. The technology that is in the world today often makes our tasks more difficult. We are exposed to programs on TV produced by the South that are very convincing. If you have never been outside Labrador, you believe that is how it is, until you go outside yourself and see it's not like that.

Having grown up in the Inuit environment, having seen what women have done and experienced, I see them as a people with great strength. I think the reason they've managed to keep their lives in order is because they never really asked for anything in the first place. I think all women everywhere should cooperate and help each other whenever they can and learn from each other's experiences. I think the strongest thing women have is their stories and their hopes. These two things alone are enough to unite women across the country and around the world. That's how I see it, and I'm still learning!

Sketch by
Kathleen Knowling

178

Wendy Williams

1991 Profile
Interview by Marian Frances White

Williams, the oldest of three sisters, was born in St. John's on August 12, 1949. After getting a Bachelor of Nursing and a Post-Graduate Diploma in Family Practice Nursing, she worked with women's health and reproductive issues. Her credits include Planned Parenthood, the Canadian Abortion Rights Action League, Transition House, and the Newfoundland and Labrador AIDS Committee. In 1990 she was appointed President of the Provincial Advisory Council on the Status of Women for a three year period. In December 1991 Wendy was sworn in as Councillor for Ward 1 in the City of St. John's.

☙ ☙ ☙

*W*omen are sexual. We have bodies, and we should know about them.

So many women don't know their own bodies. When Planned Parenthood was involved in a study on cervical caps, we met women who couldn't use a cervical cap because they had never put their hands inside their own vaginas. How many women don't do breast self-examination because touching their own bodies is not okay? To me this shows a lack of acceptance of the female body and female sexuality. I remember one woman who came into Planned Parenthood. When we were talking it came out that she did not enjoy sex. I got out *Our Bodies Our Selves* (one of the best books I know of for learning about our bodies) and showed her the clitoris. She was ecstatic and wanted to get home to share her knowledge with her sister.

I still meet women who tell me they can't wait to give "all this" up because there has been no enjoyment for them in sex. I spoke to a woman who is forty. She just had a child, and she wanted to know how soon her sex drive would come back, if ever. Was it normal to be so tired that sex was the last thing on her agenda? Yes of course it is!

When I do workshops with young teenage girls, I ask them if their mothers or fathers had talked with them about basic health information. Many times no one says yes. I think the responsibilities of a parent include giving our children both information and decision making skills. Then we must let our children use this information and these skills to make their own decisions. Children should know they can come and ask parents a question, but the trick as a parent is to know you aren't expected to have all the answers. You can suggest a trip to the public library.

Teaching aides for teenagers in schools are often not very helpful or explicit—most illustrations of females do not even identify the clitoris! I think many of the young women I work with have little understanding of their options with their sexuality, that they can say no to intercourse and have a sexual relationship without it, that they can use birth control, and that there may be times in their lives when they are not interested in sex at all.

There are classes that teach kids about ownership of their own bodies, and show them 'yes' areas and 'no' areas. While it is important for kids to understand this, if they are not also told of the beauty of their body's development, they are left with a negative image of their sexuality ... we're still not allowed to give classes that teach kids how to masturbate to orgasm ... this is perfectly natural yet children are made to feel that it is something to be ashamed of. When I talk to young women we discuss the fact that some people have partners of the same sex while others have partners of the opposite sex.

While good information is hard to find, television outlines all the bad things about female sexuality. Videos tell women we like being raped, we like being assaulted, we enjoy sex after saying no, because no means yes. There's no such thing as saying no in the media.

Our sexuality has been influenced not only by our lack of knowledge but also the organized church. The church is gradually losing its power to control sexuality. When people have been subject to very narrow definitions of sexuality they have more difficulties accepting their own sexuality if it is different from the religious definition.

As I get older, I am becoming increasingly aware that we in the women's movement have been unable to get policy makers to recognize the work that we do in the private sphere, i.e. the nurturing, the caring, the cuddling, the cleaning, the caring for the sick, as work. This to me is a major challenge for the 1990s.

I have learned two important lessons from the women with whom I have worked. The first lesson was to maintain my economic independence which nursing has allowed me to do. The other lesson was to stop and smell the roses often; to celebrate my gifts, my family, my friends and my health. Only then is my work worthwhile.

Sketch by
Kathlen Knowling

Caroline (Kay) Young

1989 Profile
Interview through letters and
phone conversations;
with help from Cathy Young
Kay Young was born Caroline
Kate Diamond on January 30,
1944 in Whitbourne, New-
foundland and moved to
Lethbridge with her parents, Wal-
lace and Nellie Diamond, when
she was a year old. She attended a
two room school until 1959 when
she moved to Clarenville to finish

high school. The following year Young entered Memorial University to study
pre-med; however, after three years she decided med school was not for her. She
worked for a year in her mother's store, then studied Business Education in
Clarenville and in 1967 returned to University. In 1968 she took up a teaching
position in her hometown—a position she continues to hold.

Young and her husband, Walter, have two daughters, Suzette and Margo.
They presently live on a two hundred acre farm in the tiny community of
Morley's Siding—about one hundred and forty miles west of St. John's. Out-
side of her teaching career and raising children, she has made presentations at
workshops for the Bonavista-Trinity-Placentia Integrated School Board and is
very active in local community groups. In 1984, when the Goose Head Farm
Women's Association formed, Young was elected Secretary and in 1986 became
President of the Association. In 1989 she was elected President of the Canadian
Farm Women's Network; in 1990 she was appointed to the Premier's Round
Table on the Environment and the Economy, and in April, 1991 Young repre-
sented Newfoundland Farm Women on a Women's Trade Mission to Norway
and Scotland. Young is the interim president for the Provincial Farm Women's
Association of Newfoundland and Labrador and a member of Winter Brook
Women's Institute.

❦ ❦ ❦

I didn't grow up around a TV and because my sister and I studied at the kitchen table, the only time my parents turned on the radio at night was to hear the Dosco News. That was break time for us. I had lots of time to daydream and living on a farm was something I used to dream about as a child. I live on a farm with my family, but because of farm financial conditions I have had to take a full time off-farm job and I am not as involved in the day-to-day operations of the farm as I would like to be. Of

181

course, I know how to milk cows, clean stalls and feed the animals but there is so much more that I want to do.

When my children were young I got involved in activities that were restricted to serving their interests; however, since '84 when I attended the first local meeting of Farm Women, I have found something that interests me a lot. It's been quite a growing experience because we are all learning how to better prepare ourselves to meet our objectives. Even though we often have disagreements I still feel we have grown stronger because of them and that we have gained a strong community spirit.

Like many women around me, I often felt that our problems were unique to Newfoundland because we live on an Island, but my work with the national group has taught me how many similar problems Canadian farmers have. By working together we are also recognizing problems that are unique to us; for example, the high cost of freight for seeds, machinery, fertilizer and hay. We are learning how to speak up for ourselves and approach government to help us overcome some of these problems. When our group formed in '84 our aims were, and still are, to educate ourselves and the public on agricultural issues, to become more assertive, to promote agriculture, to lobby government on issues of concern and to bring agriculture to the classrooms. Overall we wanted to improve our financial condition. We began to realize how many changes were needed in the agricultural industry.

Being national president of the CFWN has been very rewarding, however, because of where I live, I have had to turn down many opportunities to participate in discussions relating to policy for the industry. I often have to take time from my school teaching without pay to attend special events. For example, when I participated in the Women's Trade Mission I was granted two weeks from school and while it was an excellent experience, it provided me with no monetary gains and the time lost will actually affect my pension. I was granted Ministerial leave for a round table meeting to attend the Calgary constitutional conference and I felt honoured that my contribution to that conference led to my name being put forward to attend the major constitutional conference held in Vancouver, but I had to decline.

Women have always been involved in issues surrounding the farm, but as with most groups if it is mixed, the men usually dominate the floor. When women did attend meetings most felt excluded from major decision making and were generally over-shadowed by men. Most of us have now done public speaking and workshops on parliamentary issues, so we have a better knowledge of when to speak, and what to say when we do. The public does not appear to recognize farmers as business people who have invested hundreds of thousands of dollars into their operations. Farmers are not getting a fair return for their invested dollars. Why? One reason is due to the fact that often labour is not included in production costs. The farmer may take a small salary and pay hired help, but the spouse and children are seldom recognized financially. Often it's a triple work day for the spouse who works on and off the farm and keeps house as well.

The Farm Women's Association have lobbied governments on issues such as a better licensing policy for farm equipment and gained that in '87. Recently we presented a proposal to the Dept. of Development to have a farm woman go on their next North Sea Tour to determine the effects the off-shore oil industry might have on the future of Newfoundland agriculture. We have been successful in lobbying the government to have CN Marine give dairy cows coming in from Nova Scotia priority. Often the animals would have to wait twenty-four to forty-eight hours in North Sydney and arrive at our farms in real poor condition because of stress— this was a case where our transportation system needed to be improved.

Over the past three years, five farm women groups have sprung up and recently we formed our first provincial association.

Yet, the only affiliation we have with any mainland agricultural group is the "Canadian Farm Women's Network" which we use to lobby for change and improvements. However, now that the Provincial Federation of Agriculture has been revived, we hope that all farmers will use it as a vehicle for change. In Newfoundland, agriculture provides seasonal employment and full-time employment for thousands. We are presently self-sufficient in eggs and soon will be in milk, but there could be expansion in greenhouse and berry production as well as dairy and vegetables.

Although the first settlers came to this province to fish, they tried to cultivate the soil, but merchants and ship owners became increasingly anxious over the power the inhabitants might gain through settlement and often the early homesteads, including gardens, were destroyed. The fishery has had a powerful influence to the point where agriculture has always been a neglected industry. Today we are still at a disadvantage because farmers cannot even get unemployment benefits in the off-season, whereas those who fish can. This is not a big issue for most of us because we are not looking to be unemployed, but we have to recognize that not having that benefit places us in a vulnerable position. Less than three per cent of the province's land is suitable for farming; that amounts to approximately one hundred thousand hectares but we are still in the pioneering stages because only eight thousand hectares are used for commercial agricultural products. We need more funding to do research because as long as we are underdeveloped, our supply will be low and our dependence on imports will remain high.

Through our association we are learning that women can speak with one voice and by doing that we are putting ourselves and our industry on a higher level than it ever has been. We are becoming recognized as farmers without having to lean on our husbands. Not too long ago women found it difficult to start a business of their own, so we are gaining footing all the time and making our mark by standing up for ourselves. We are also trying to improve day care and care for the elderly. Through all this, we are learning how to cope with the stress of farm life, but we realize any gains we make will be beneficial for the industry as a whole.

Individually there are many rewards as well. For myself I feel I now have more compassion for the problems other farmers face and I realize that we cannot go very far if we live in isolation—that goes for individuals as well as groups. My involvement with the Farm Women's Association has opened new doors for me and has had a positive effect on my work. It has taught me to stand up for my beliefs and my rights. It's a lot of hard work, but that's nothing new to Newfoundland women. We welcome the challenge!

KATHLEEN KNOWLING

Afterword

*W*hile this *Almanac* compendium had a beginning with the first edition in 1987, there is no finite ending. It is a gratifying fact that the ever changing lives of these women continue independent of the life of this book. In essence, the individual profiles could be expanded to form many books. And while there are any number of remarkable women in this province to profile, I'm sure you will agree that these women are representative of the finest kind you will encounter anywhere. I encourage all of you to go further with any of these stories and create plays, songs or other artistic forms. Use this research as a base from where to dig even deeper into the lives of our mothers and our foremothers.